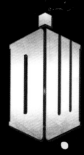

BBC

DOCTOR WHO

VOLUME 1: **THE HYPOTHETICAL GENTLEMAN**

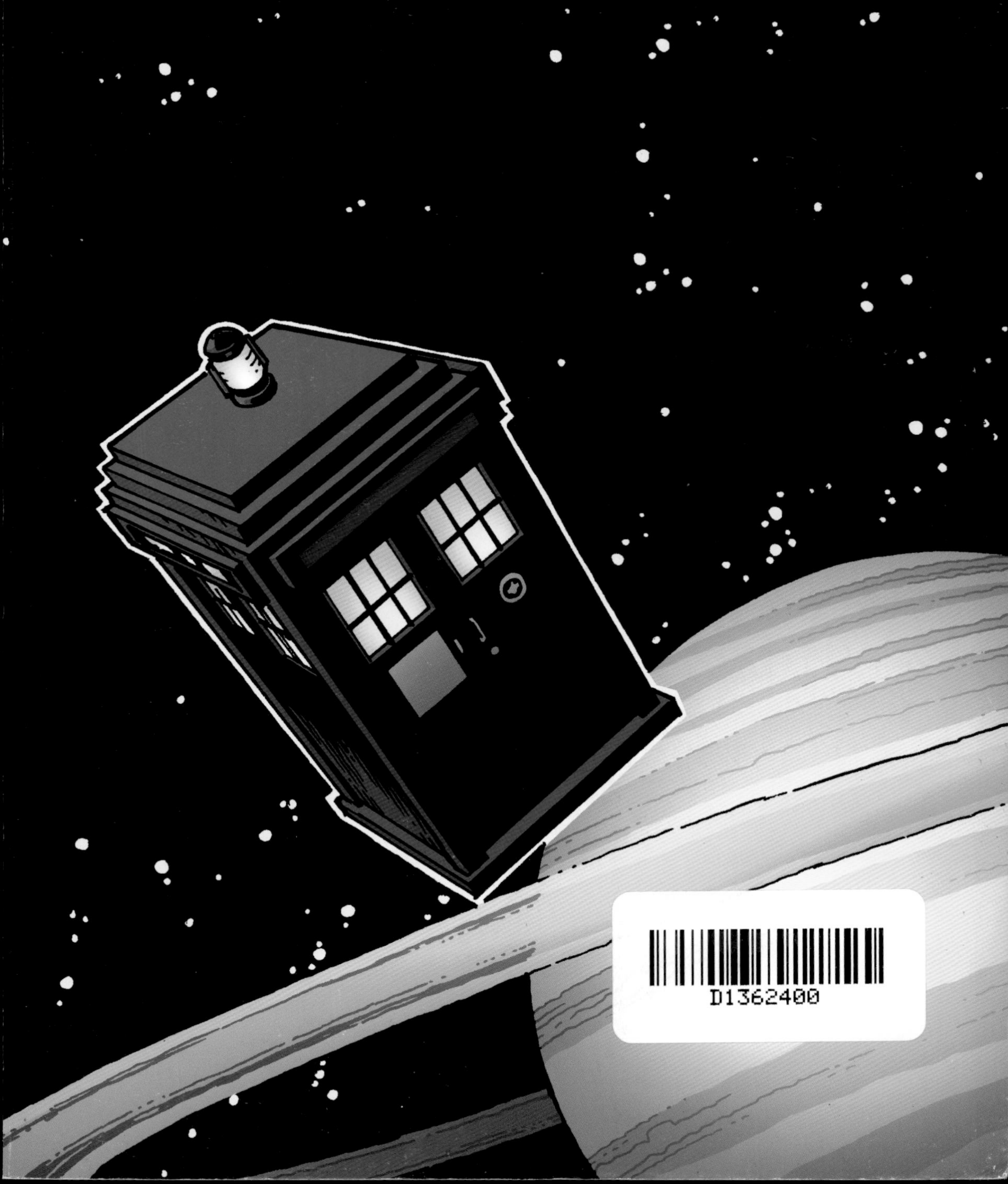

Cover by
Mark Buckingham
Cover Colors by
Charlie Kirchoff
Collection Edits by
Justin Eisinger and
Alonzo Simon
Collection Design by
Tom B. Long

Special thanks to Kate Bush, Georgie Britton, Caroline Skinner, Denise Paul,
and Ed Casey at BBC Worldwide for their invaluable assistance.

ISBN: 978-1-61377-579-0

16 15 14 13   2 3 4 5

IDW founded by Ted Adams, Alex Garner, Kris Oprisko, and Robbie Robbins

IDW®

Ted Adams, CEO & Publisher
Greg Goldstein, President & COO
Robbie Robbins, EVP/Sr. Graphic Artist
Chris Ryall, Chief Creative Officer/Editor-in-Chief
Matthew Ruzicka, CPA, Chief Financial Officer
Alan Payne, VP of Sales
Dirk Wood, VP of Marketing
Lorelei Bunjes, VP of Digital Services

Become our fan on Facebook **facebook.com/idwpublishing**
Follow us on Twitter **@idwpublishing**
Check us out on YouTube **youtube.com/idwpublishing**
www.IDWPUBLISHING.COM

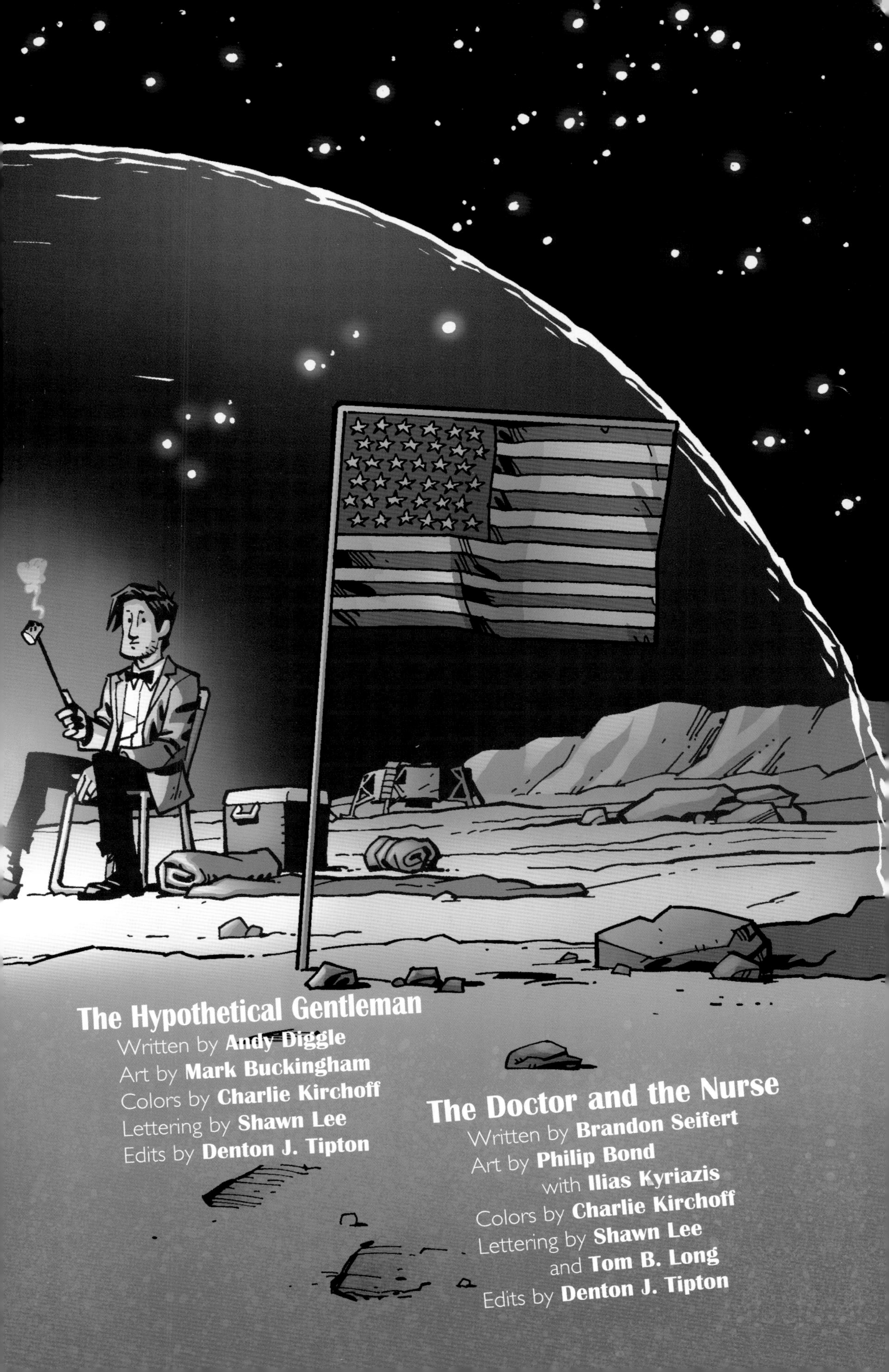

The Hypothetical Gentleman

Written by **Andy Diggle**
Art by **Mark Buckingham**
Colors by **Charlie Kirchoff**
Lettering by **Shawn Lee**
Edits by **Denton J. Tipton**

The Doctor and the Nurse

Written by **Brandon Seifert**
Art by **Philip Bond**
with **Ilias Kyriazis**
Colors by **Charlie Kirchoff**
Lettering by **Shawn Lee**
and **Tom B. Long**
Edits by **Denton J. Tipton**

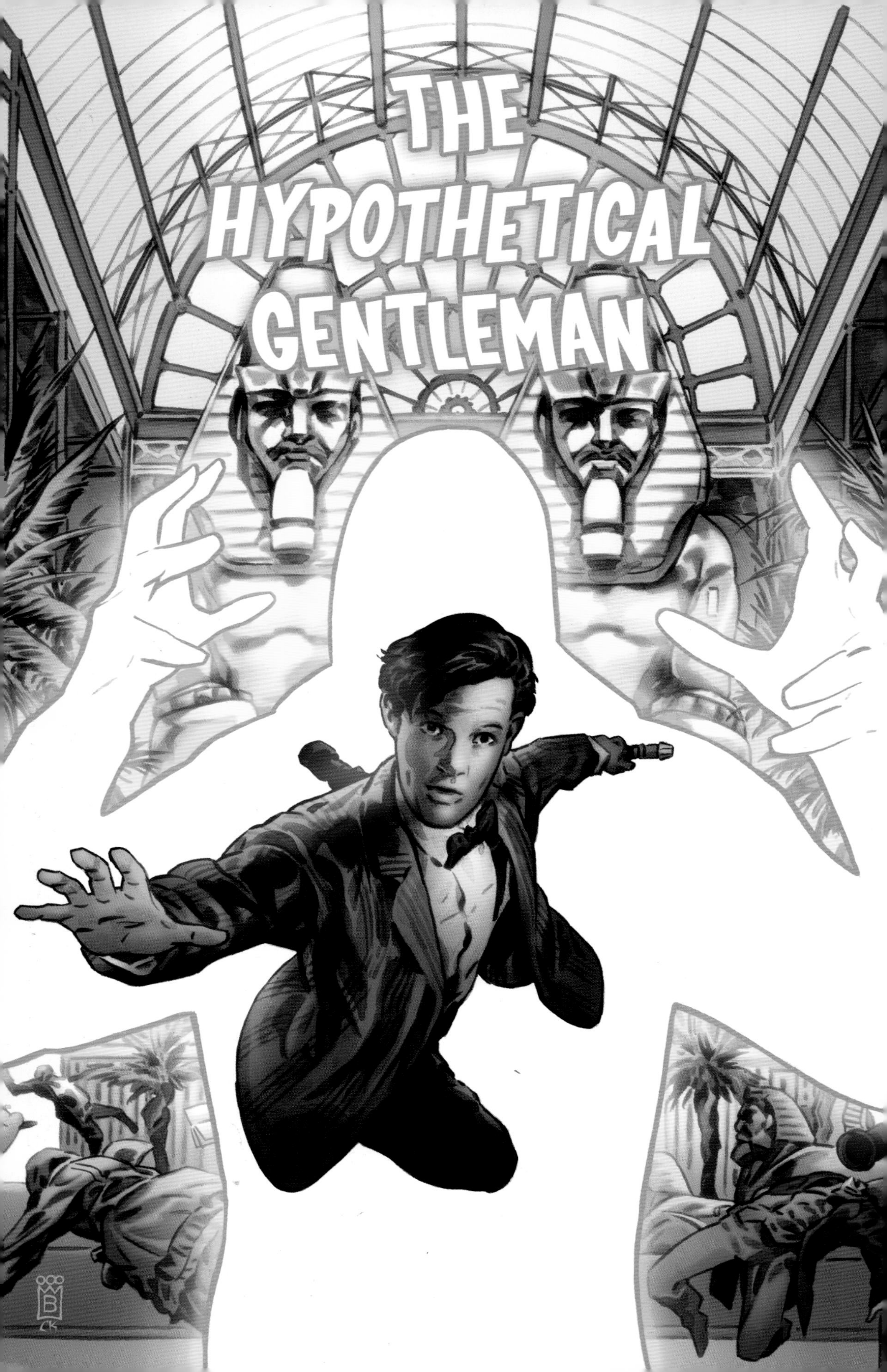
THE
HYPOTHETICAL
GENTLEMAN

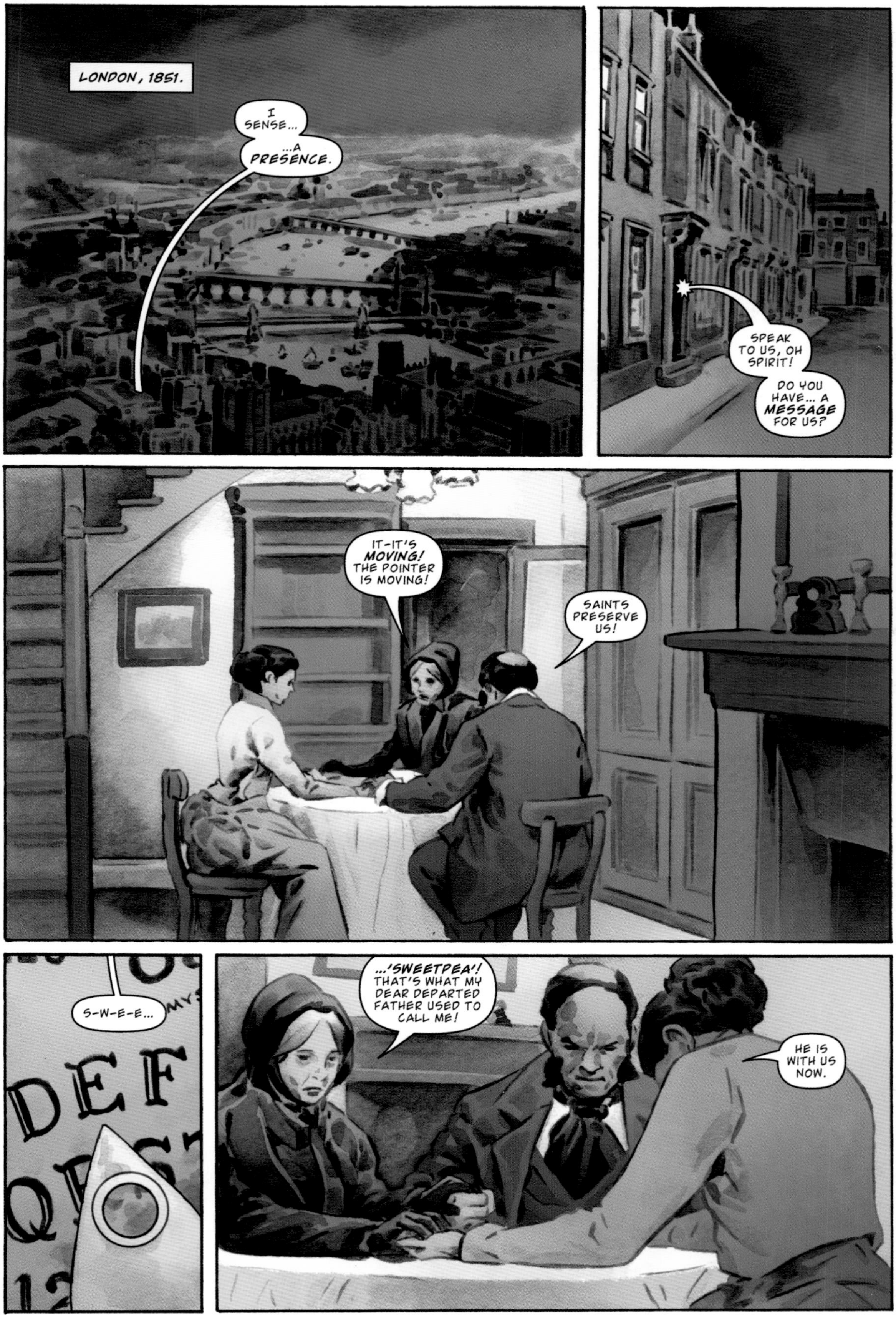
LONDON, 1851.
I SENSE...
...A PRESENCE.
SPEAK TO US, OH SPIRIT!
DO YOU HAVE... A MESSAGE FOR US?
IT-IT'S MOVING! THE POINTER IS MOVING!
SAINTS PRESERVE US!
S-W-E-E...
...'SWEETPEA'! THAT'S WHAT MY DEAR DEPARTED FATHER USED TO CALL ME!
HE IS WITH US NOW.

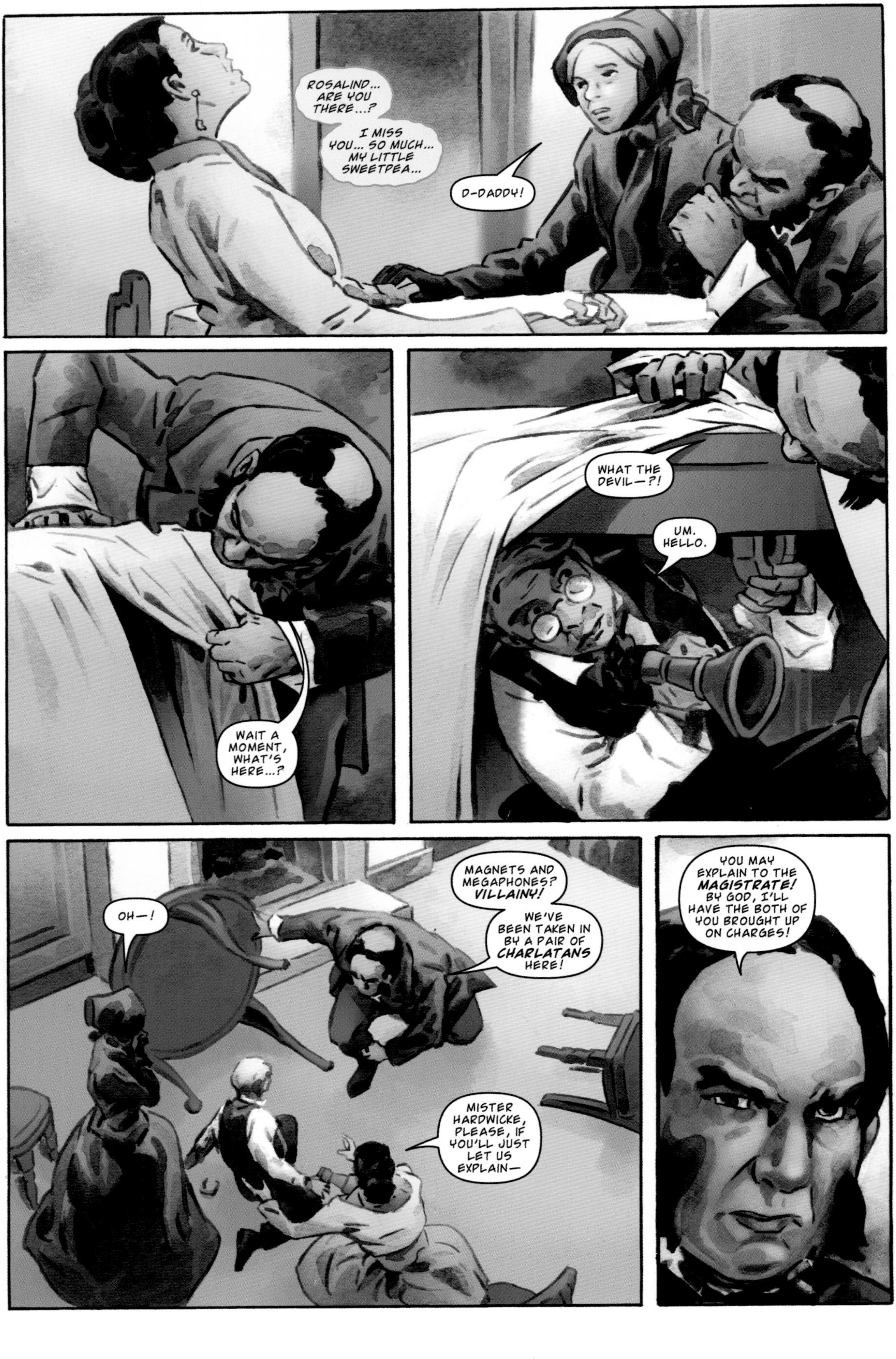
ROSALIND... ARE YOU THERE...?
I MISS YOU... SO MUCH... MY LITTLE SWEETPEA...
D-DADDY!
WAIT A MOMENT, WHAT'S HERE...?
WHAT THE DEVIL—?!
UM. HELLO.
OH—!
MAGNETS AND MEGAPHONES? VILLAINY!
WE'VE BEEN TAKEN IN BY A PAIR OF CHARLATANS HERE!
MISTER HARDWICKE, PLEASE, IF YOU'LL JUST LET US EXPLAIN—
YOU MAY EXPLAIN TO THE MAGISTRATE! BY GOD, I'LL HAVE THE BOTH OF YOU BROUGHT UP ON CHARGES!

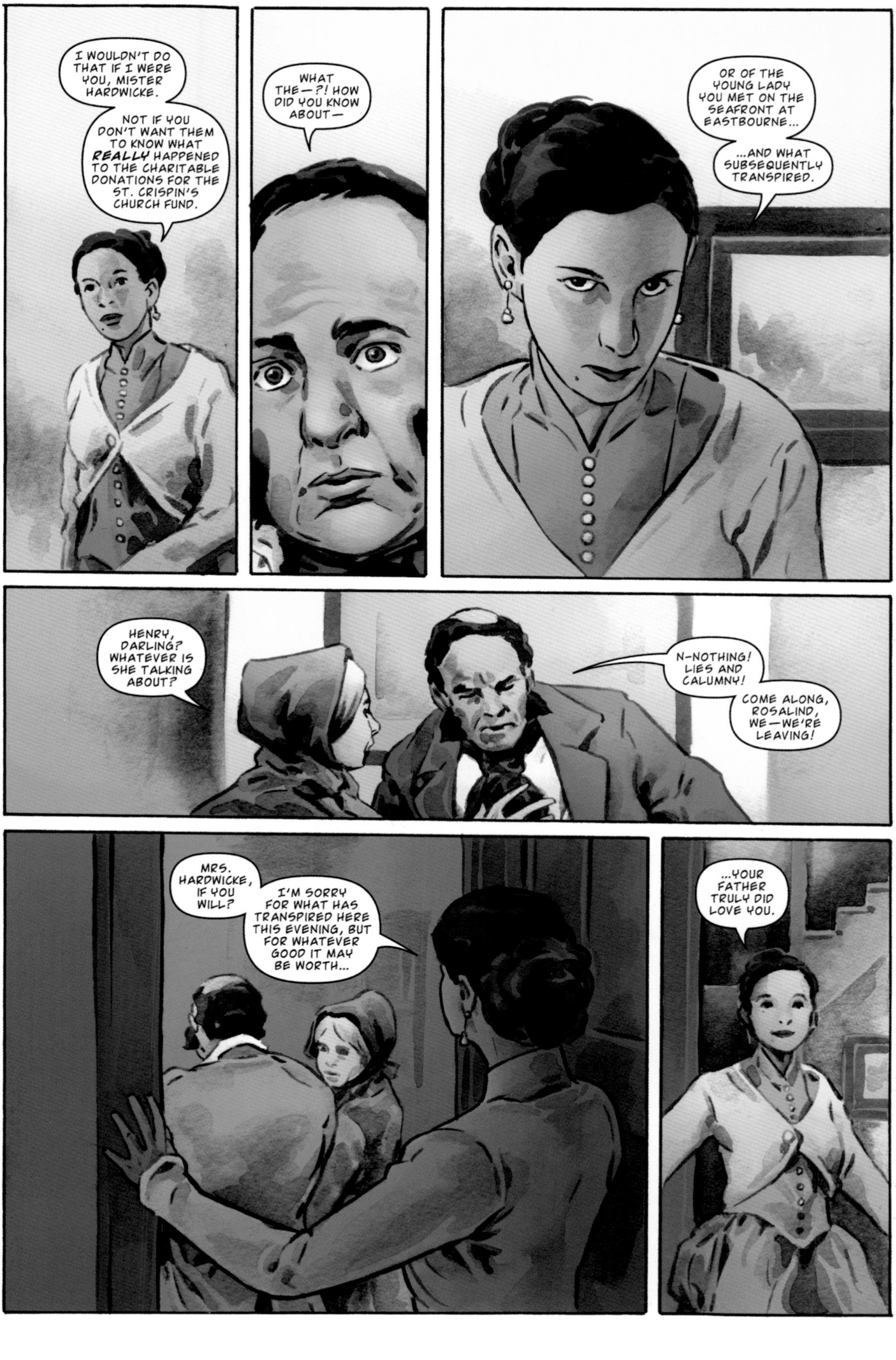
I WOULDN'T DO THAT IF I WERE YOU, MISTER HARDWICKE.
NOT IF YOU DON'T WANT THEM TO KNOW WHAT REALLY HAPPENED TO THE CHARITABLE DONATIONS FOR THE ST. CRISPIN'S CHURCH FUND.
WHAT THE—?! HOW DID YOU KNOW ABOUT—
OR OF THE YOUNG LADY YOU MET ON THE SEAFRONT AT EASTBOURNE...
...AND WHAT SUBSEQUENTLY TRANSPIRED.
HENRY, DARLING? WHATEVER IS SHE TALKING ABOUT?
N-NOTHING! LIES AND CALUMNY!
COME ALONG, ROSALIND, WE—WE'RE LEAVING!
MRS. HARDWICKE, IF YOU WILL?
I'M SORRY FOR WHAT HAS TRANSPIRED HERE THIS EVENING, BUT FOR WHATEVER GOOD IT MAY BE WORTH...
...YOUR FATHER TRULY DID LOVE YOU.

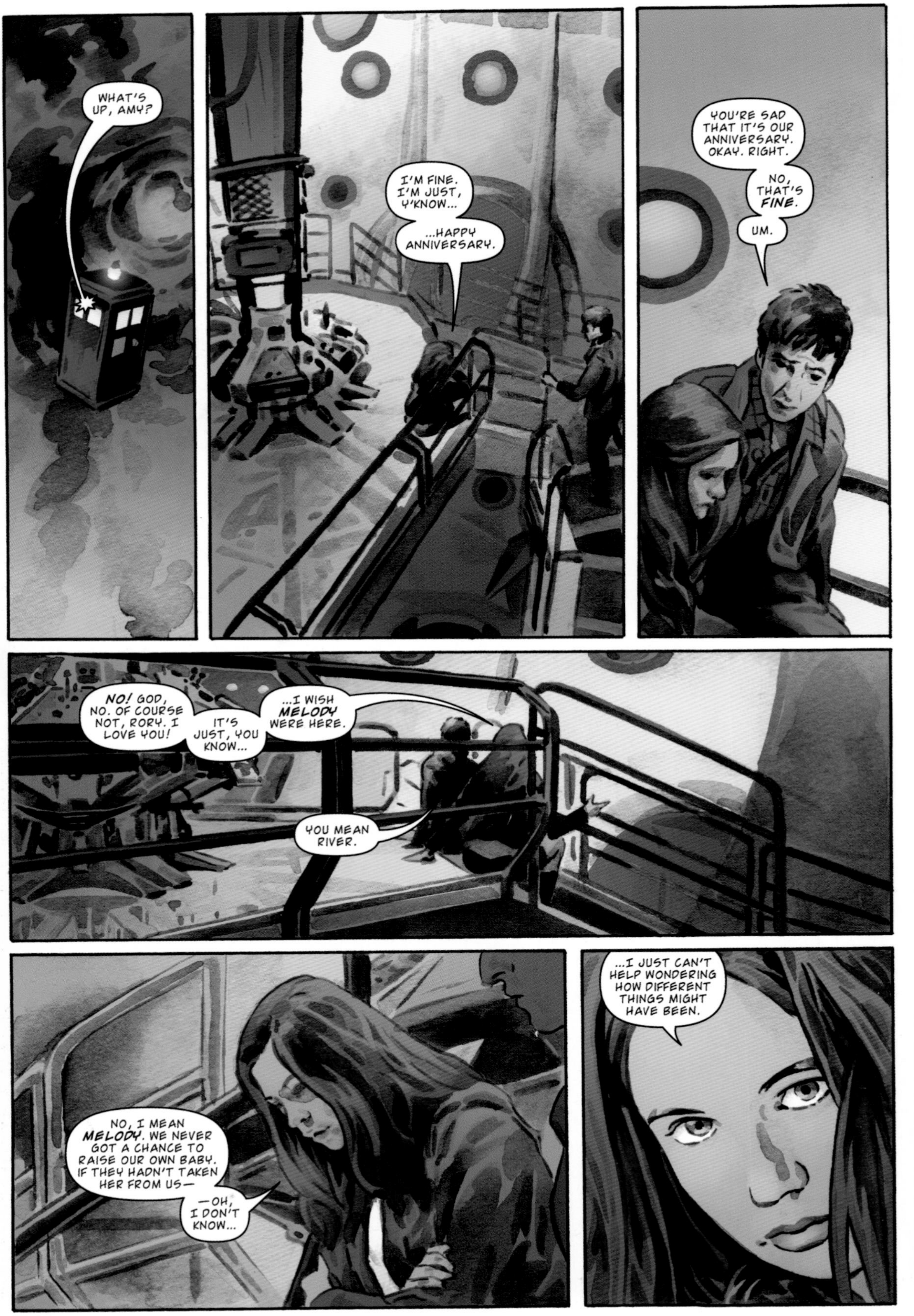
WHAT'S UP, AMY?
I'M FINE. I'M JUST, Y'KNOW...
...HAPPY ANNIVERSARY.
YOU'RE SAD THAT IT'S OUR ANNIVERSARY. OKAY. RIGHT.
NO, THAT'S FINE.
UM.
NO! GOD, NO. OF COURSE NOT, RORY. I LOVE YOU!
IT'S JUST, YOU KNOW...
...I WISH MELODY WERE HERE.
YOU MEAN RIVER.
NO, I MEAN MELODY. WE NEVER GOT A CHANCE TO RAISE OUR OWN BABY. IF THEY HADN'T TAKEN HER FROM US—
—OH, I DON'T KNOW...
...I JUST CAN'T HELP WONDERING HOW DIFFERENT THINGS MIGHT HAVE BEEN.

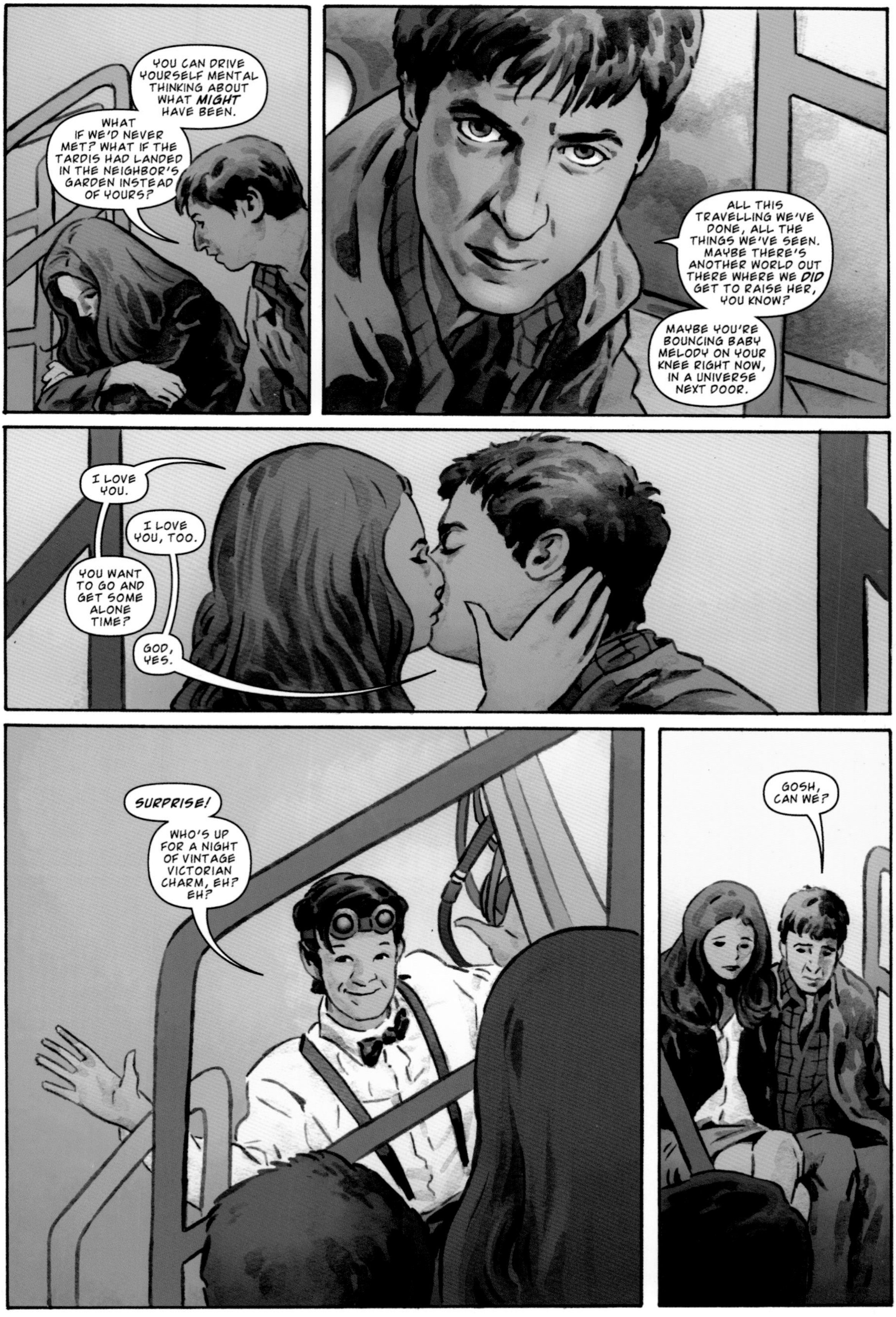
YOU CAN DRIVE YOURSELF MENTAL THINKING ABOUT WHAT MIGHT HAVE BEEN.
WHAT IF WE'D NEVER MET? WHAT IF THE TARDIS HAD LANDED IN THE NEIGHBOR'S GARDEN INSTEAD OF YOURS?
ALL THIS TRAVELLING WE'VE DONE, ALL THE THINGS WE'VE SEEN. MAYBE THERE'S ANOTHER WORLD OUT THERE WHERE WE DID GET TO RAISE HER, YOU KNOW?
MAYBE YOU'RE BOUNCING BABY MELODY ON YOUR KNEE RIGHT NOW, IN A UNIVERSE NEXT DOOR.
I LOVE YOU.
I LOVE YOU, TOO.
YOU WANT TO GO AND GET SOME ALONE TIME?
GOD, YES.
SURPRISE!
WHO'S UP FOR A NIGHT OF VINTAGE VICTORIAN CHARM, EH? EH?
GOSH, CAN WE?

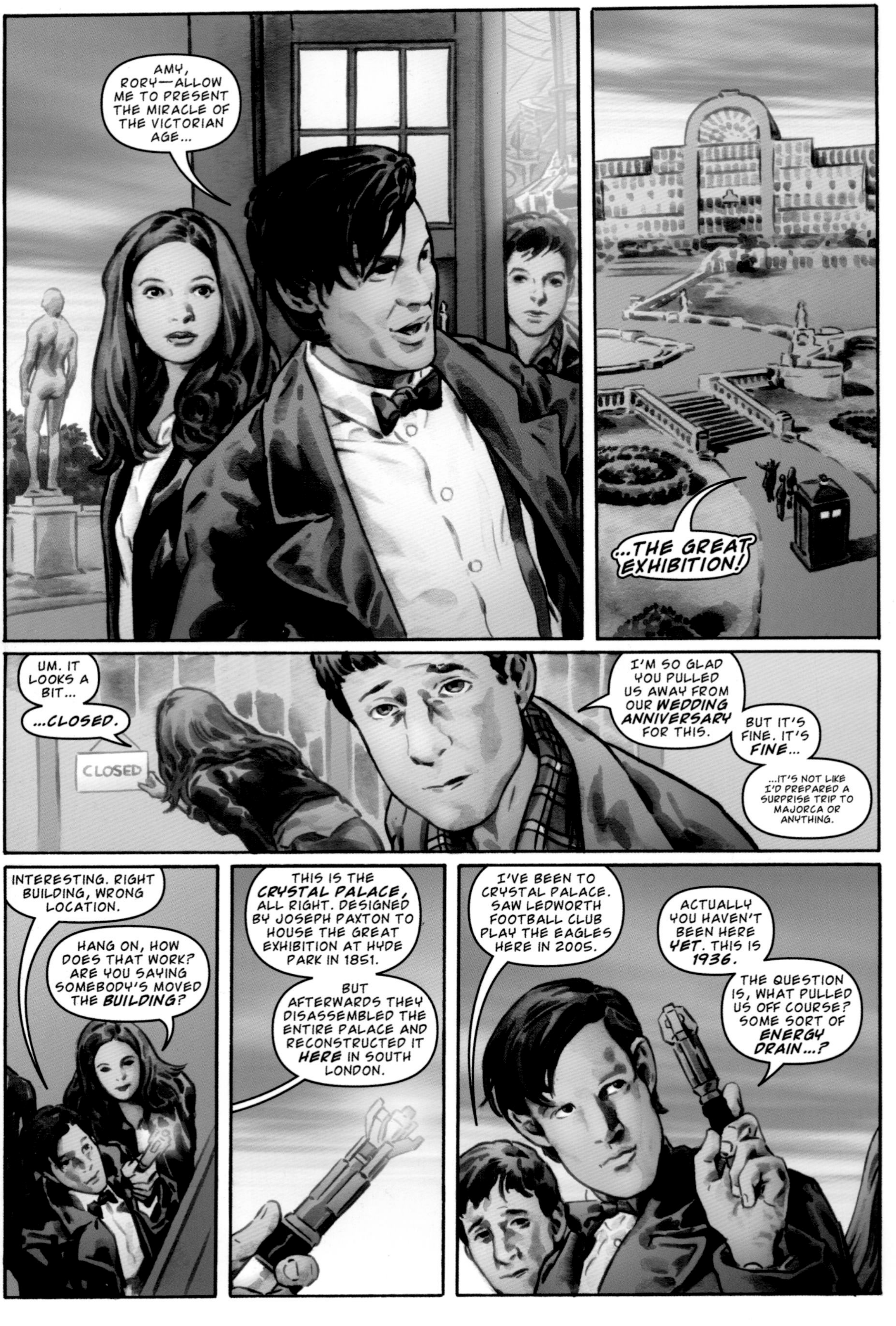
AMY, RORY—ALLOW ME TO PRESENT THE MIRACLE OF THE VICTORIAN AGE...
...THE GREAT EXHIBITION!
UM. IT LOOKS A BIT...
...CLOSED.
CLOSED
I'M SO GLAD YOU PULLED US AWAY FROM OUR WEDDING ANNIVERSARY FOR THIS.
BUT IT'S FINE. IT'S FINE...
...IT'S NOT LIKE I'D PREPARED A SURPRISE TRIP TO MAJORCA OR ANYTHING.
INTERESTING. RIGHT BUILDING, WRONG LOCATION.
HANG ON, HOW DOES THAT WORK? ARE YOU SAYING SOMEBODY'S MOVED THE BUILDING?
THIS IS THE CRYSTAL PALACE, ALL RIGHT. DESIGNED BY JOSEPH PAXTON TO HOUSE THE GREAT EXHIBITION AT HYDE PARK IN 1851.
BUT AFTERWARDS THEY DISASSEMBLED THE ENTIRE PALACE AND RECONSTRUCTED IT HERE IN SOUTH LONDON.
I'VE BEEN TO CRYSTAL PALACE. SAW LEDWORTH FOOTBALL CLUB PLAY THE EAGLES HERE IN 2005.
ACTUALLY YOU HAVEN'T BEEN HERE YET. THIS IS 1936.
THE QUESTION IS, WHAT PULLED US OFF COURSE? SOME SORT OF ENERGY DRAIN...?

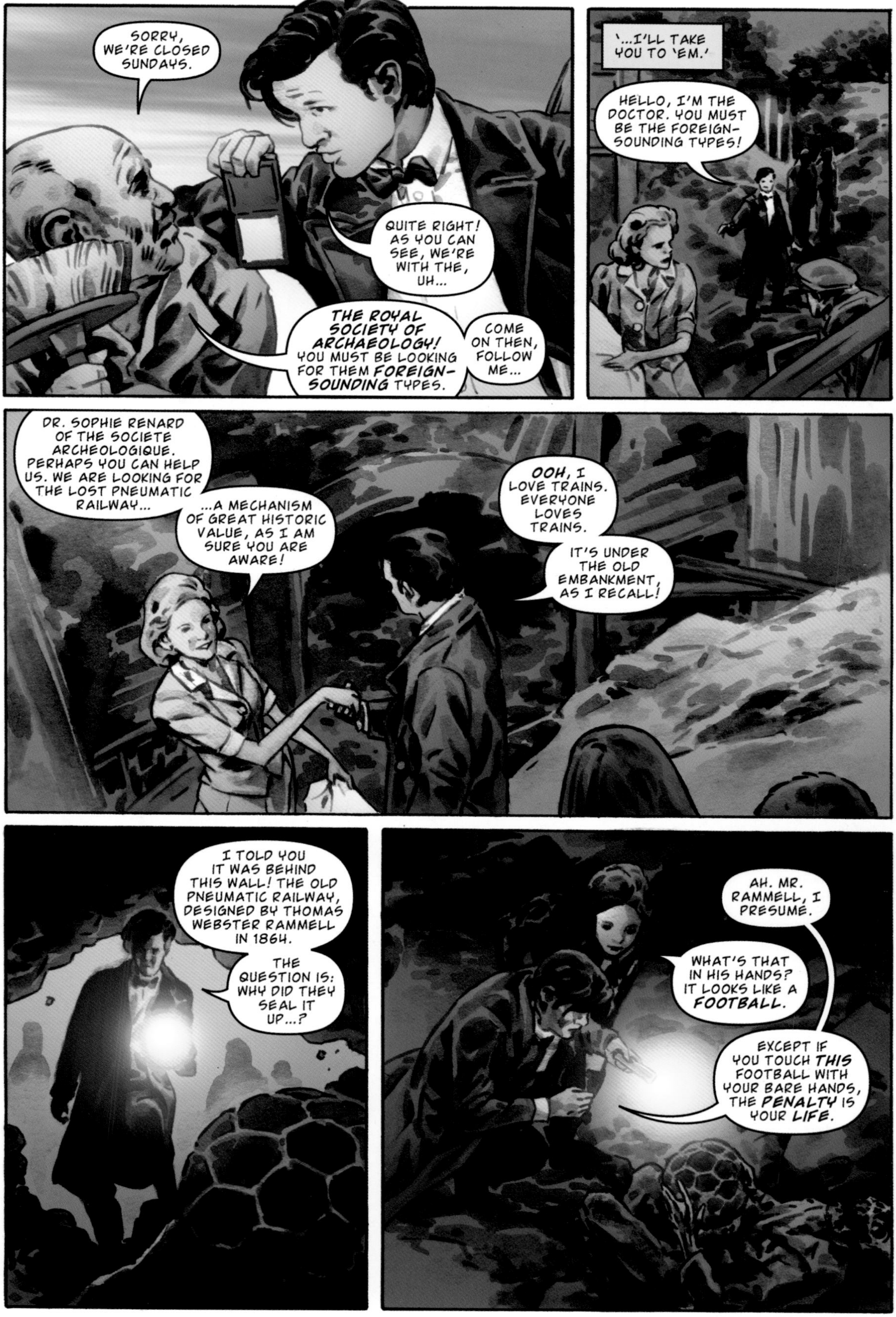
SORRY, WE'RE CLOSED SUNDAYS.
QUITE RIGHT! AS YOU CAN SEE, WE'RE WITH THE, UH...
THE ROYAL SOCIETY OF ARCHAEOLOGY! YOU MUST BE LOOKING FOR THEM FOREIGN-SOUNDING TYPES.
COME ON THEN, FOLLOW ME...
'...I'LL TAKE YOU TO 'EM.'
HELLO, I'M THE DOCTOR. YOU MUST BE THE FOREIGN-SOUNDING TYPES!
DR. SOPHIE RENARD OF THE SOCIETE ARCHEOLOGIQUE. PERHAPS YOU CAN HELP US. WE ARE LOOKING FOR THE LOST PNEUMATIC RAILWAY...
...A MECHANISM OF GREAT HISTORIC VALUE, AS I AM SURE YOU ARE AWARE!
OOH, I LOVE TRAINS. EVERYONE LOVES TRAINS.
IT'S UNDER THE OLD EMBANKMENT, AS I RECALL!
I TOLD YOU IT WAS BEHIND THIS WALL! THE OLD PNEUMATIC RAILWAY, DESIGNED BY THOMAS WEBSTER RAMMELL IN 1864.
THE QUESTION IS: WHY DID THEY SEAL IT UP...?
AH. MR. RAMMELL, I PRESUME.
WHAT'S THAT IN HIS HANDS? IT LOOKS LIKE A FOOTBALL.
EXCEPT IF YOU TOUCH THIS FOOTBALL WITH YOUR BARE HANDS, THE PENALTY IS YOUR LIFE.

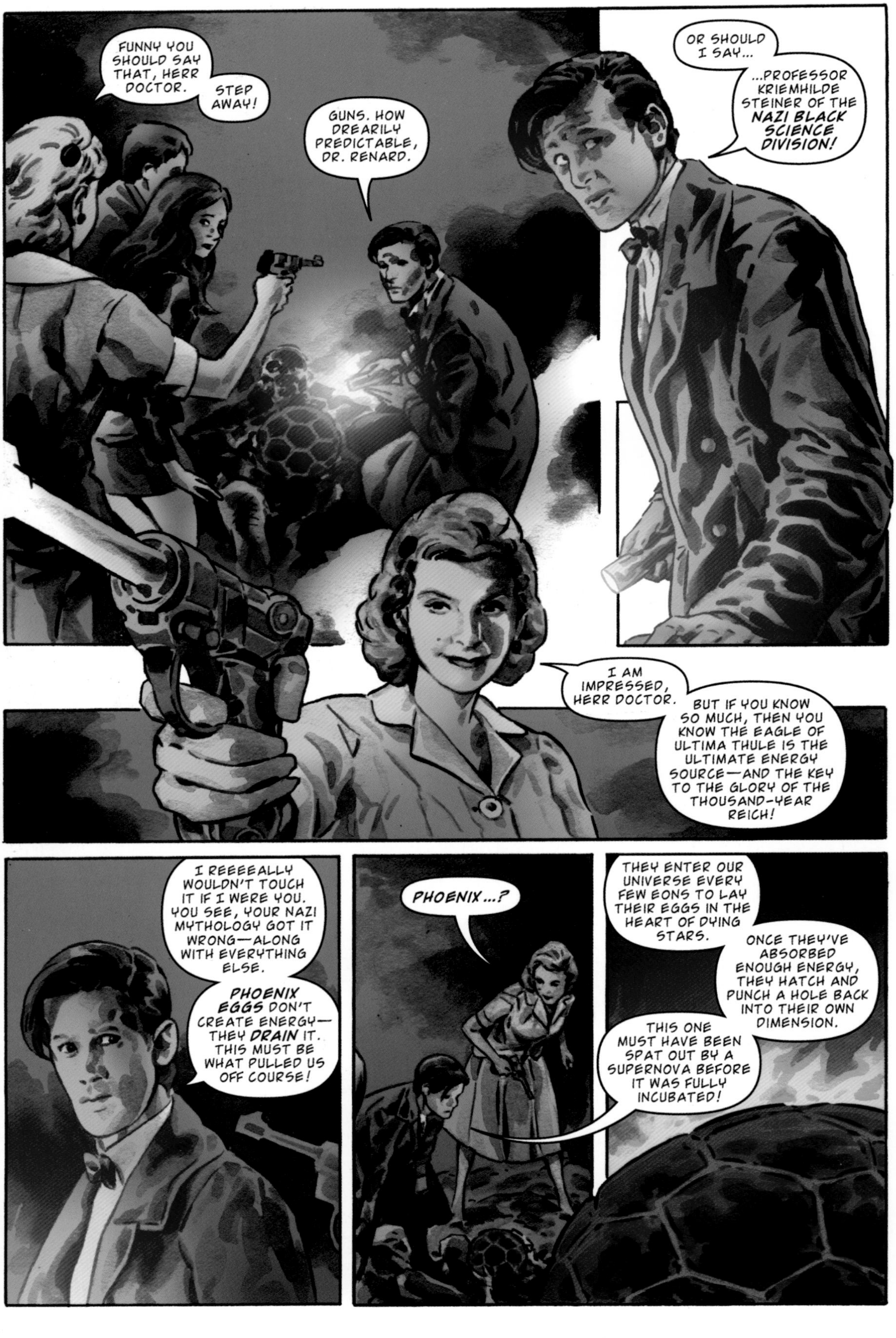
FUNNY YOU SHOULD SAY THAT, HERR DOCTOR.
STEP AWAY!
GUNS. HOW DREARILY PREDICTABLE, DR. RENARD.
OR SHOULD I SAY...
...PROFESSOR KRIEMHILDE STEINER OF THE NAZI BLACK SCIENCE DIVISION!
I AM IMPRESSED, HERR DOCTOR.
BUT IF YOU KNOW SO MUCH, THEN YOU KNOW THE EAGLE OF ULTIMA THULE IS THE ULTIMATE ENERGY SOURCE—AND THE KEY TO THE GLORY OF THE THOUSAND-YEAR REICH!
I REEEEALLY WOULDN'T TOUCH IT IF I WERE YOU. YOU SEE, YOUR NAZI MYTHOLOGY GOT IT WRONG—ALONG WITH EVERYTHING ELSE.
PHOENIX EGGS DON'T CREATE ENERGY—THEY DRAIN IT. THIS MUST BE WHAT PULLED US OFF COURSE!
PHOENIX...?
THEY ENTER OUR UNIVERSE EVERY FEW EONS TO LAY THEIR EGGS IN THE HEART OF DYING STARS.
ONCE THEY'VE ABSORBED ENOUGH ENERGY, THEY HATCH AND PUNCH A HOLE BACK INTO THEIR OWN DIMENSION.
THIS ONE MUST HAVE BEEN SPAT OUT BY A SUPERNOVA BEFORE IT WAS FULLY INCUBATED!

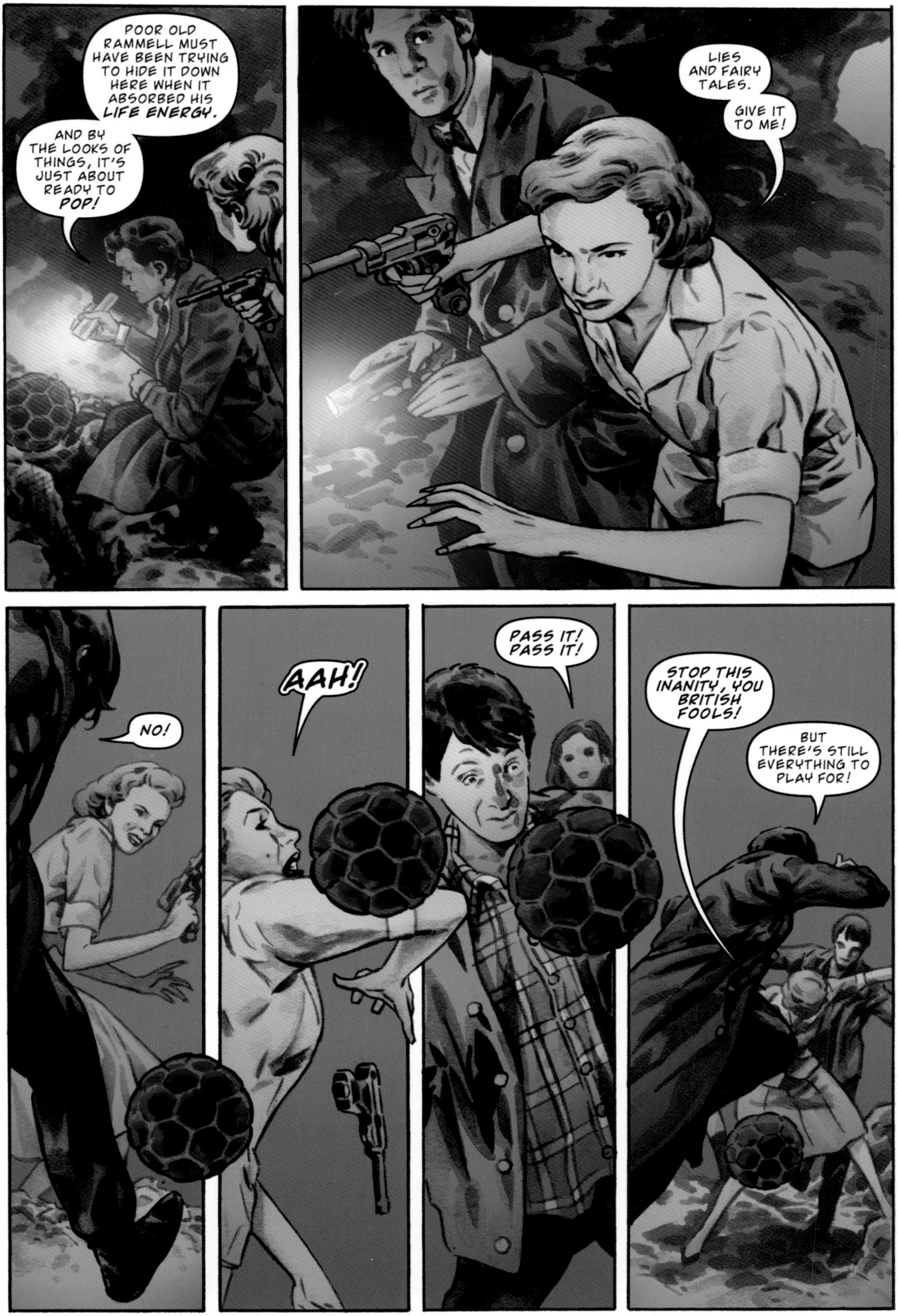
POOR OLD RAMMELL MUST HAVE BEEN TRYING TO HIDE IT DOWN HERE WHEN IT ABSORBED HIS LIFE ENERGY.
AND BY THE LOOKS OF THINGS, IT'S JUST ABOUT READY TO POP!
LIES AND FAIRY TALES.
GIVE IT TO ME!
NO!
AAH!
PASS IT! PASS IT!
STOP THIS INANITY, YOU BRITISH FOOLS!
BUT THERE'S STILL EVERYTHING TO PLAY FOR!

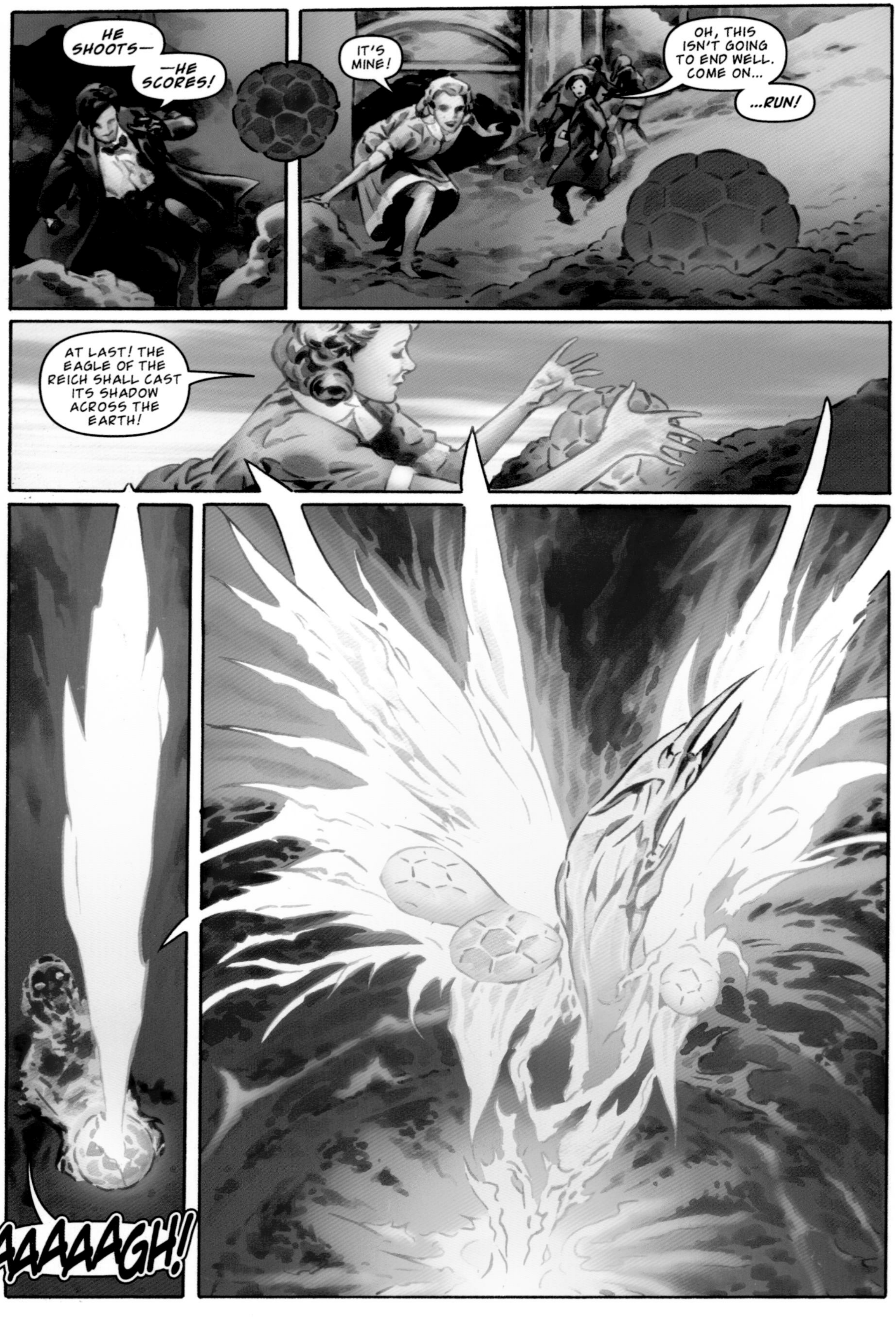
HE SHOOTS—
—HE SCORES!
IT'S MINE!
OH, THIS ISN'T GOING TO END WELL. COME ON...
...RUN!
AT LAST! THE EAGLE OF THE REICH SHALL CAST ITS SHADOW ACROSS THE EARTH!
AAAAAGH!

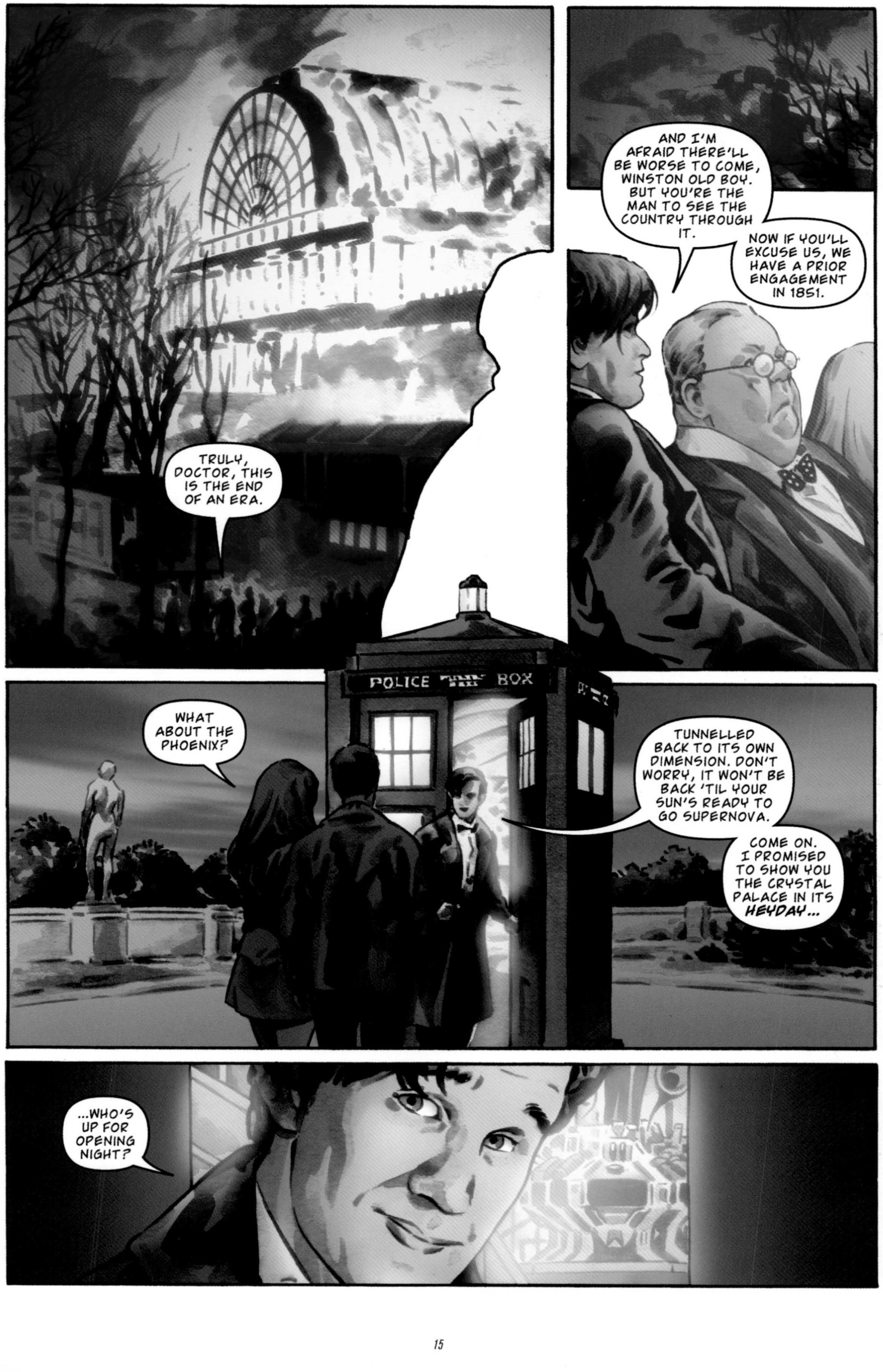
TRULY, DOCTOR, THIS IS THE END OF AN ERA.
AND I'M AFRAID THERE'LL BE WORSE TO COME, WINSTON OLD BOY. BUT YOU'RE THE MAN TO SEE THE COUNTRY THROUGH IT.
NOW IF YOU'LL EXCUSE US, WE HAVE A PRIOR ENGAGEMENT IN 1851.
POLICE BOX
WHAT ABOUT THE PHOENIX?
TUNNELLED BACK TO ITS OWN DIMENSION. DON'T WORRY, IT WON'T BE BACK 'TIL YOUR SUN'S READY TO GO SUPERNOVA.
COME ON. I PROMISED TO SHOW YOU THE CRYSTAL PALACE IN ITS ***HEYDAY...***
...WHO'S UP FOR OPENING NIGHT?

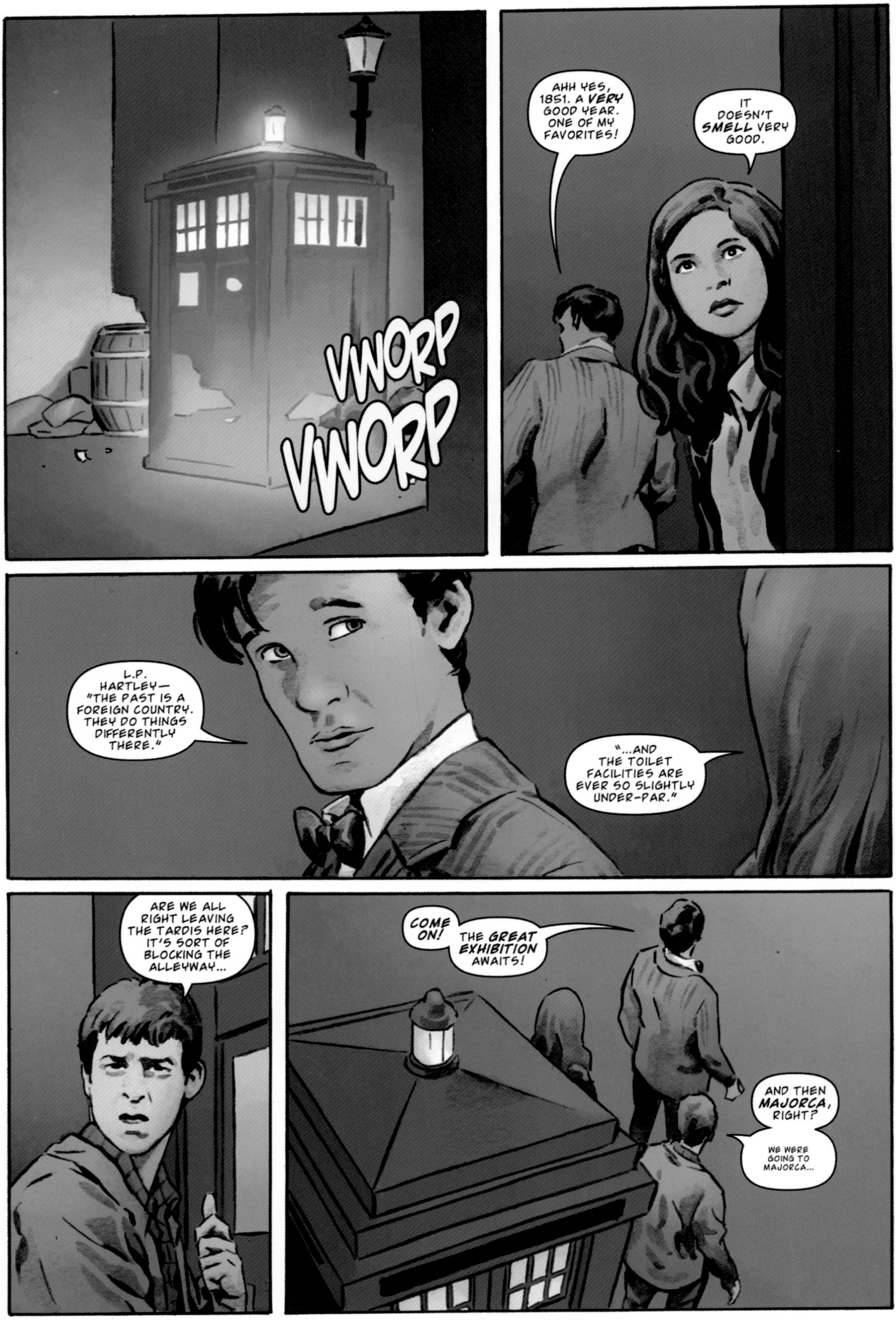
VWORP
VWORP
AHH YES, 1851. A VERY GOOD YEAR. ONE OF MY FAVORITES!
IT DOESN'T SMELL VERY GOOD.
L.P. HARTLEY— "THE PAST IS A FOREIGN COUNTRY. THEY DO THINGS DIFFERENTLY THERE."
"...AND THE TOILET FACILITIES ARE EVER SO SLIGHTLY UNDER-PAR."
ARE WE ALL RIGHT LEAVING THE TARDIS HERE? IT'S SORT OF BLOCKING THE ALLEYWAY...
COME ON!
THE GREAT EXHIBITION AWAITS!
AND THEN MAJORCA, RIGHT?
WE WERE GOING TO MAJORCA...

I'M SORRY, CHARLES. I'M SO SORRY.
HUSH, EMILY DARLING. YOU'VE NOTHING TO APOLOGISE FOR.
BUT IT'S BEEN A YEAR NOW SINCE OUR... VISITATION. WE'VE POURED EVERY LAST PENNY INTO THAT INFERNAL MACHINE, AND FOR WHAT?
I'VE REDUCED US TO THIS. PARLOUR TRICKS, LIES AND DECEITFULNESS.
YOU HAVE A GIFT, EMILY. AN AMAZING, GOD-GIVEN GIFT.
WE HAVE TO TRUST THAT HE WILL REVEAL HIS PURPOSE TO US IN TIME.
NNGH.
GUHH—
EMILY—?

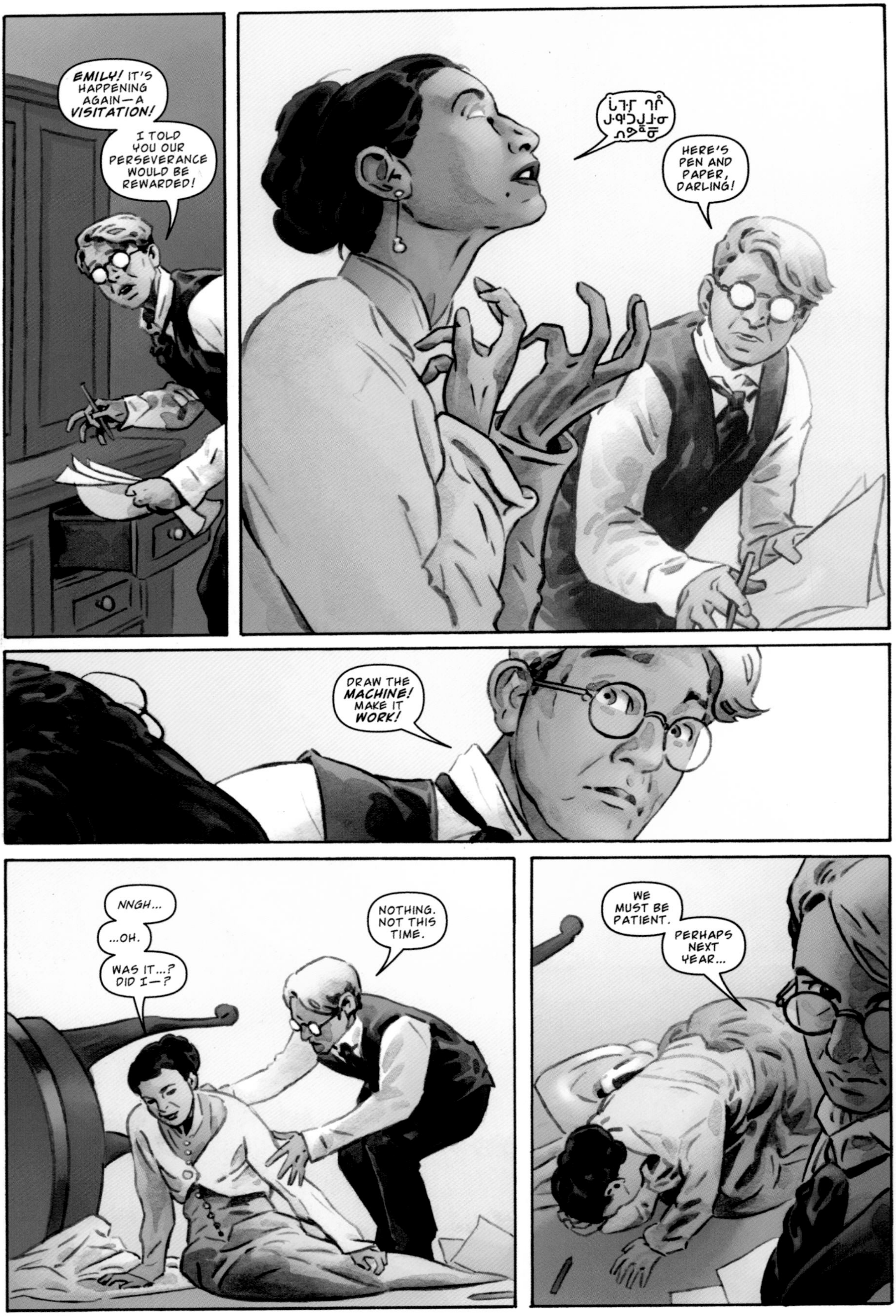
EMILY! IT'S HAPPENING AGAIN—A VISITATION!
I TOLD YOU OUR PERSEVERANCE WOULD BE REWARDED!
HERE'S PEN AND PAPER, DARLING!
DRAW THE MACHINE! MAKE IT WORK!
NNGH...
...OH.
WAS IT...? DID I—?
NOTHING. NOT THIS TIME.
WE MUST BE PATIENT.
PERHAPS NEXT YEAR...

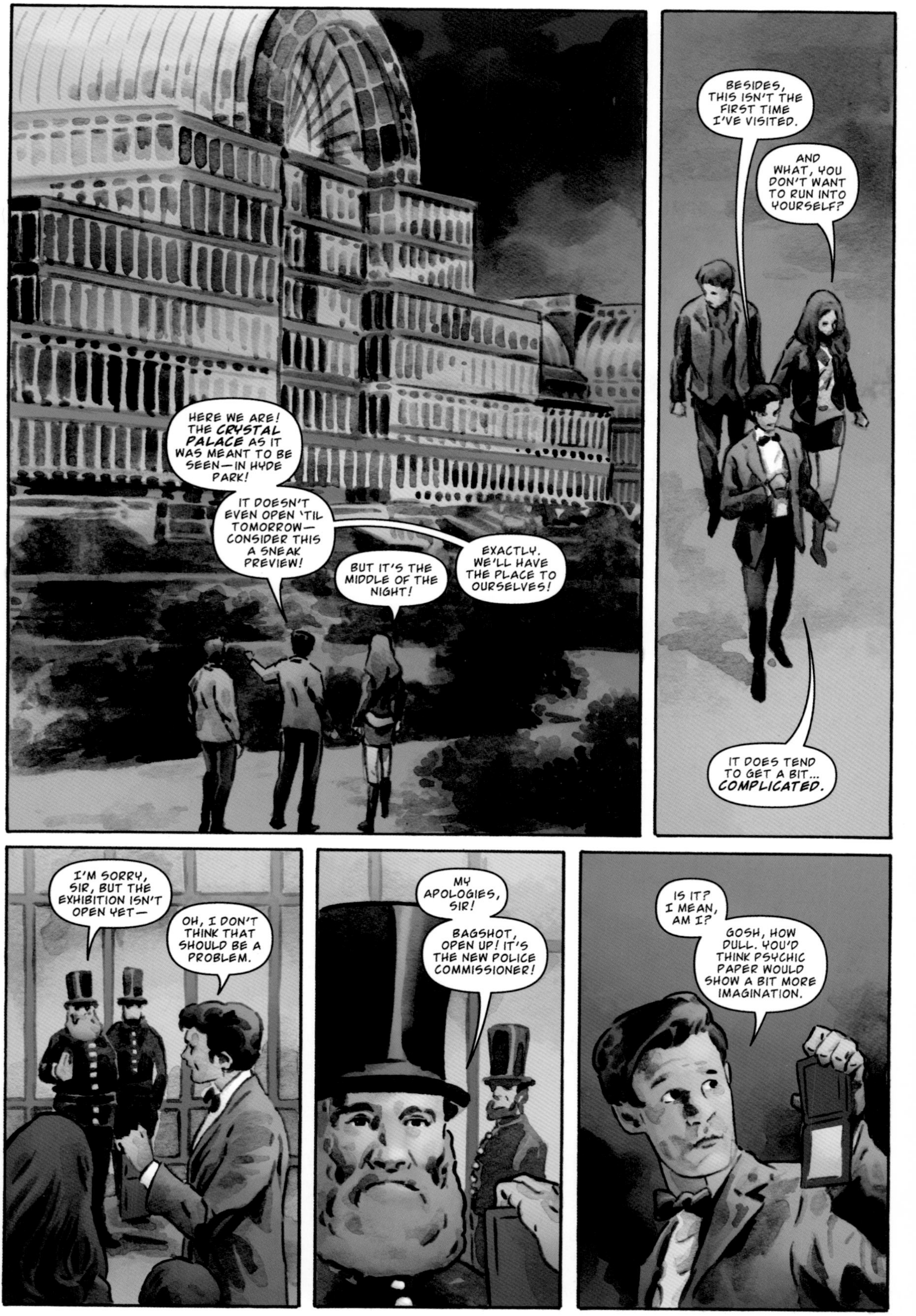
HERE WE ARE! THE CRYSTAL PALACE AS IT WAS MEANT TO BE SEEN—IN HYDE PARK!
IT DOESN'T EVEN OPEN 'TIL TOMORROW—CONSIDER THIS A SNEAK PREVIEW!
BUT IT'S THE MIDDLE OF THE NIGHT!
EXACTLY. WE'LL HAVE THE PLACE TO OURSELVES!
BESIDES, THIS ISN'T THE FIRST TIME I'VE VISITED.
AND WHAT, YOU DON'T WANT TO RUN INTO YOURSELF?
IT DOES TEND TO GET A BIT... COMPLICATED.
I'M SORRY, SIR, BUT THE EXHIBITION ISN'T OPEN YET—
OH, I DON'T THINK THAT SHOULD BE A PROBLEM.
MY APOLOGIES, SIR!
BAGSHOT, OPEN UP! IT'S THE NEW POLICE COMMISSIONER!
IS IT? I MEAN, AM I?
GOSH, HOW DULL. YOU'D THINK PSYCHIC PAPER WOULD SHOW A BIT MORE IMAGINATION.

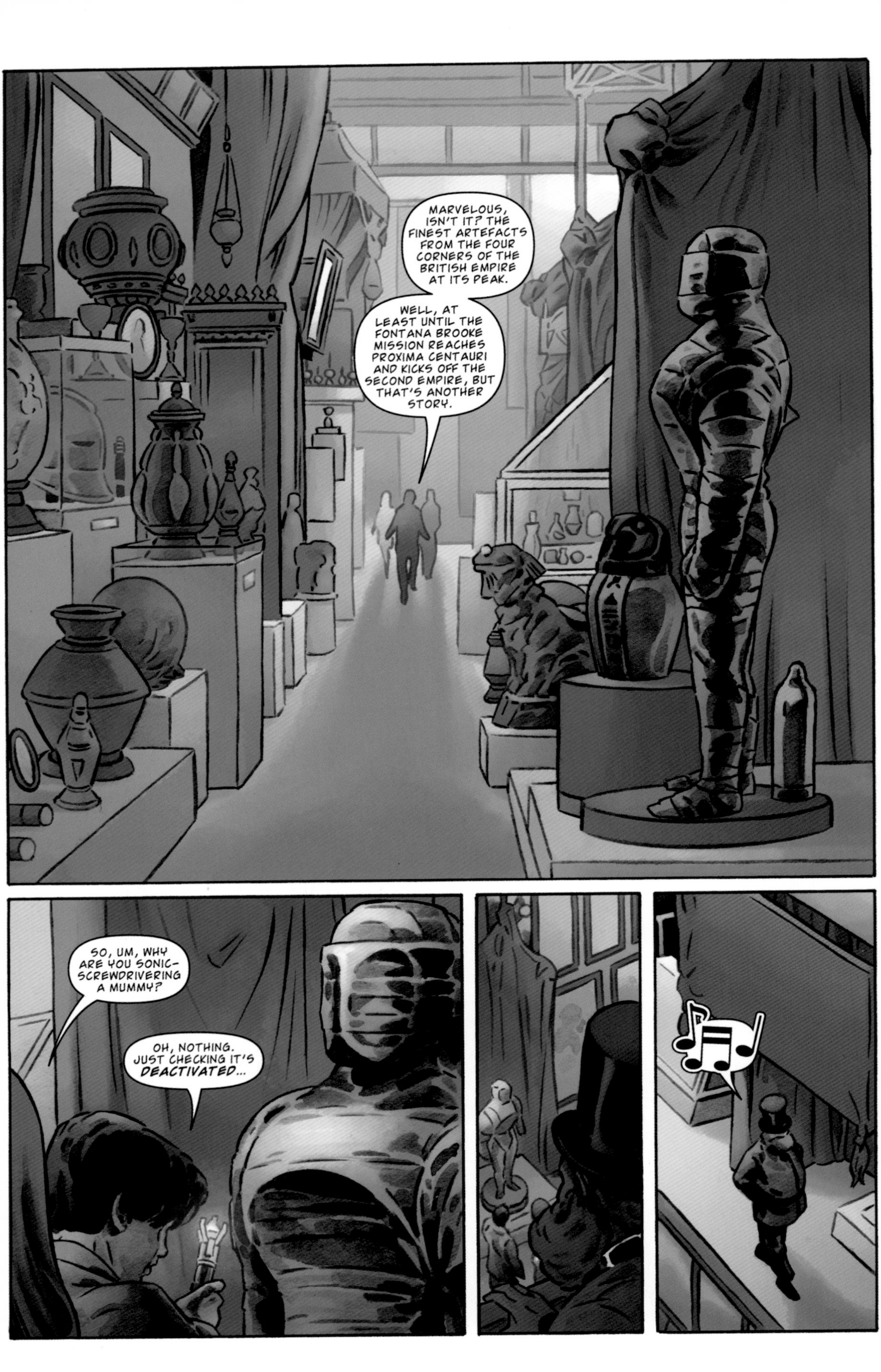
MARVELOUS, ISN'T IT? THE FINEST ARTEFACTS FROM THE FOUR CORNERS OF THE BRITISH EMPIRE AT ITS PEAK.
WELL, AT LEAST UNTIL THE FONTANA BROOKE MISSION REACHES PROXIMA CENTAURI AND KICKS OFF THE SECOND EMPIRE, BUT THAT'S ANOTHER STORY.
SO, UM, WHY ARE YOU SONIC-SCREWDRIVERING A MUMMY?
OH, NOTHING. JUST CHECKING IT'S *DEACTIVATED*...

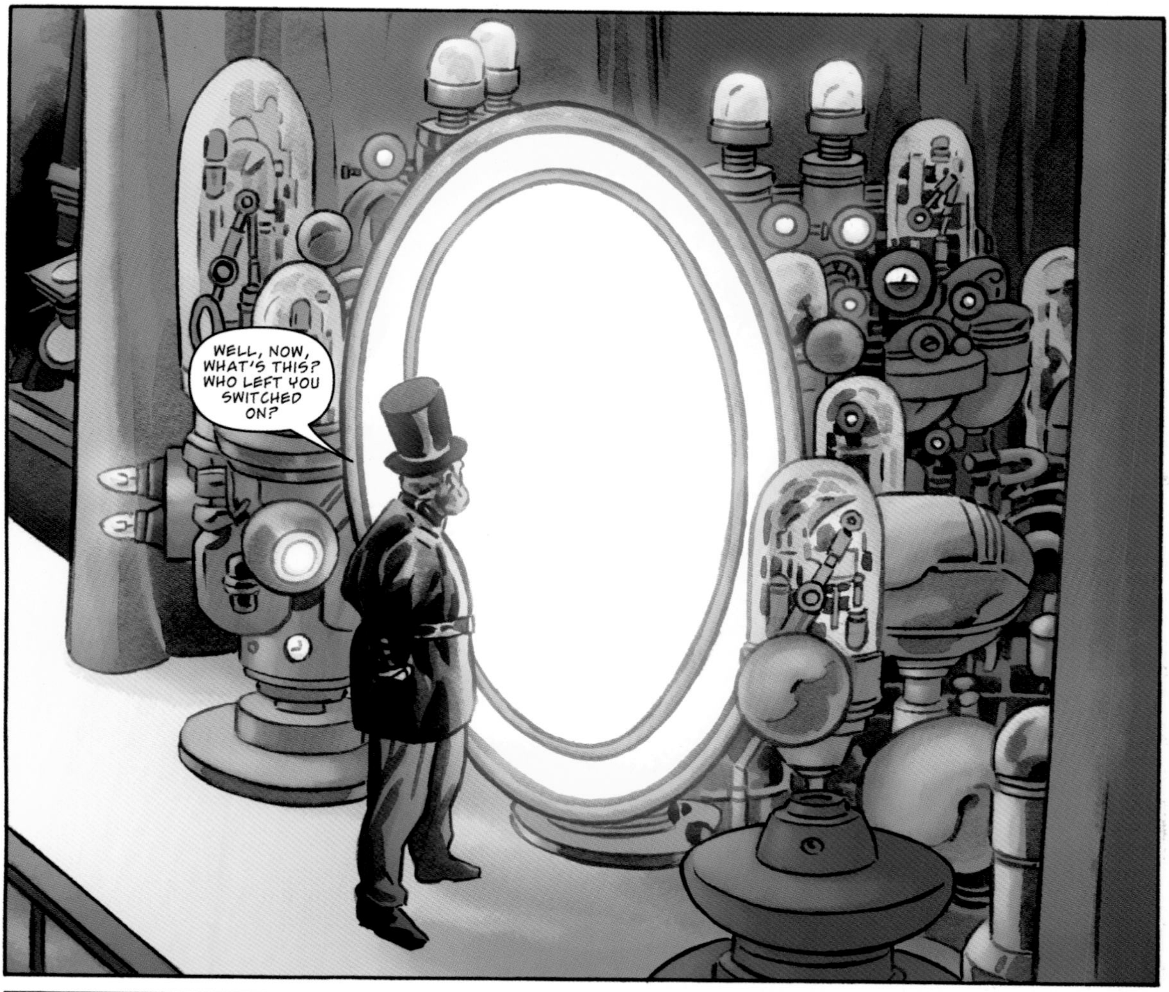
WELL, NOW, WHAT'S THIS? WHO LEFT YOU SWITCHED ON?

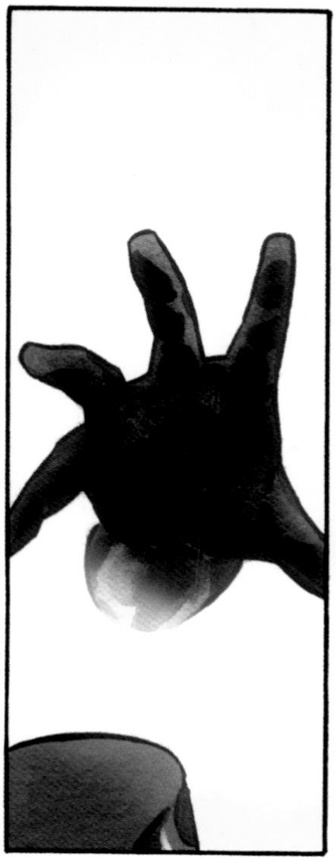

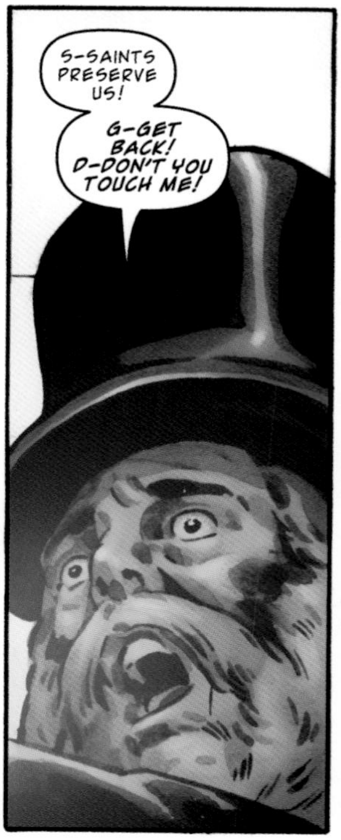
S-SAINTS PRESERVE US!
G-GET BACK! D-DON'T YOU TOUCH ME!

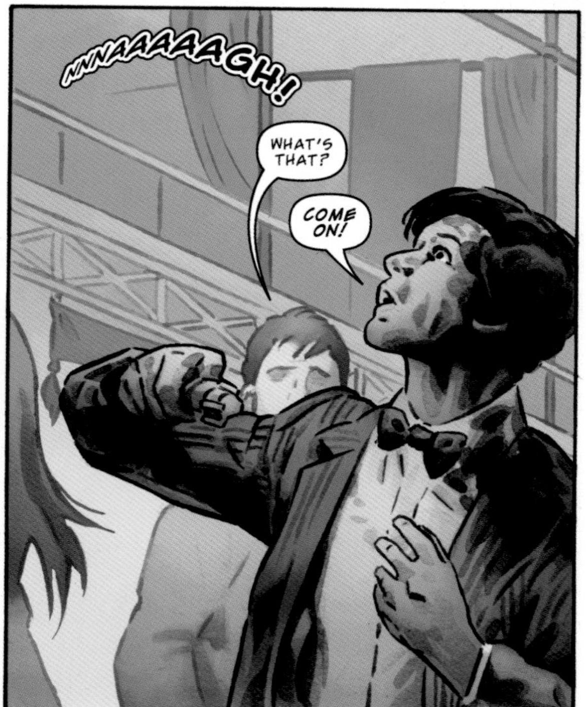
NNNAAAAAAGH!
WHAT'S THAT?
COME ON!

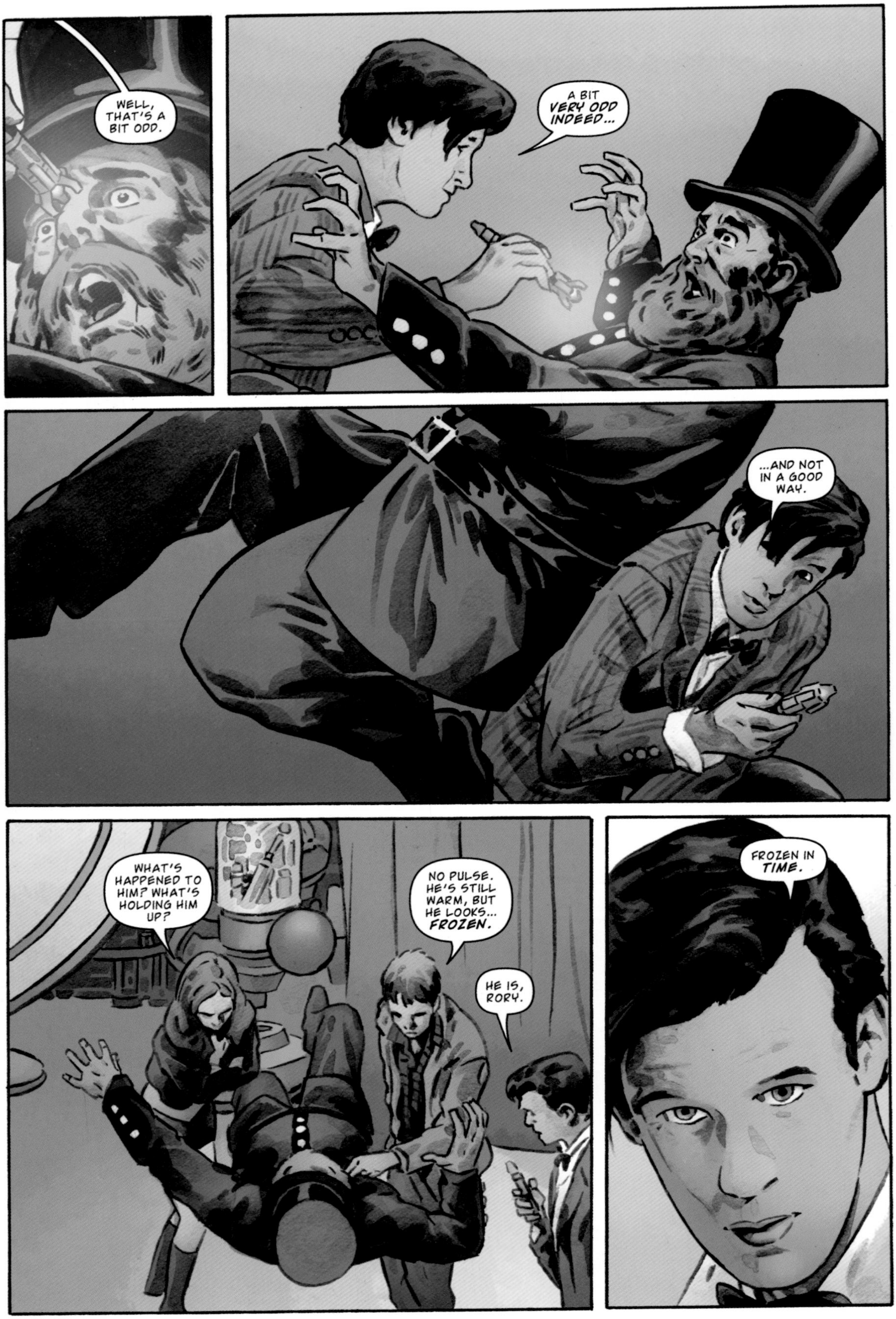
WELL, THAT'S A BIT ODD.
A BIT VERY ODD INDEED...
...AND NOT IN A GOOD WAY.
WHAT'S HAPPENED TO HIM? WHAT'S HOLDING HIM UP?
NO PULSE. HE'S STILL WARM, BUT HE LOOKS... FROZEN.
HE IS, RORY.
FROZEN IN TIME.

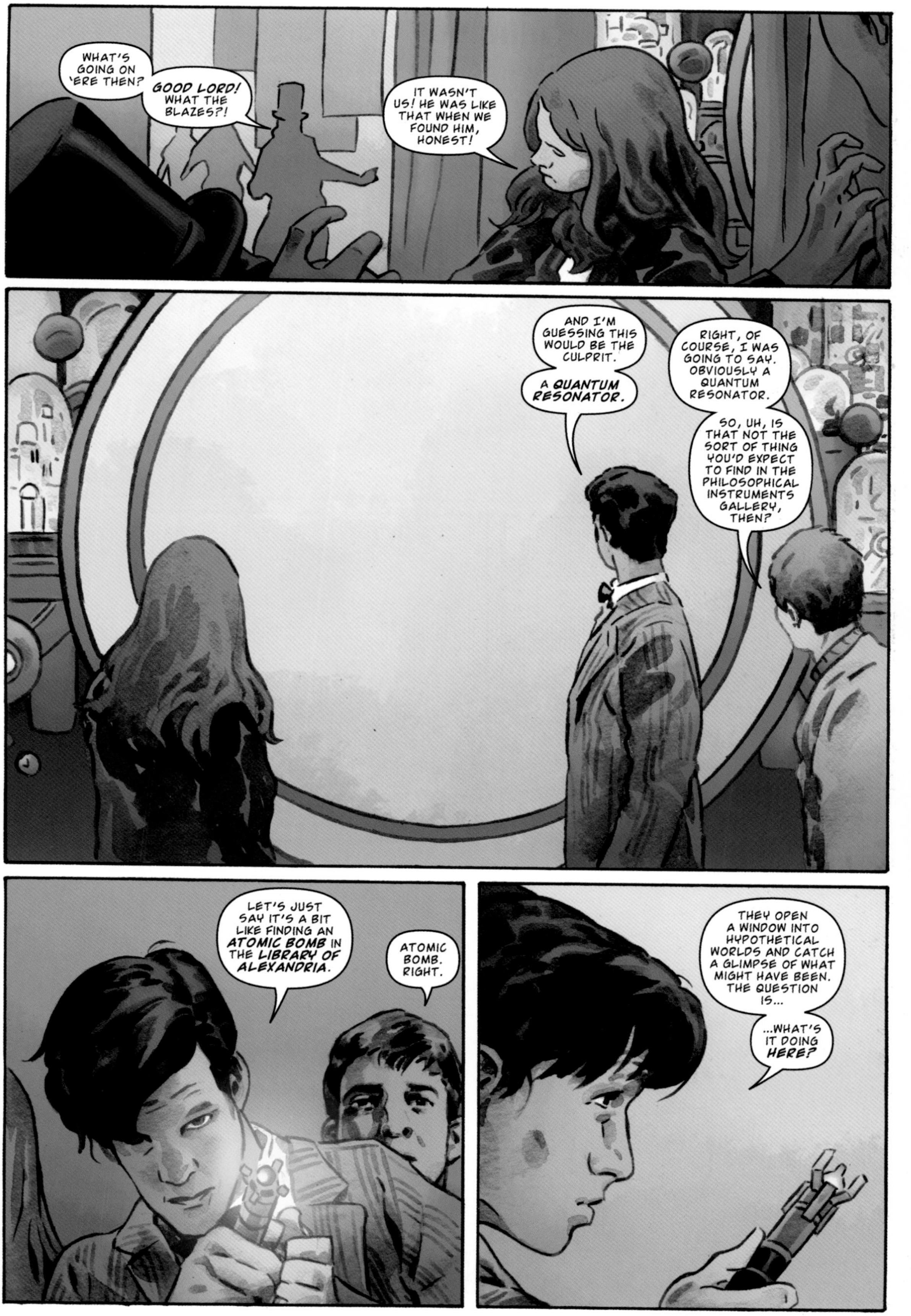
WHAT'S GOING ON 'ERE THEN?
GOOD LORD! WHAT THE BLAZES?!
IT WASN'T US! HE WAS LIKE THAT WHEN WE FOUND HIM, HONEST!
AND I'M GUESSING THIS WOULD BE THE CULPRIT.
A QUANTUM RESONATOR.
RIGHT, OF COURSE, I WAS GOING TO SAY. OBVIOUSLY A QUANTUM RESONATOR.
SO, UH, IS THAT NOT THE SORT OF THING YOU'D EXPECT TO FIND IN THE PHILOSOPHICAL INSTRUMENTS GALLERY, THEN?
LET'S JUST SAY IT'S A BIT LIKE FINDING AN ATOMIC BOMB IN THE LIBRARY OF ALEXANDRIA.
ATOMIC BOMB. RIGHT.
THEY OPEN A WINDOW INTO HYPOTHETICAL WORLDS AND CATCH A GLIMPSE OF WHAT MIGHT HAVE BEEN. THE QUESTION IS...
...WHAT'S IT DOING HERE?

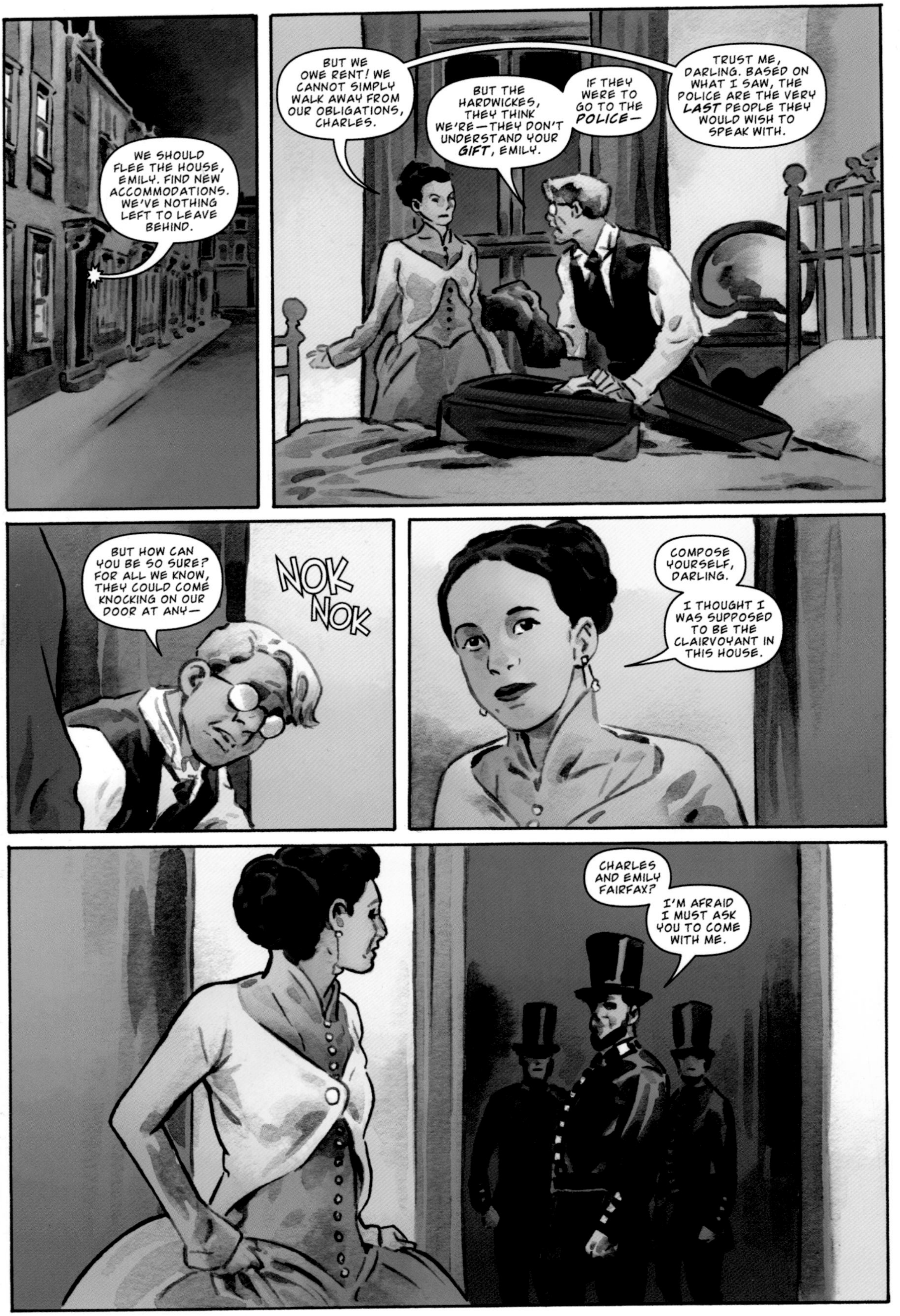
WE SHOULD FLEE THE HOUSE, EMILY. FIND NEW ACCOMMODATIONS. WE'VE NOTHING LEFT TO LEAVE BEHIND.
BUT WE OWE RENT! WE CANNOT SIMPLY WALK AWAY FROM OUR OBLIGATIONS, CHARLES.
BUT THE HARDWICKES, THEY THINK WE'RE—THEY DON'T UNDERSTAND YOUR GIFT, EMILY.
IF THEY WERE TO GO TO THE POLICE—
TRUST ME, DARLING. BASED ON WHAT I SAW, THE POLICE ARE THE VERY LAST PEOPLE THEY WOULD WISH TO SPEAK WITH.
BUT HOW CAN YOU BE SO SURE? FOR ALL WE KNOW, THEY COULD COME KNOCKING ON OUR DOOR AT ANY—
NOK NOK
COMPOSE YOURSELF, DARLING.
I THOUGHT I WAS SUPPOSED TO BE THE CLAIRVOYANT IN THIS HOUSE.
CHARLES AND EMILY FAIRFAX?
I'M AFRAID I MUST ASK YOU TO COME WITH ME.

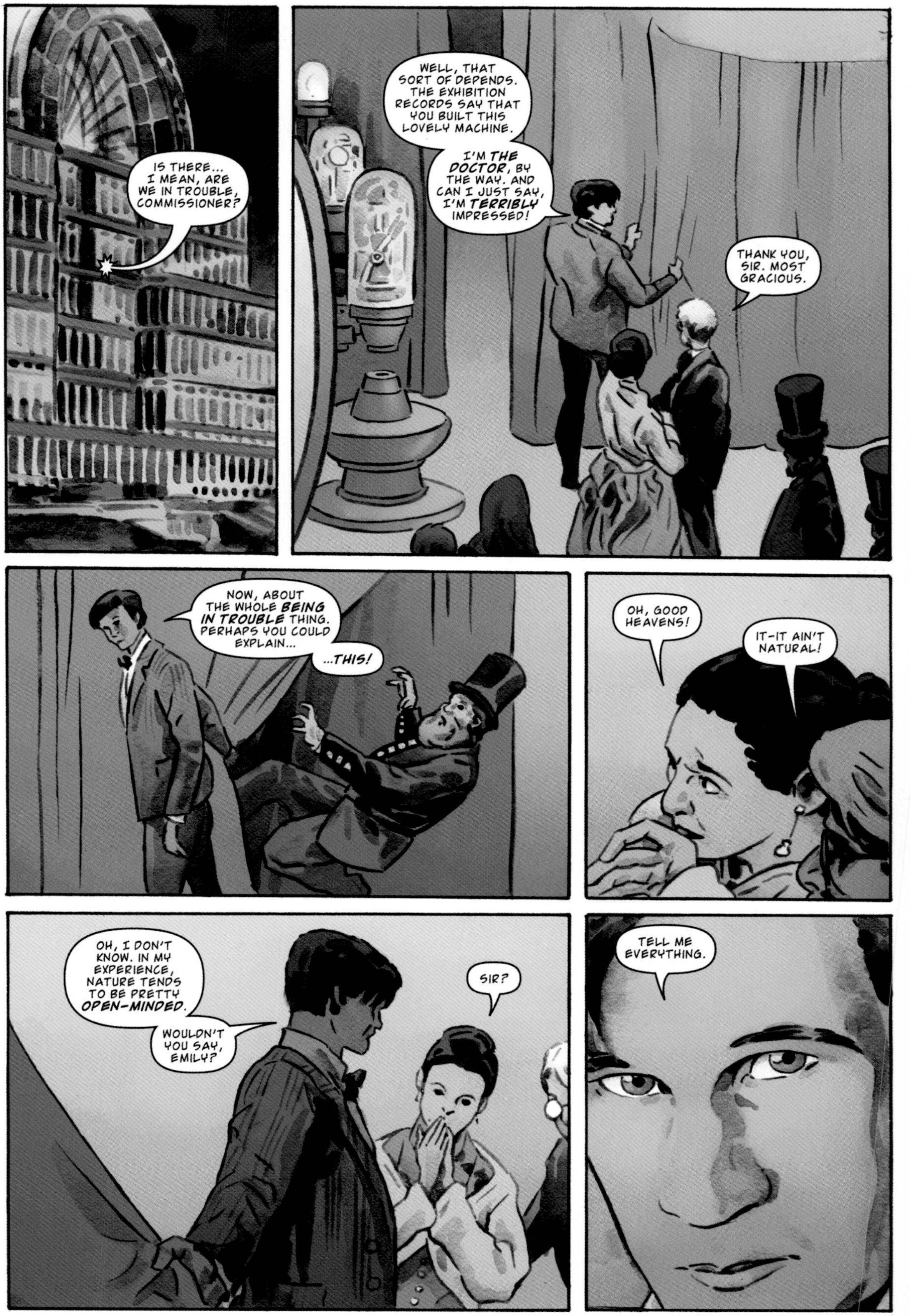
IS THERE... I MEAN, ARE WE IN TROUBLE, COMMISSIONER?
WELL, THAT SORT OF DEPENDS. THE EXHIBITION RECORDS SAY THAT YOU BUILT THIS LOVELY MACHINE.
I'M THE DOCTOR, BY THE WAY. AND CAN I JUST SAY, I'M TERRIBLY IMPRESSED!
THANK YOU, SIR. MOST GRACIOUS.
NOW, ABOUT THE WHOLE BEING IN TROUBLE THING. PERHAPS YOU COULD EXPLAIN...
...THIS!
OH, GOOD HEAVENS!
IT-IT AIN'T NATURAL!
OH, I DON'T KNOW. IN MY EXPERIENCE, NATURE TENDS TO BE PRETTY OPEN-MINDED.
WOULDN'T YOU SAY, EMILY?
SIR?
TELL ME EVERYTHING.

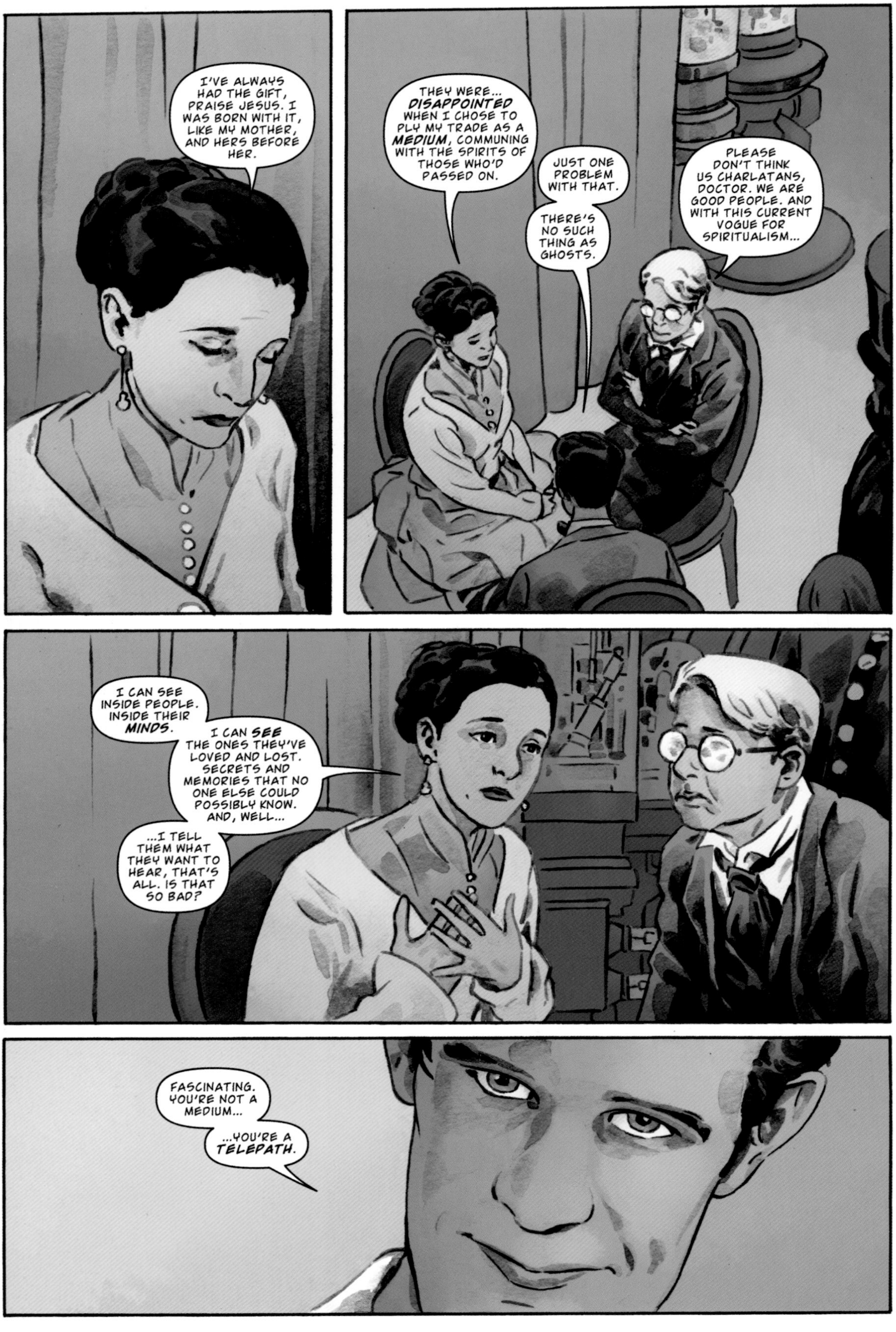

I'VE ALWAYS HAD THE GIFT, PRAISE JESUS. I WAS BORN WITH IT, LIKE MY MOTHER, AND HERS BEFORE HER.
THEY WERE... DISAPPOINTED WHEN I CHOSE TO PLY MY TRADE AS A MEDIUM, COMMUNING WITH THE SPIRITS OF THOSE WHO'D PASSED ON.
JUST ONE PROBLEM WITH THAT.
THERE'S NO SUCH THING AS GHOSTS.
PLEASE DON'T THINK US CHARLATANS, DOCTOR. WE ARE GOOD PEOPLE. AND WITH THIS CURRENT VOGUE FOR SPIRITUALISM...
I CAN SEE INSIDE PEOPLE. INSIDE THEIR MINDS.
I CAN SEE THE ONES THEY'VE LOVED AND LOST. SECRETS AND MEMORIES THAT NO ONE ELSE COULD POSSIBLY KNOW. AND, WELL...
...I TELL THEM WHAT THEY WANT TO HEAR, THAT'S ALL. IS THAT SO BAD?
FASCINATING. YOU'RE NOT A MEDIUM...
...YOU'RE A TELEPATH.

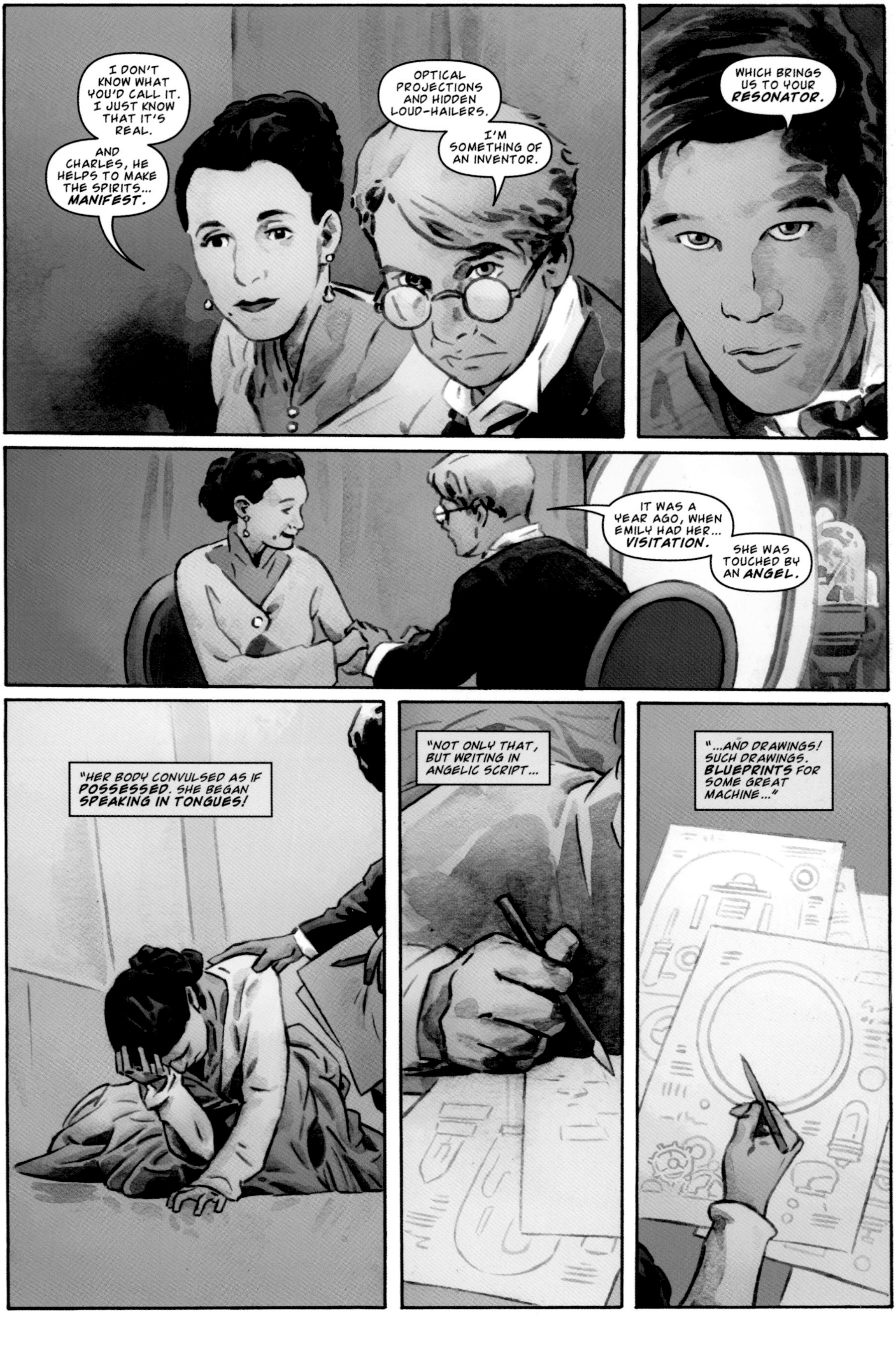
I DON'T KNOW WHAT YOU'D CALL IT. I JUST KNOW THAT IT'S REAL.
AND CHARLES, HE HELPS TO MAKE THE SPIRITS... MANIFEST.
OPTICAL PROJECTIONS AND HIDDEN LOUD-HAILERS.
I'M SOMETHING OF AN INVENTOR.
WHICH BRINGS US TO YOUR RESONATOR.
IT WAS A YEAR AGO, WHEN EMILY HAD HER... VISITATION.
SHE WAS TOUCHED BY AN ANGEL.
"HER BODY CONVULSED AS IF POSSESSED. SHE BEGAN SPEAKING IN TONGUES!
"NOT ONLY THAT, BUT WRITING IN ANGELIC SCRIPT...
"...AND DRAWINGS! SUCH DRAWINGS. BLUEPRINTS FOR SOME GREAT MACHINE..."

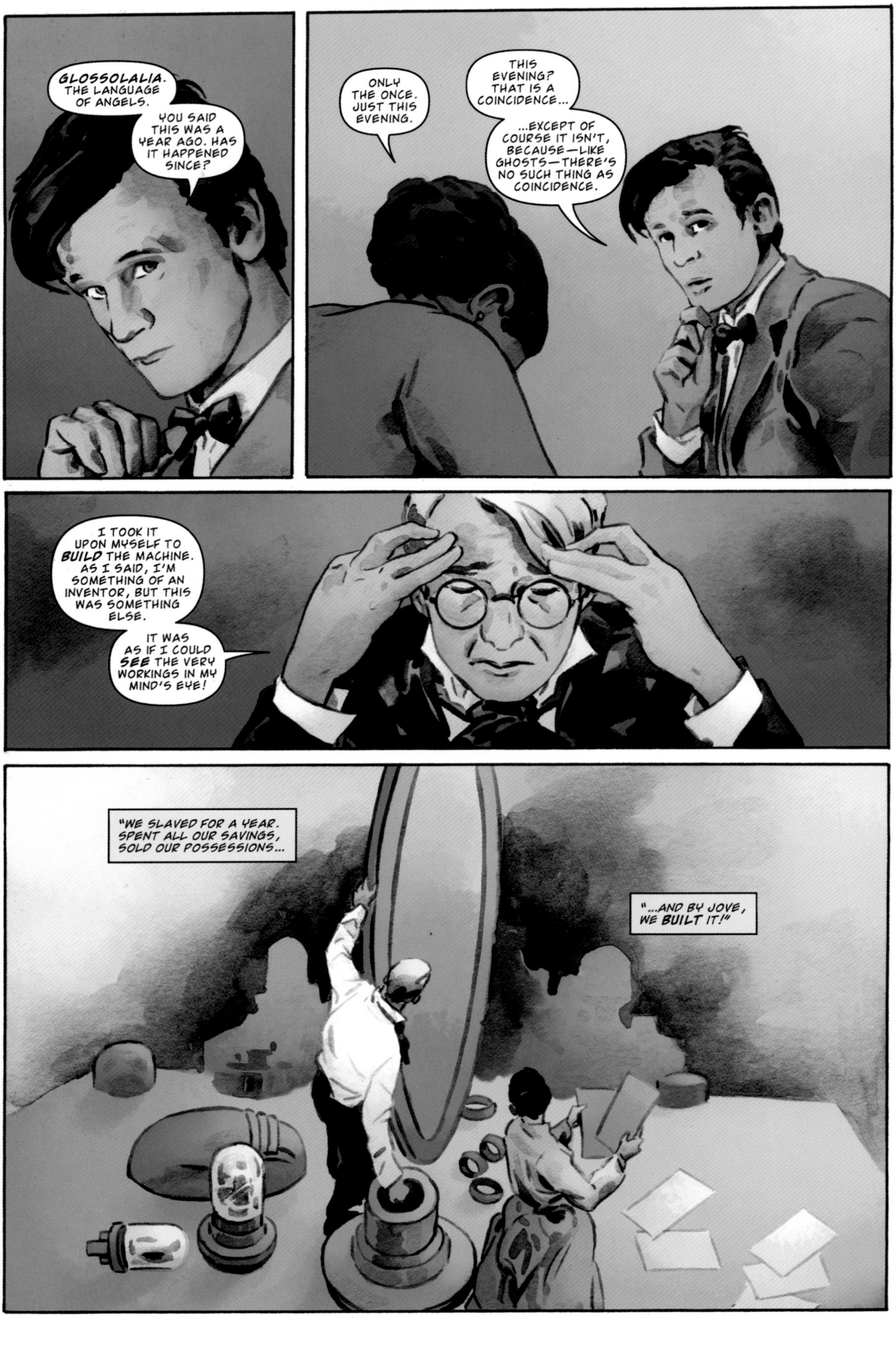
GLOSSOLALIA. THE LANGUAGE OF ANGELS.
YOU SAID THIS WAS A YEAR AGO. HAS IT HAPPENED SINCE?
ONLY THE ONCE. JUST THIS EVENING.
THIS EVENING? THAT IS A COINCIDENCE...
...EXCEPT OF COURSE IT ISN'T, BECAUSE—LIKE GHOSTS—THERE'S NO SUCH THING AS COINCIDENCE.
I TOOK IT UPON MYSELF TO BUILD THE MACHINE. AS I SAID, I'M SOMETHING OF AN INVENTOR, BUT THIS WAS SOMETHING ELSE.
IT WAS AS IF I COULD SEE THE VERY WORKINGS IN MY MIND'S EYE!
"WE SLAVED FOR A YEAR. SPENT ALL OUR SAVINGS, SOLD OUR POSSESSIONS...
"...AND BY JOVE, WE BUILT IT!"

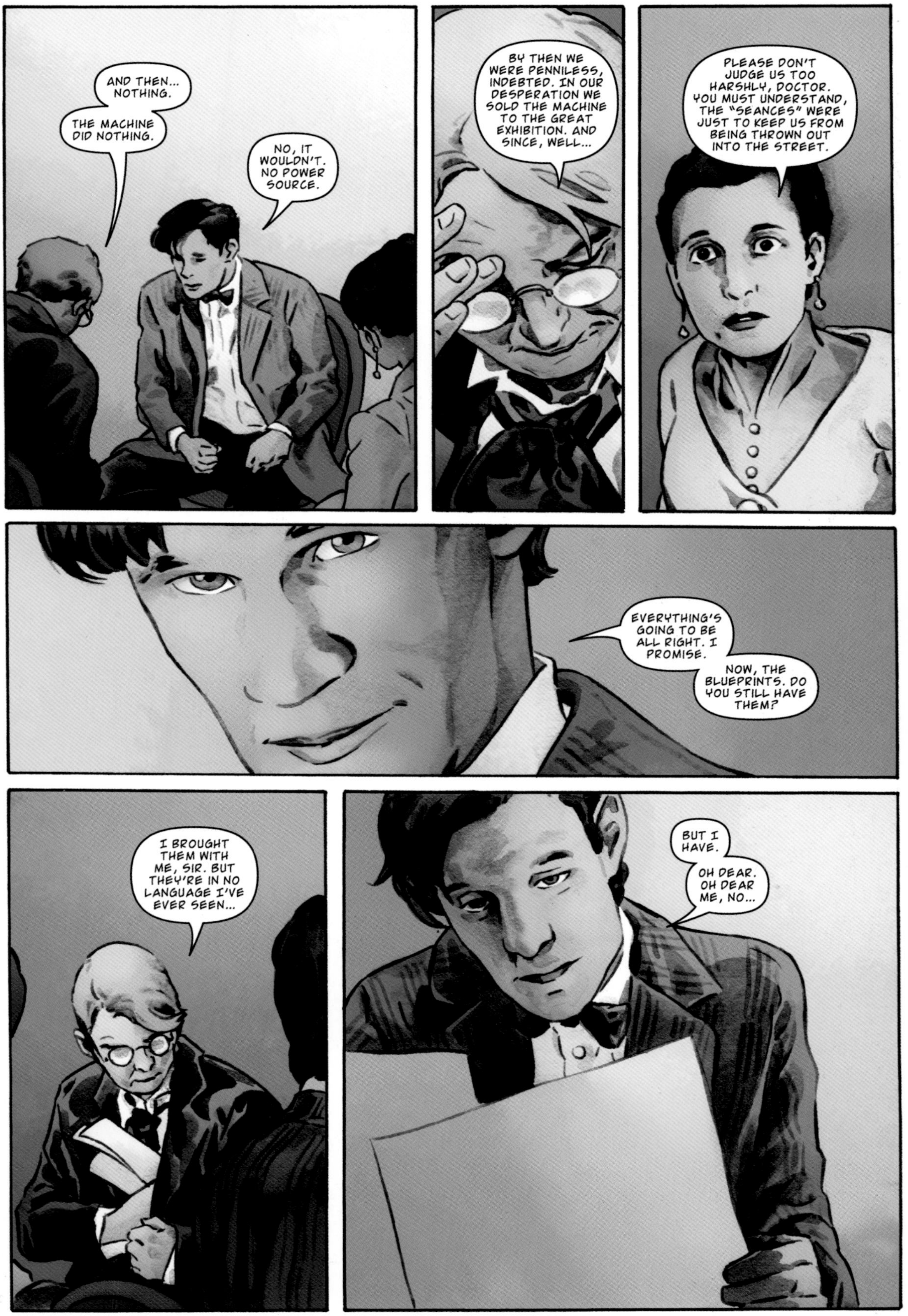
AND THEN... NOTHING.
THE MACHINE DID NOTHING.
NO, IT WOULDN'T. NO POWER SOURCE.
BY THEN WE WERE PENNILESS, INDEBTED. IN OUR DESPERATION WE SOLD THE MACHINE TO THE GREAT EXHIBITION. AND SINCE, WELL...
PLEASE DON'T JUDGE US TOO HARSHLY, DOCTOR. YOU MUST UNDERSTAND, THE "SEANCES" WERE JUST TO KEEP US FROM BEING THROWN OUT INTO THE STREET.
EVERYTHING'S GOING TO BE ALL RIGHT. I PROMISE.
NOW, THE BLUEPRINTS. DO YOU STILL HAVE THEM?
I BROUGHT THEM WITH ME, SIR. BUT THEY'RE IN NO LANGUAGE I'VE EVER SEEN...
BUT I HAVE.
OH DEAR. OH DEAR ME, NO...

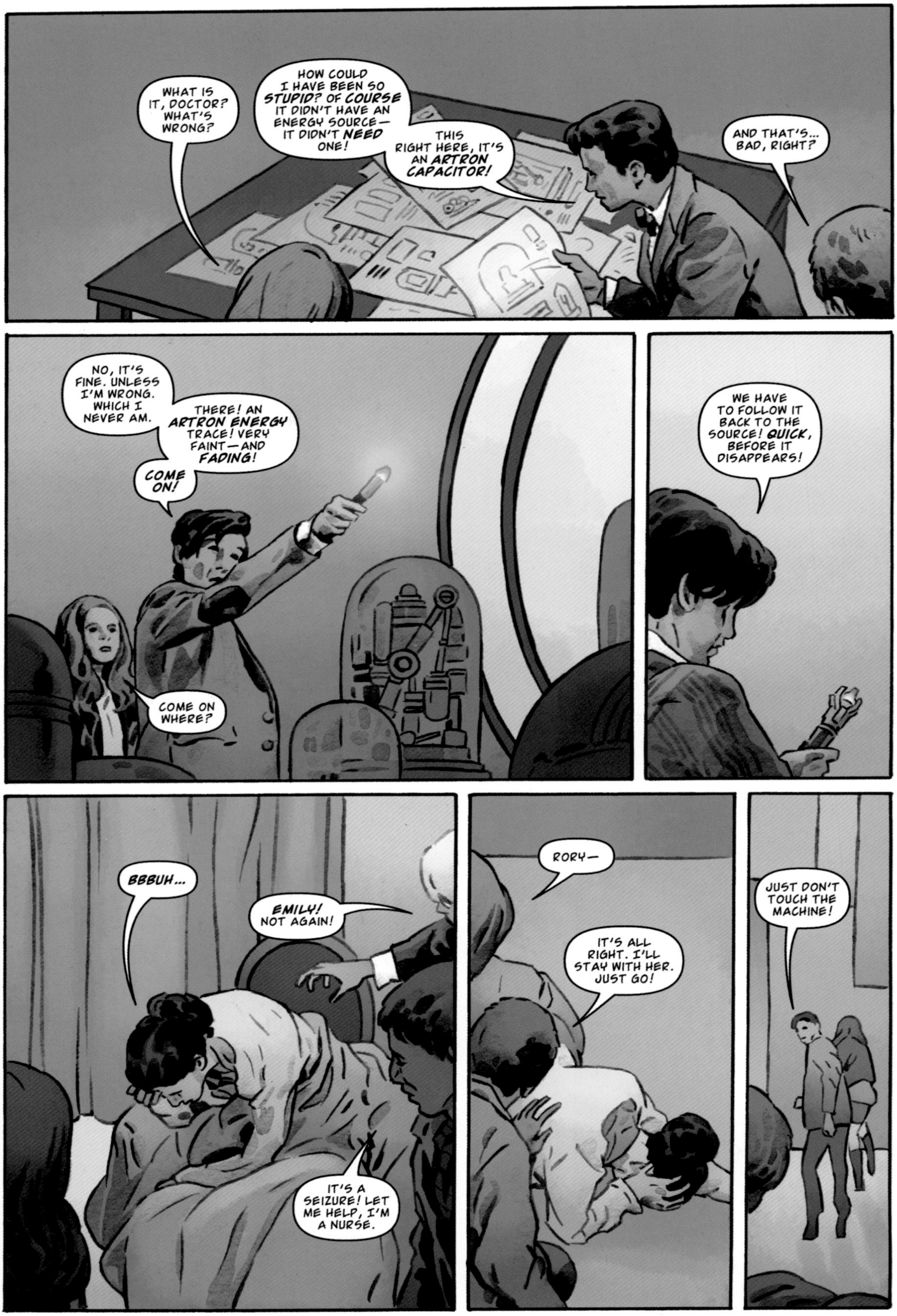
WHAT IS IT, DOCTOR? WHAT'S WRONG?
HOW COULD I HAVE BEEN SO STUPID? OF COURSE IT DIDN'T HAVE AN ENERGY SOURCE— IT DIDN'T NEED ONE!
THIS RIGHT HERE, IT'S AN ARTRON CAPACITOR!
AND THAT'S... BAD, RIGHT?
NO, IT'S FINE. UNLESS I'M WRONG. WHICH I NEVER AM.
THERE! AN ARTRON ENERGY TRACE! VERY FAINT—AND FADING!
COME ON!
COME ON WHERE?
WE HAVE TO FOLLOW IT BACK TO THE SOURCE! QUICK, BEFORE IT DISAPPEARS!
BBBUH...
EMILY! NOT AGAIN!
IT'S A SEIZURE! LET ME HELP, I'M A NURSE.
RORY—
IT'S ALL RIGHT. I'LL STAY WITH HER. JUST GO!
JUST DON'T TOUCH THE MACHINE!

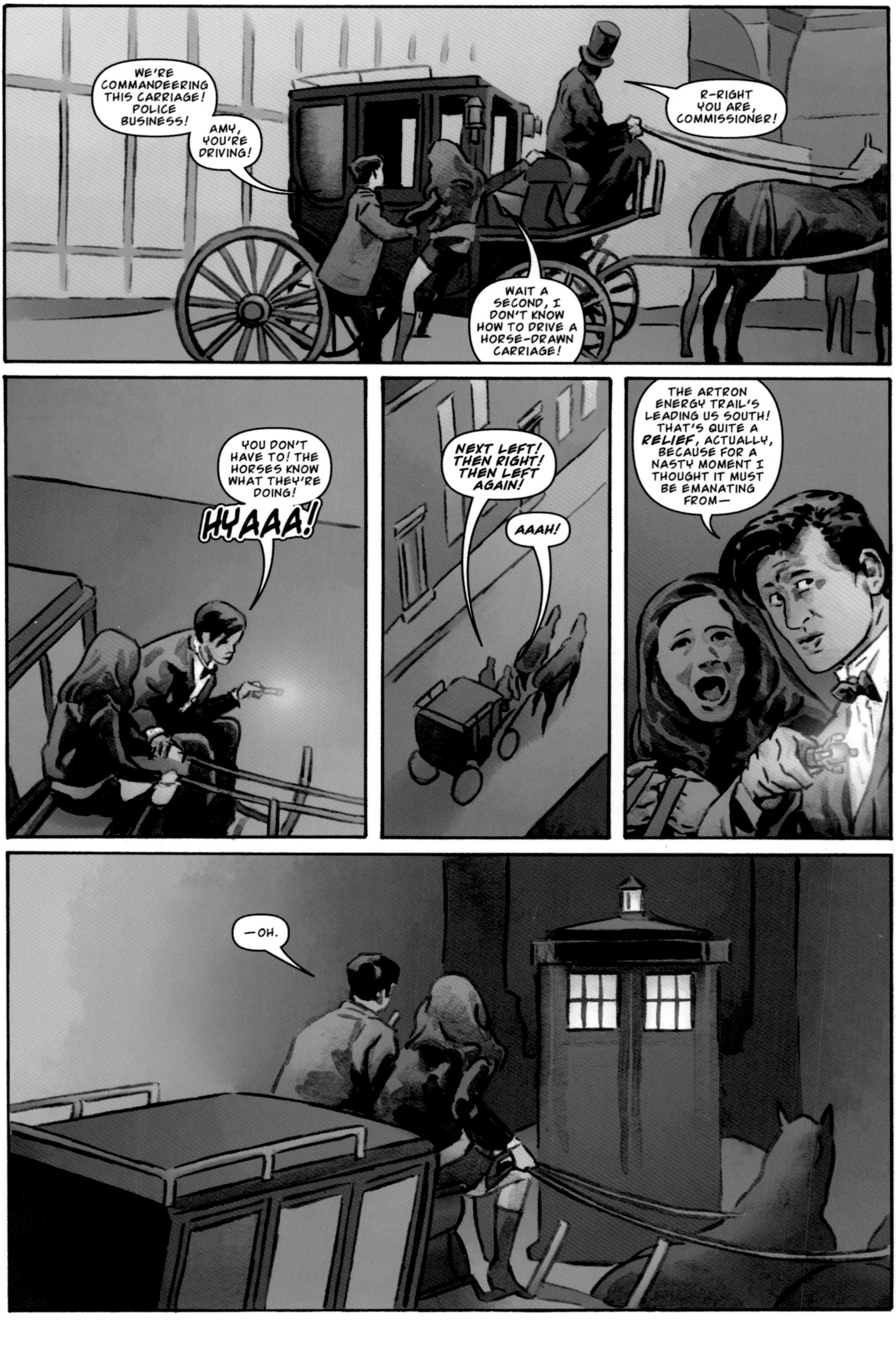
WE'RE COMMANDEERING THIS CARRIAGE! POLICE BUSINESS!
AMY, YOU'RE DRIVING!
R-RIGHT YOU ARE, COMMISSIONER!
WAIT A SECOND, I DON'T KNOW HOW TO DRIVE A HORSE-DRAWN CARRIAGE!
YOU DON'T HAVE TO! THE HORSES KNOW WHAT THEY'RE DOING!
HYAAA!
NEXT LEFT! THEN RIGHT! THEN LEFT AGAIN!
AAAH!
THE ARTRON ENERGY TRAIL'S LEADING US SOUTH! THAT'S QUITE A RELIEF, ACTUALLY, BECAUSE FOR A NASTY MOMENT I THOUGHT IT MUST BE EMANATING FROM—
—OH.

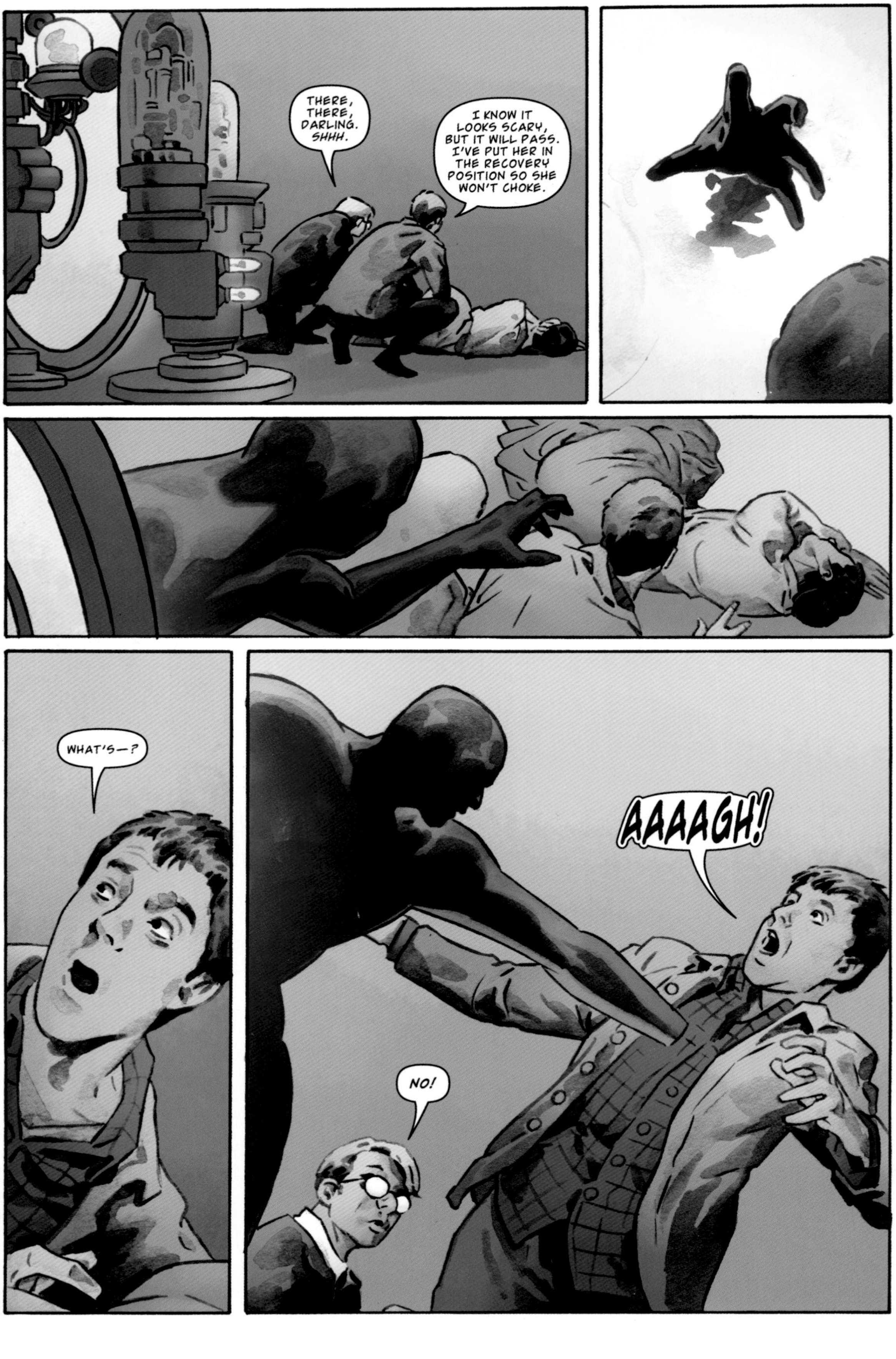
THERE, THERE, DARLING. SHHH.
I KNOW IT LOOKS SCARY, BUT IT WILL PASS. I'VE PUT HER IN THE RECOVERY POSITION SO SHE WON'T CHOKE.
WHAT'S—?
AAAAGH!
NO!

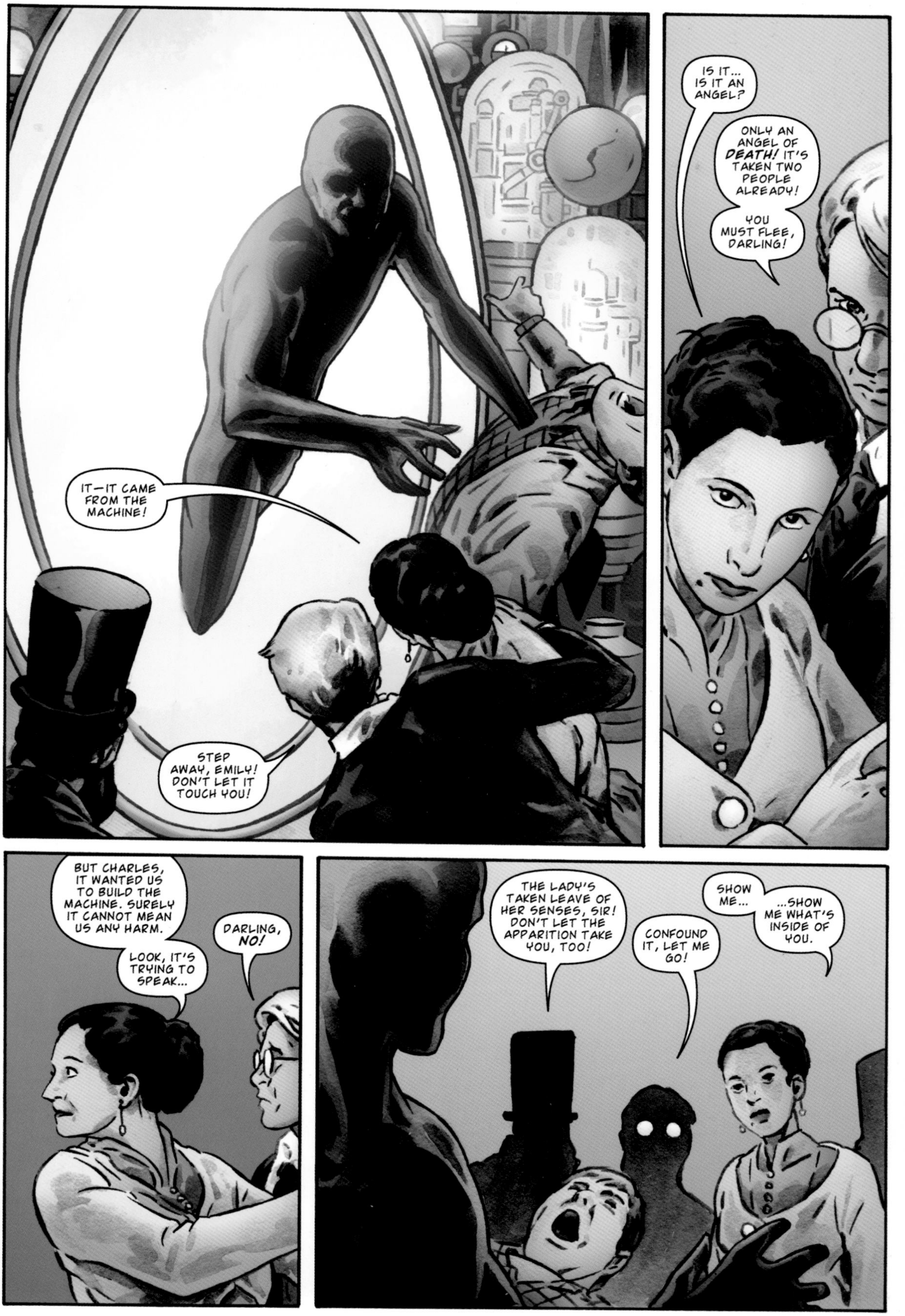
IT—IT CAME FROM THE MACHINE!
STEP AWAY, EMILY! DON'T LET IT TOUCH YOU!
IS IT... IS IT AN ANGEL?
ONLY AN ANGEL OF DEATH! IT'S TAKEN TWO PEOPLE ALREADY!
YOU MUST FLEE, DARLING!
BUT CHARLES, IT WANTED US TO BUILD THE MACHINE. SURELY IT CANNOT MEAN US ANY HARM.
LOOK, IT'S TRYING TO SPEAK...
DARLING, NO!
THE LADY'S TAKEN LEAVE OF HER SENSES, SIR! DON'T LET THE APPARITION TAKE YOU, TOO!
CONFOUND IT, LET ME GO!
SHOW ME...
...SHOW ME WHAT'S INSIDE OF YOU.

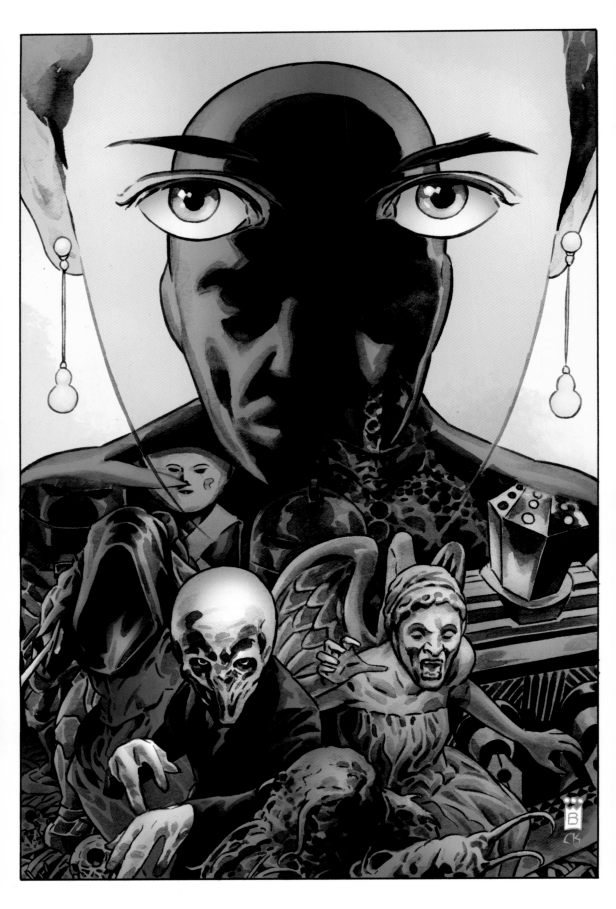

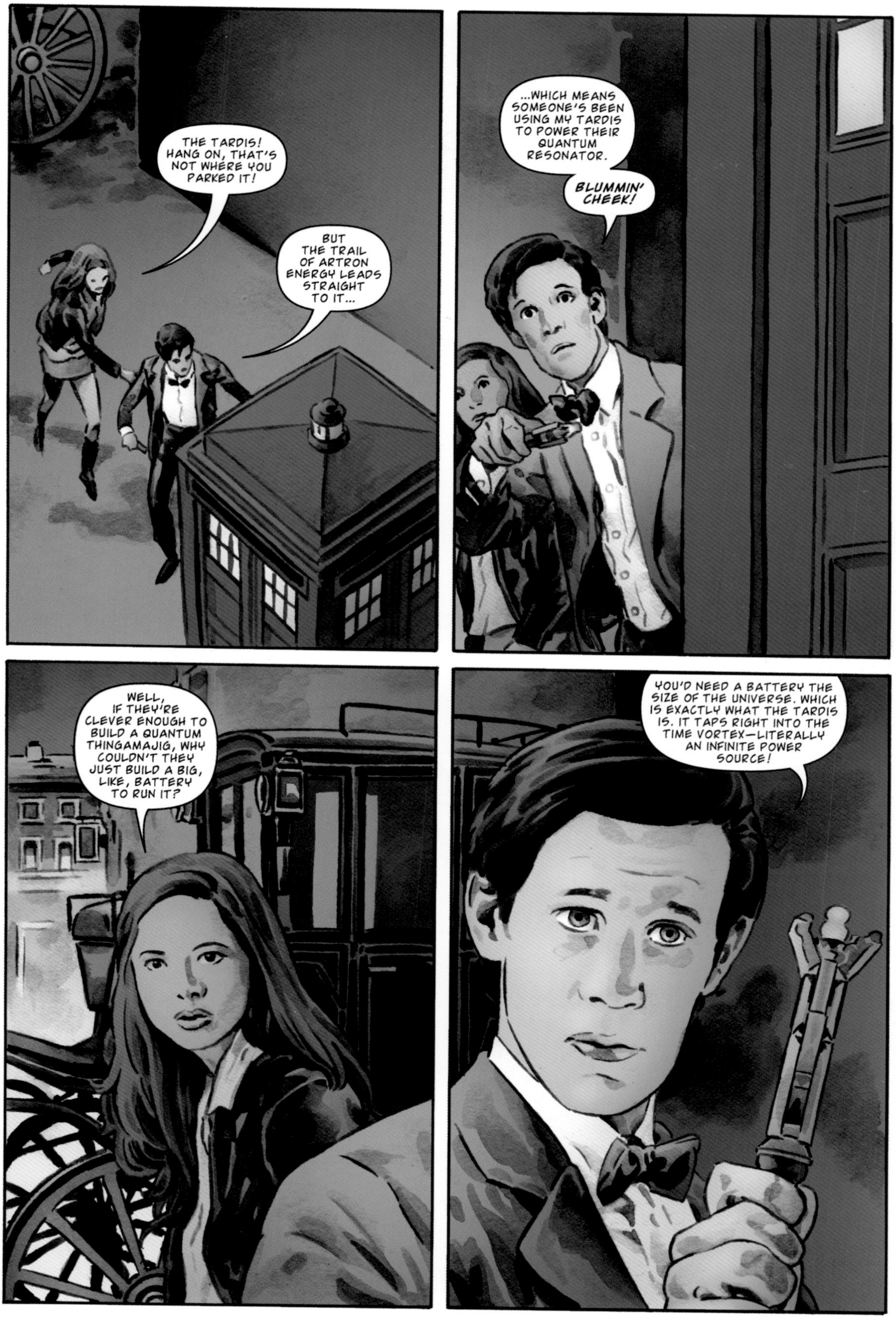
THE TARDIS! HANG ON, THAT'S NOT WHERE YOU PARKED IT!
BUT THE TRAIL OF ARTRON ENERGY LEADS STRAIGHT TO IT...
...WHICH MEANS SOMEONE'S BEEN USING MY TARDIS TO POWER THEIR QUANTUM RESONATOR.
BLUMMIN' CHEEK!
WELL, IF THEY'RE CLEVER ENOUGH TO BUILD A QUANTUM THINGAMAJIG, WHY COULDN'T THEY JUST BUILD A BIG, LIKE, BATTERY TO RUN IT?
YOU'D NEED A BATTERY THE SIZE OF THE UNIVERSE. WHICH IS EXACTLY WHAT THE TARDIS IS. IT TAPS RIGHT INTO THE TIME VORTEX—LITERALLY AN INFINITE POWER SOURCE!

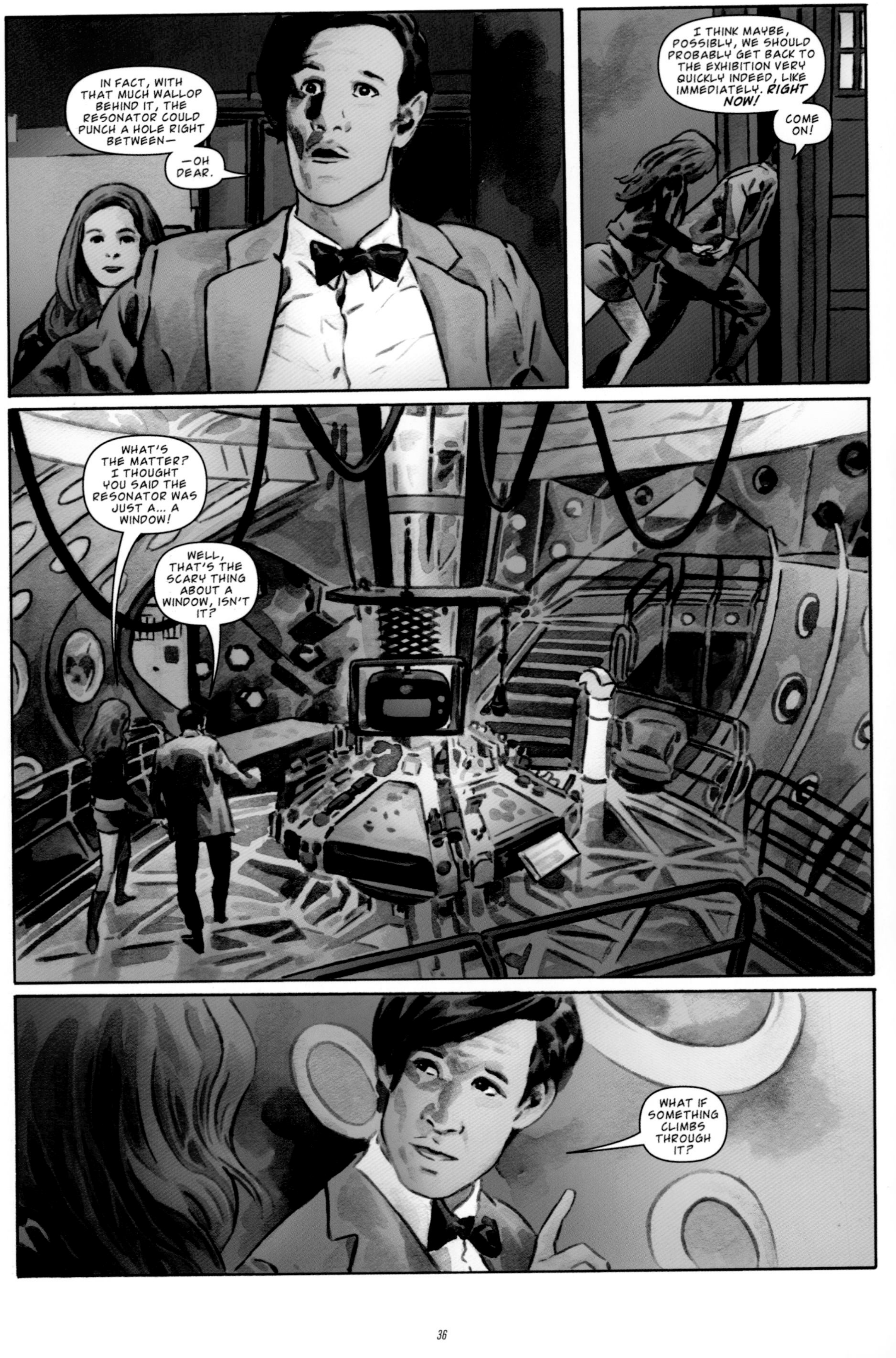
IN FACT, WITH THAT MUCH WALLOP BEHIND IT, THE RESONATOR COULD PUNCH A HOLE RIGHT BETWEEN—
—OH DEAR.
I THINK MAYBE, POSSIBLY, WE SHOULD PROBABLY GET BACK TO THE EXHIBITION VERY QUICKLY INDEED, LIKE IMMEDIATELY. **RIGHT NOW!**
COME ON!
WHAT'S THE MATTER? I THOUGHT YOU SAID THE RESONATOR WAS JUST A... A WINDOW!
WELL, THAT'S THE SCARY THING ABOUT A WINDOW, ISN'T IT?
WHAT IF SOMETHING CLIMBS THROUGH IT?

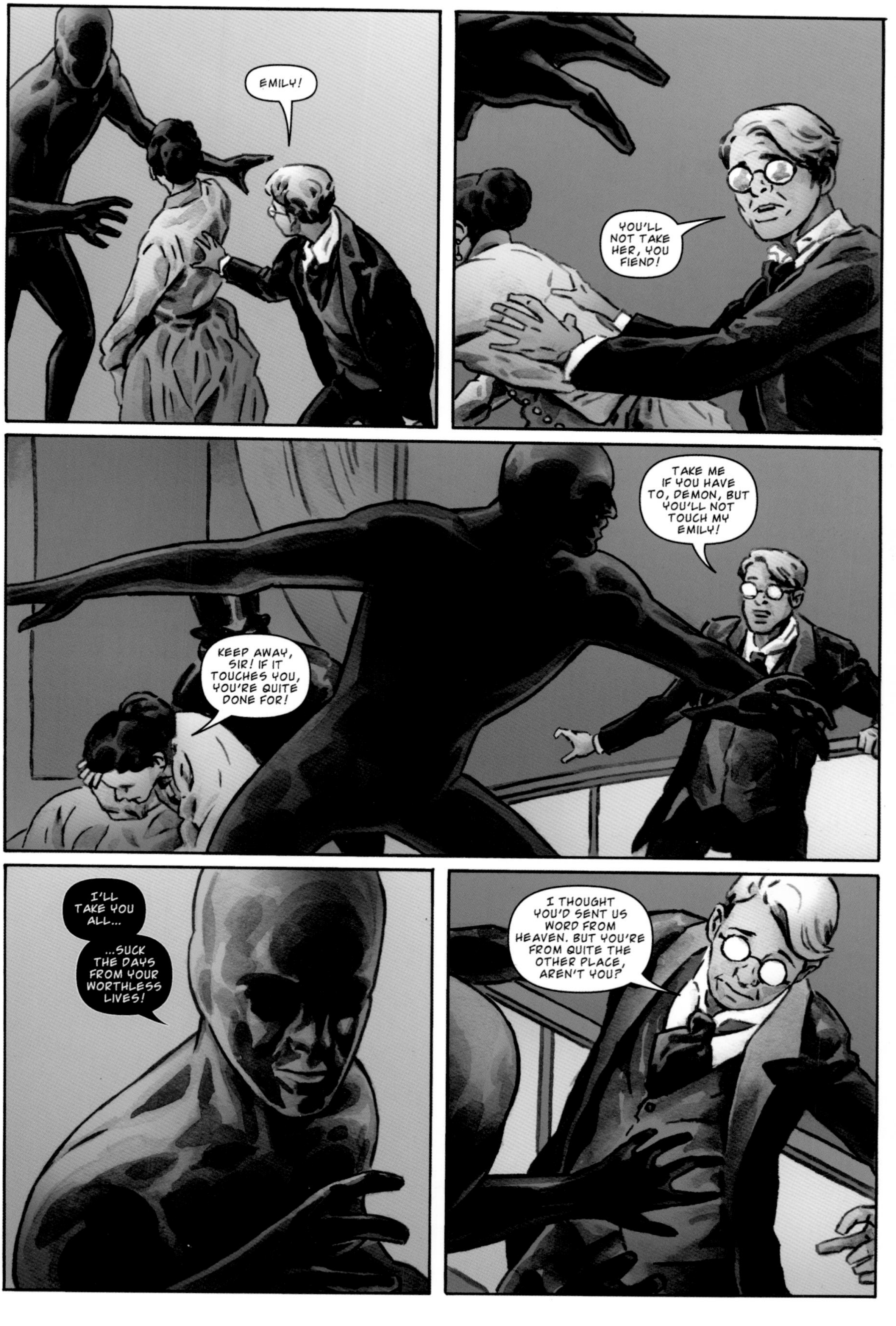
EMILY!
YOU'LL NOT TAKE HER, YOU FIEND!
TAKE ME IF YOU HAVE TO, DEMON, BUT YOU'LL NOT TOUCH MY EMILY!
KEEP AWAY, SIR! IF IT TOUCHES YOU, YOU'RE QUITE DONE FOR!
I'LL TAKE YOU ALL...
...SUCK THE DAYS FROM YOUR WORTHLESS LIVES!
I THOUGHT YOU'D SENT US WORD FROM HEAVEN. BUT YOU'RE FROM QUITE THE OTHER PLACE, AREN'T YOU?

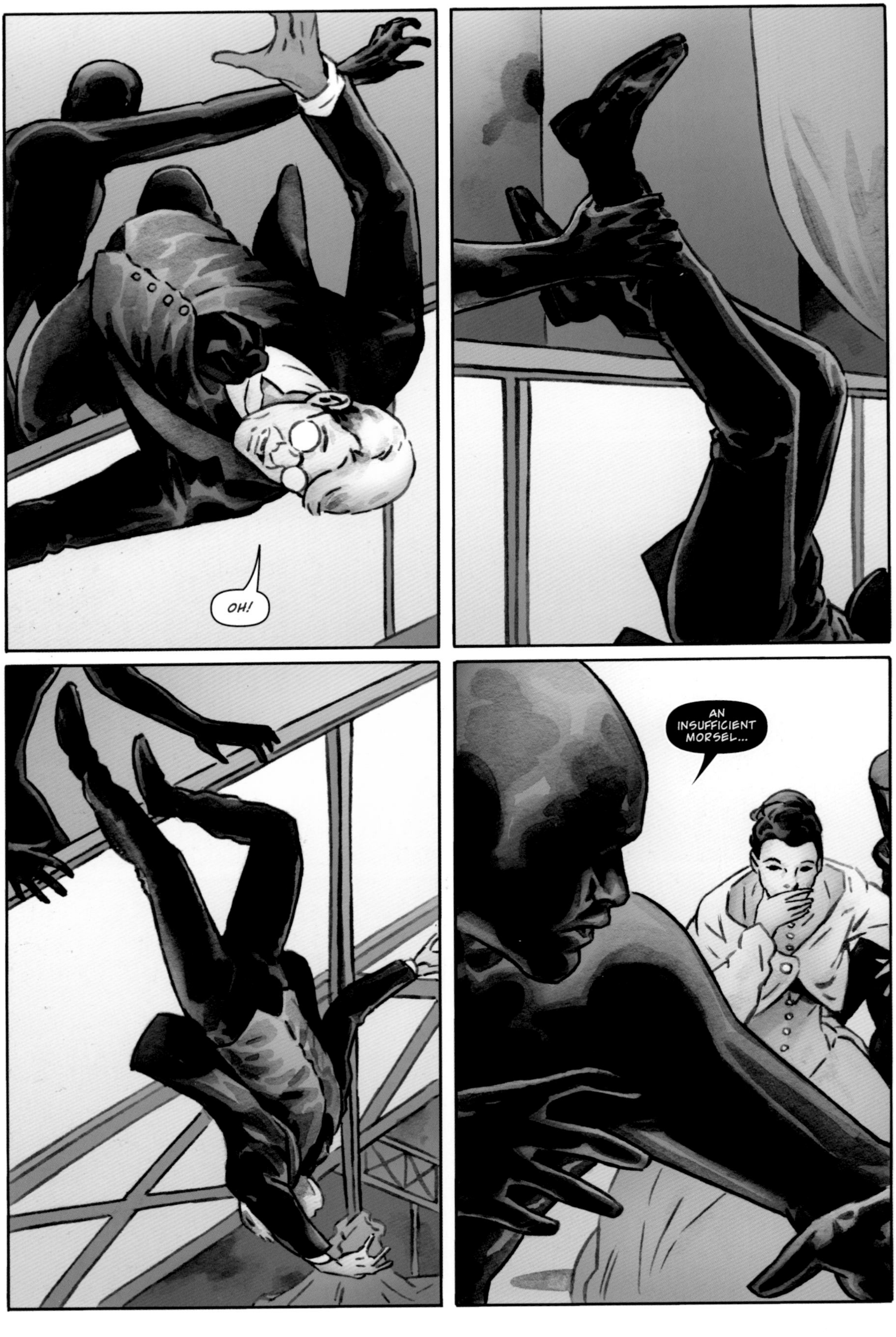
OH!
AN INSUFFICIENT MORSEL...

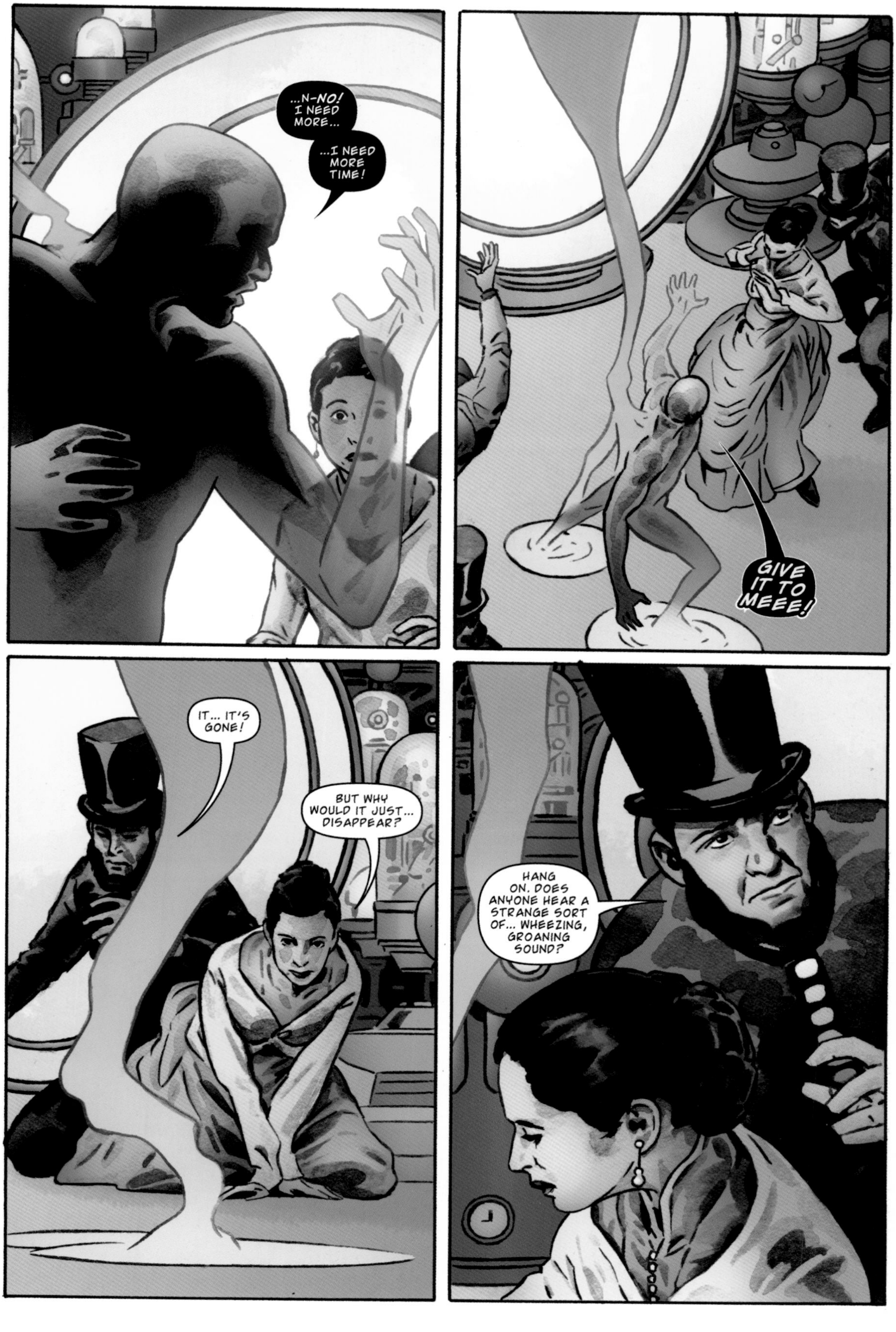
...N-NO! I NEED MORE...
...I NEED MORE TIME!
GIVE IT TO MEEE!
IT... IT'S GONE!
BUT WHY WOULD IT JUST... DISAPPEAR?
HANG ON. DOES ANYONE HEAR A STRANGE SORT OF... WHEEZING, GROANING SOUND?

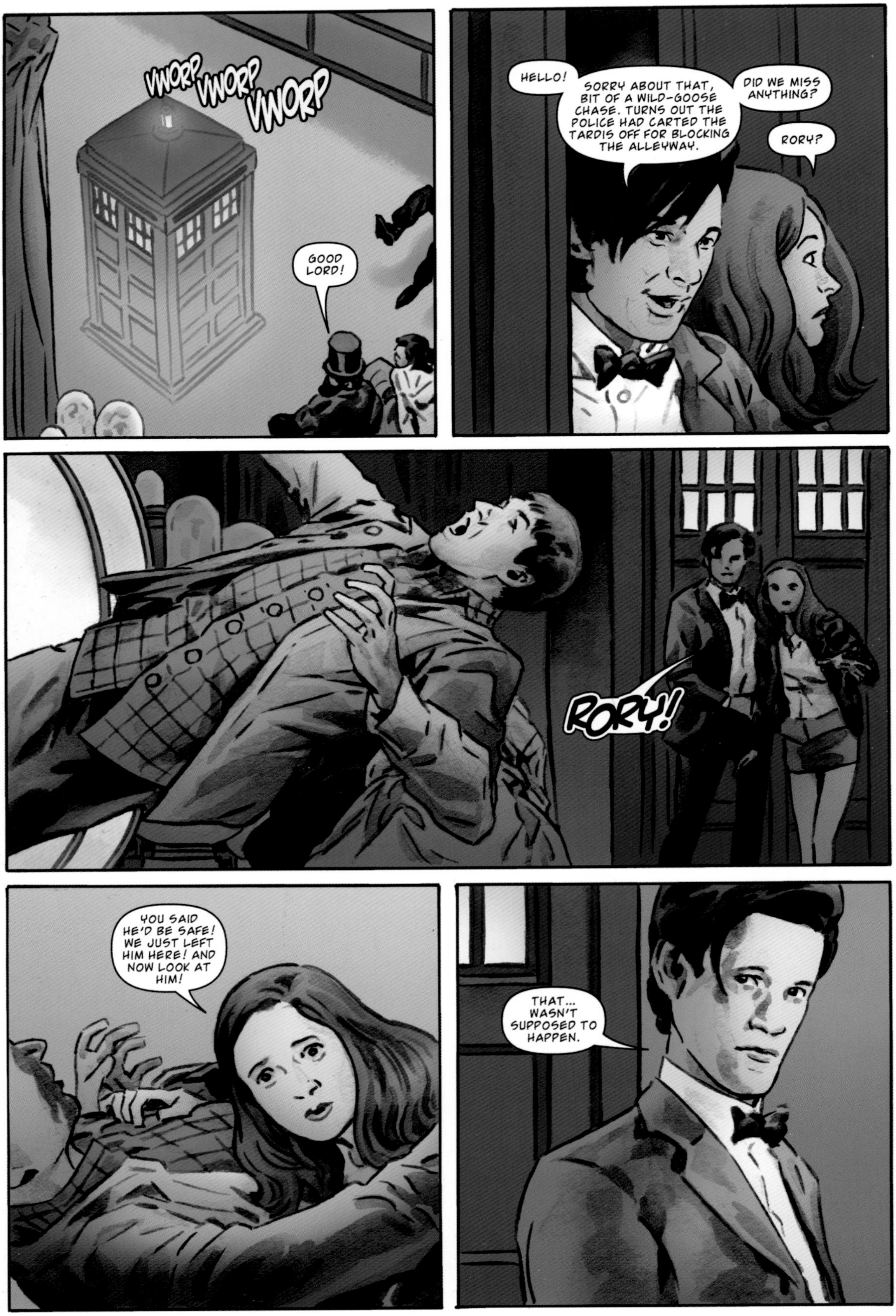
VWORP VWORP VWORP
GOOD LORD!
HELLO!
SORRY ABOUT THAT, BIT OF A WILD-GOOSE CHASE. TURNS OUT THE POLICE HAD CARTED THE TARDIS OFF FOR BLOCKING THE ALLEYWAY.
DID WE MISS ANYTHING?
RORY?
RORY!
YOU SAID HE'D BE SAFE! WE JUST LEFT HIM HERE! AND NOW LOOK AT HIM!
THAT... WASN'T SUPPOSED TO HAPPEN.

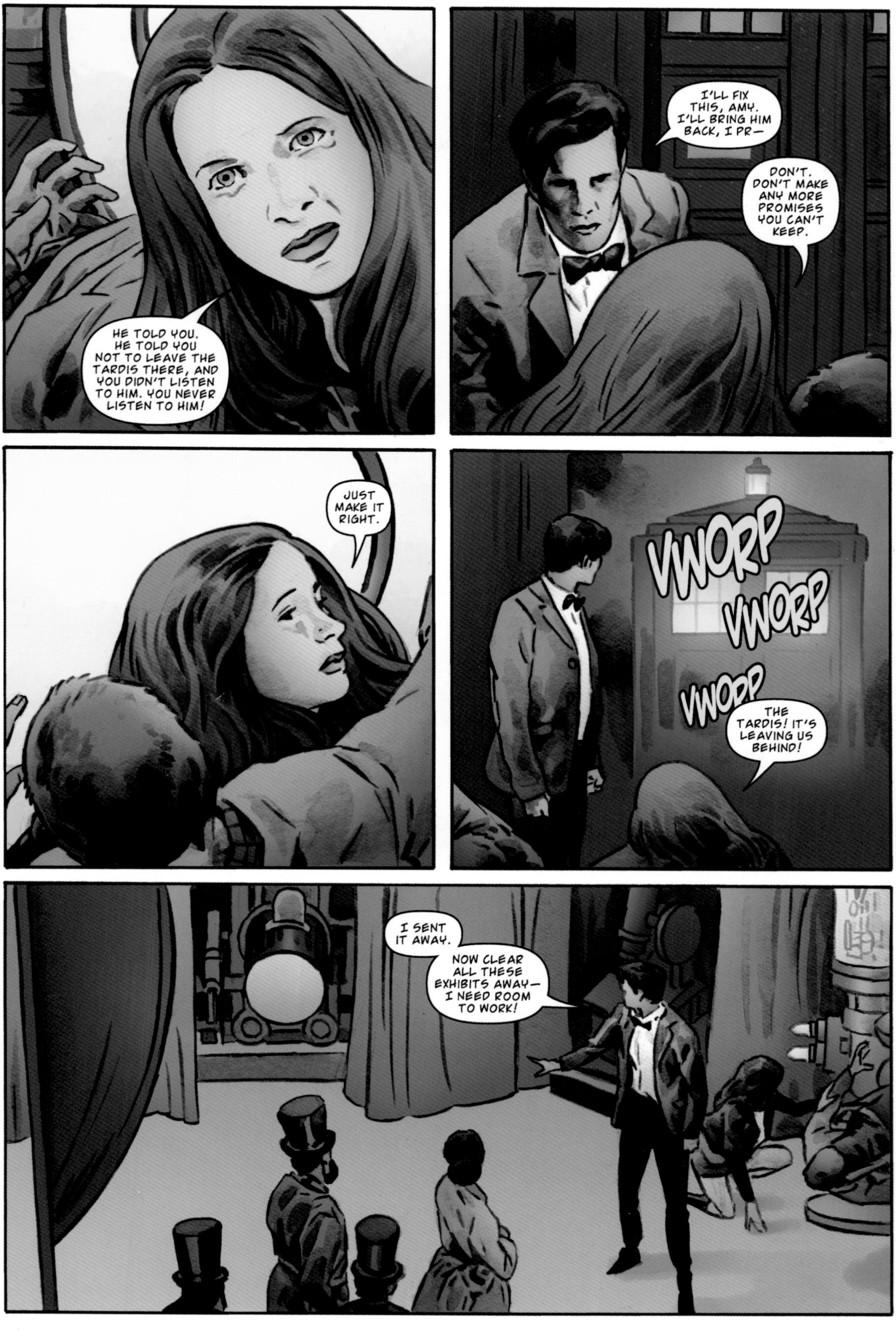
HE TOLD YOU. HE TOLD YOU NOT TO LEAVE THE TARDIS THERE, AND YOU DIDN'T LISTEN TO HIM. YOU NEVER LISTEN TO HIM!
I'LL FIX THIS, AMY. I'LL BRING HIM BACK, I PR—
DON'T. DON'T MAKE ANY MORE PROMISES YOU CAN'T KEEP.
JUST MAKE IT RIGHT.
VWORP
VWORP
VWORP
THE TARDIS! IT'S LEAVING US BEHIND!
I SENT IT AWAY.
NOW CLEAR ALL THESE EXHIBITS AWAY— I NEED ROOM TO WORK!

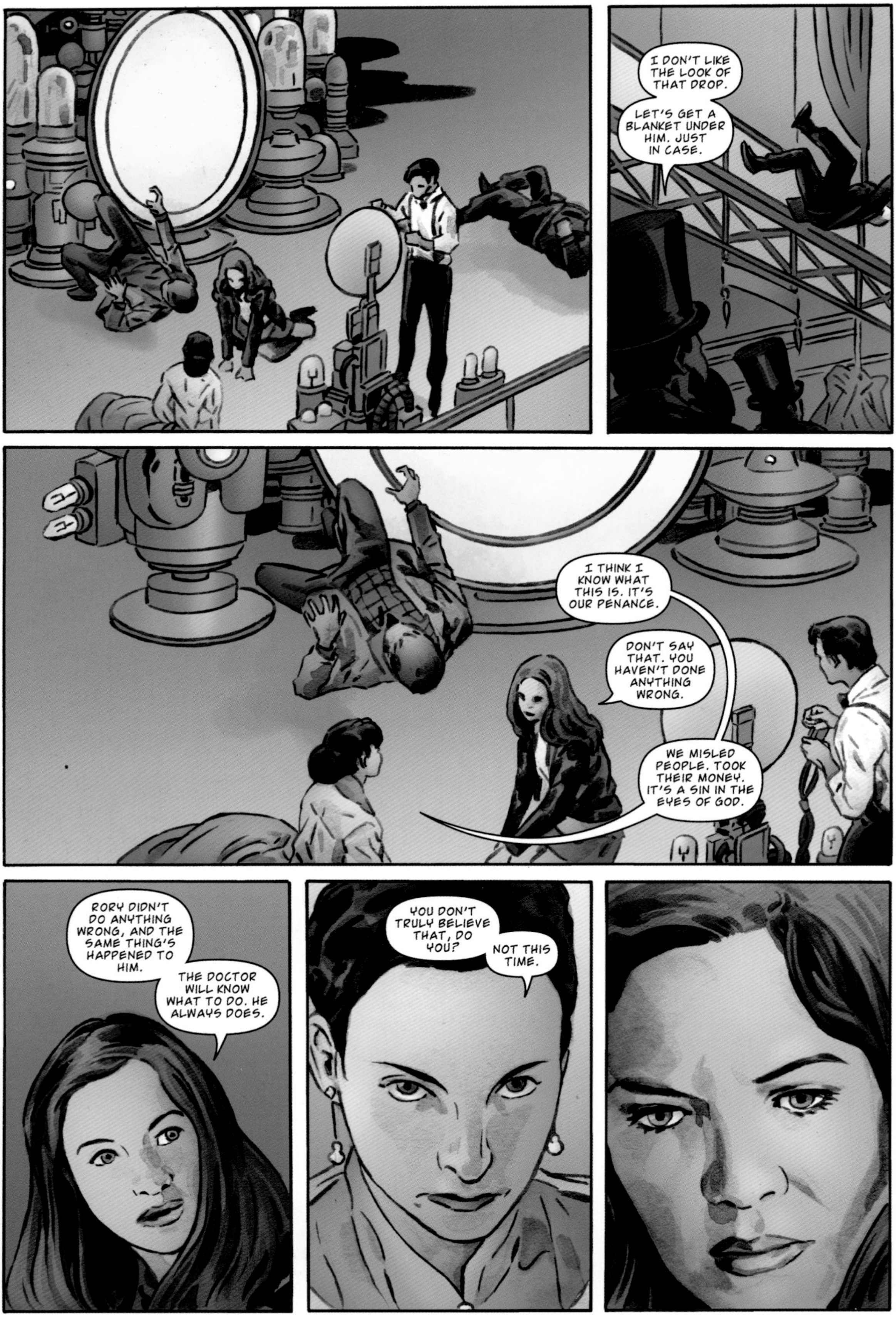
I DON'T LIKE THE LOOK OF THAT DROP.
LET'S GET A BLANKET UNDER HIM. JUST IN CASE.
I THINK I KNOW WHAT THIS IS. IT'S OUR PENANCE.
DON'T SAY THAT. YOU HAVEN'T DONE ANYTHING WRONG.
WE MISLED PEOPLE. TOOK THEIR MONEY. IT'S A SIN IN THE EYES OF GOD.
RORY DIDN'T DO ANYTHING WRONG, AND THE SAME THING'S HAPPENED TO HIM.
THE DOCTOR WILL KNOW WHAT TO DO. HE ALWAYS DOES.
YOU DON'T TRULY BELIEVE THAT, DO YOU?
NOT THIS TIME.

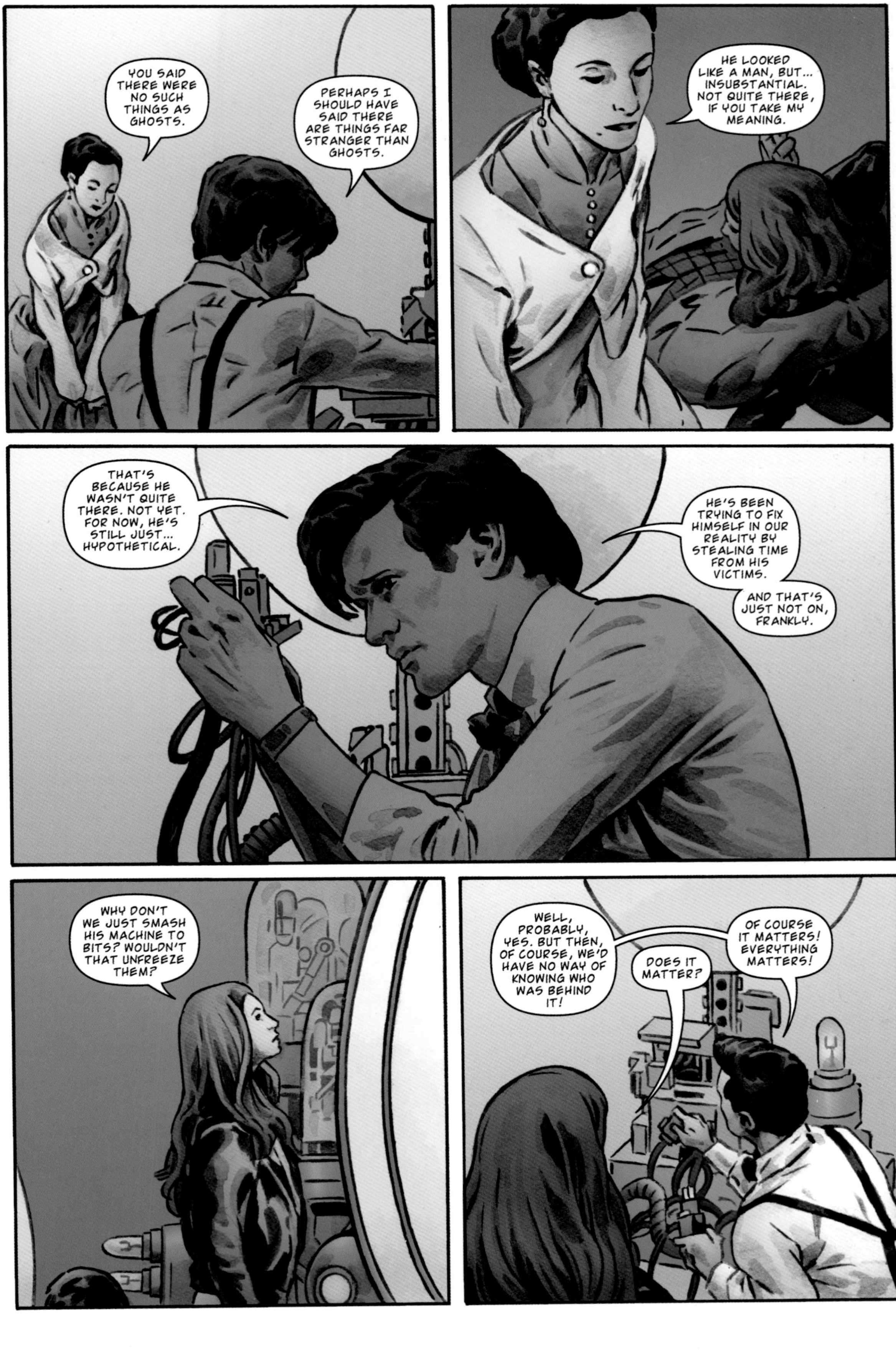
YOU SAID THERE WERE NO SUCH THINGS AS GHOSTS.
PERHAPS I SHOULD HAVE SAID THERE ARE THINGS FAR STRANGER THAN GHOSTS.
HE LOOKED LIKE A MAN, BUT... INSUBSTANTIAL. NOT QUITE THERE, IF YOU TAKE MY MEANING.
THAT'S BECAUSE HE WASN'T QUITE THERE. NOT YET. FOR NOW, HE'S STILL JUST... HYPOTHETICAL.
HE'S BEEN TRYING TO FIX HIMSELF IN OUR REALITY BY STEALING TIME FROM HIS VICTIMS.
AND THAT'S JUST NOT ON, FRANKLY.
WHY DON'T WE JUST SMASH HIS MACHINE TO BITS? WOULDN'T THAT UNFREEZE THEM?
WELL, PROBABLY, YES. BUT THEN, OF COURSE, WE'D HAVE NO WAY OF KNOWING WHO WAS BEHIND IT!
DOES IT MATTER?
OF COURSE IT MATTERS! EVERYTHING MATTERS!

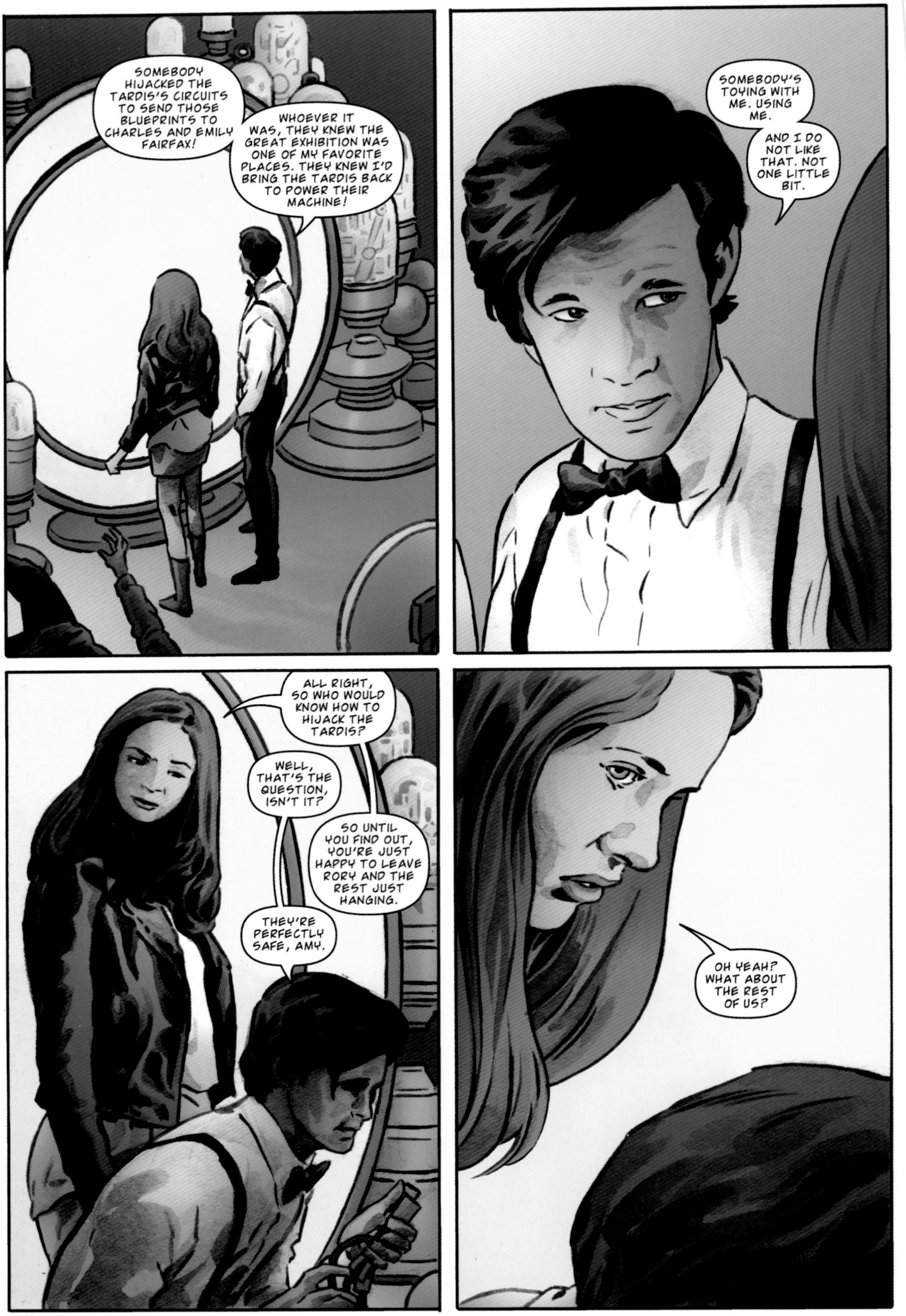
SOMEBODY HIJACKED THE TARDIS'S CIRCUITS TO SEND THOSE BLUEPRINTS TO CHARLES AND EMILY FAIRFAX!
WHOEVER IT WAS, THEY KNEW THE GREAT EXHIBITION WAS ONE OF MY FAVORITE PLACES. THEY KNEW I'D BRING THE TARDIS BACK TO POWER THEIR MACHINE!
SOMEBODY'S TOYING WITH ME. USING ME.
AND I DO NOT LIKE THAT. NOT ONE LITTLE BIT.
ALL RIGHT, SO WHO WOULD KNOW HOW TO HIJACK THE TARDIS?
WELL, THAT'S THE QUESTION, ISN'T IT?
SO UNTIL YOU FIND OUT, YOU'RE JUST HAPPY TO LEAVE RORY AND THE REST JUST HANGING.
THEY'RE PERFECTLY SAFE, AMY.
OH YEAH? WHAT ABOUT THE REST OF US?

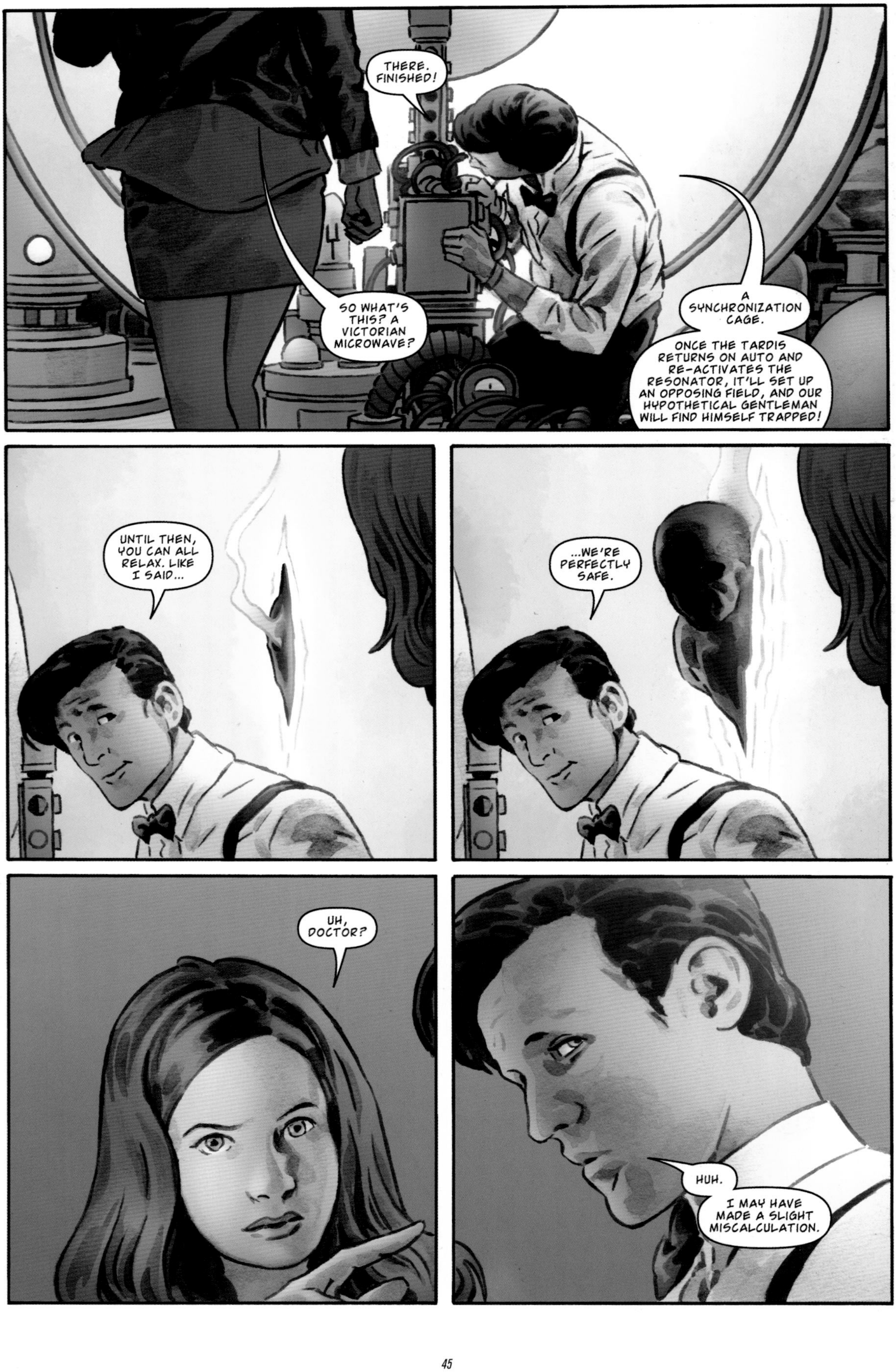
THERE. FINISHED!
SO WHAT'S THIS? A VICTORIAN MICROWAVE?
A SYNCHRONIZATION CAGE.
ONCE THE TARDIS RETURNS ON AUTO AND RE-ACTIVATES THE RESONATOR, IT'LL SET UP AN OPPOSING FIELD, AND OUR HYPOTHETICAL GENTLEMAN WILL FIND HIMSELF TRAPPED!
UNTIL THEN, YOU CAN ALL RELAX. LIKE I SAID...
...WE'RE PERFECTLY SAFE.
UH, DOCTOR?
HUH.
I MAY HAVE MADE A SLIGHT MISCALCULATION.

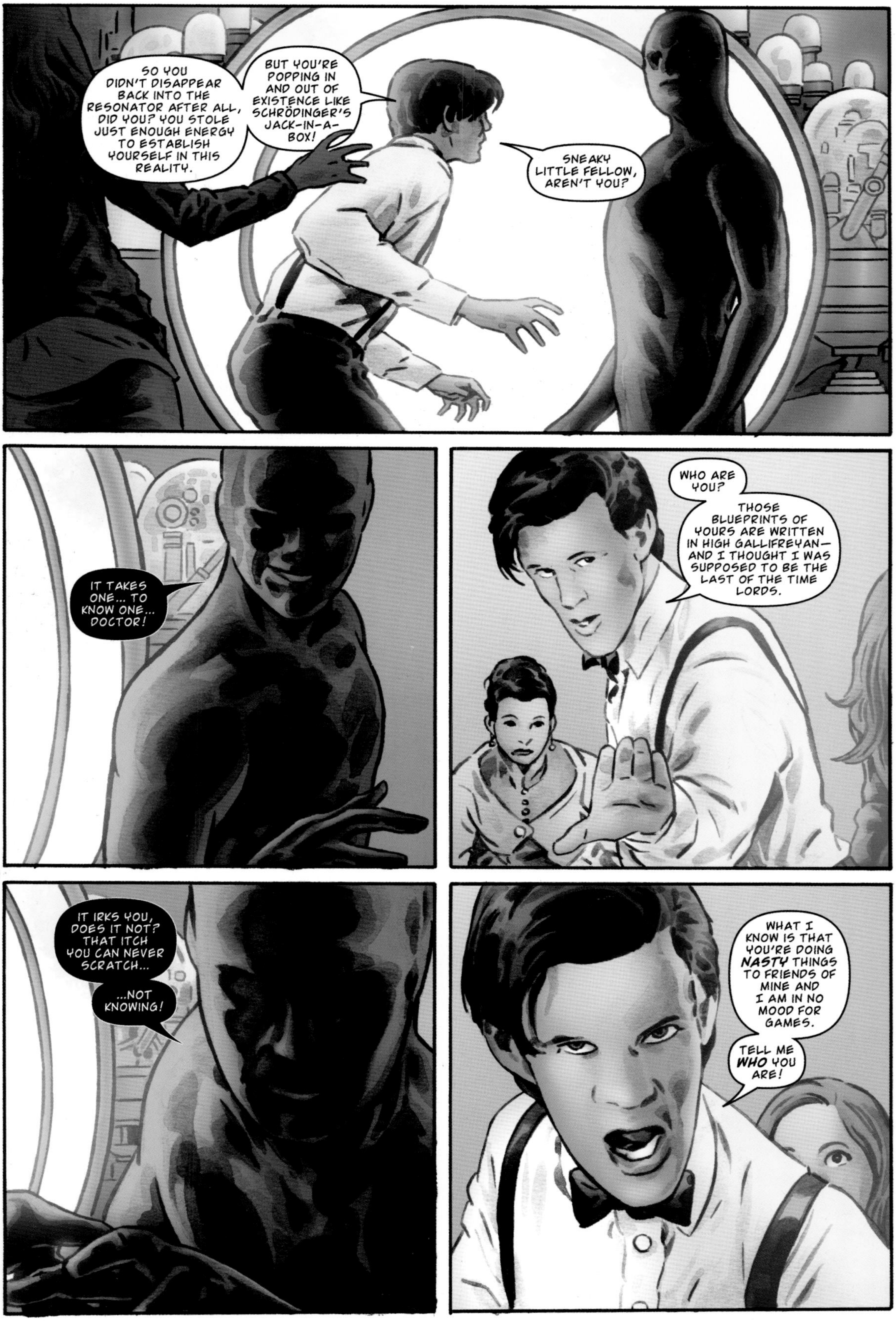
SO YOU DIDN'T DISAPPEAR BACK INTO THE RESONATOR AFTER ALL, DID YOU? YOU STOLE JUST ENOUGH ENERGY TO ESTABLISH YOURSELF IN THIS REALITY.
BUT YOU'RE POPPING IN AND OUT OF EXISTENCE LIKE SCHRÖDINGER'S JACK-IN-A-BOX!
SNEAKY LITTLE FELLOW, AREN'T YOU?
IT TAKES ONE... TO KNOW ONE... DOCTOR!
WHO ARE YOU?
THOSE BLUEPRINTS OF YOURS ARE WRITTEN IN HIGH GALLIFREYAN—AND I THOUGHT I WAS SUPPOSED TO BE THE LAST OF THE TIME LORDS.
IT IRKS YOU, DOES IT NOT? THAT ITCH YOU CAN NEVER SCRATCH...
...NOT KNOWING!
WHAT I KNOW IS THAT YOU'RE DOING NASTY THINGS TO FRIENDS OF MINE AND I AM IN NO MOOD FOR GAMES.
TELL ME WHO YOU ARE!

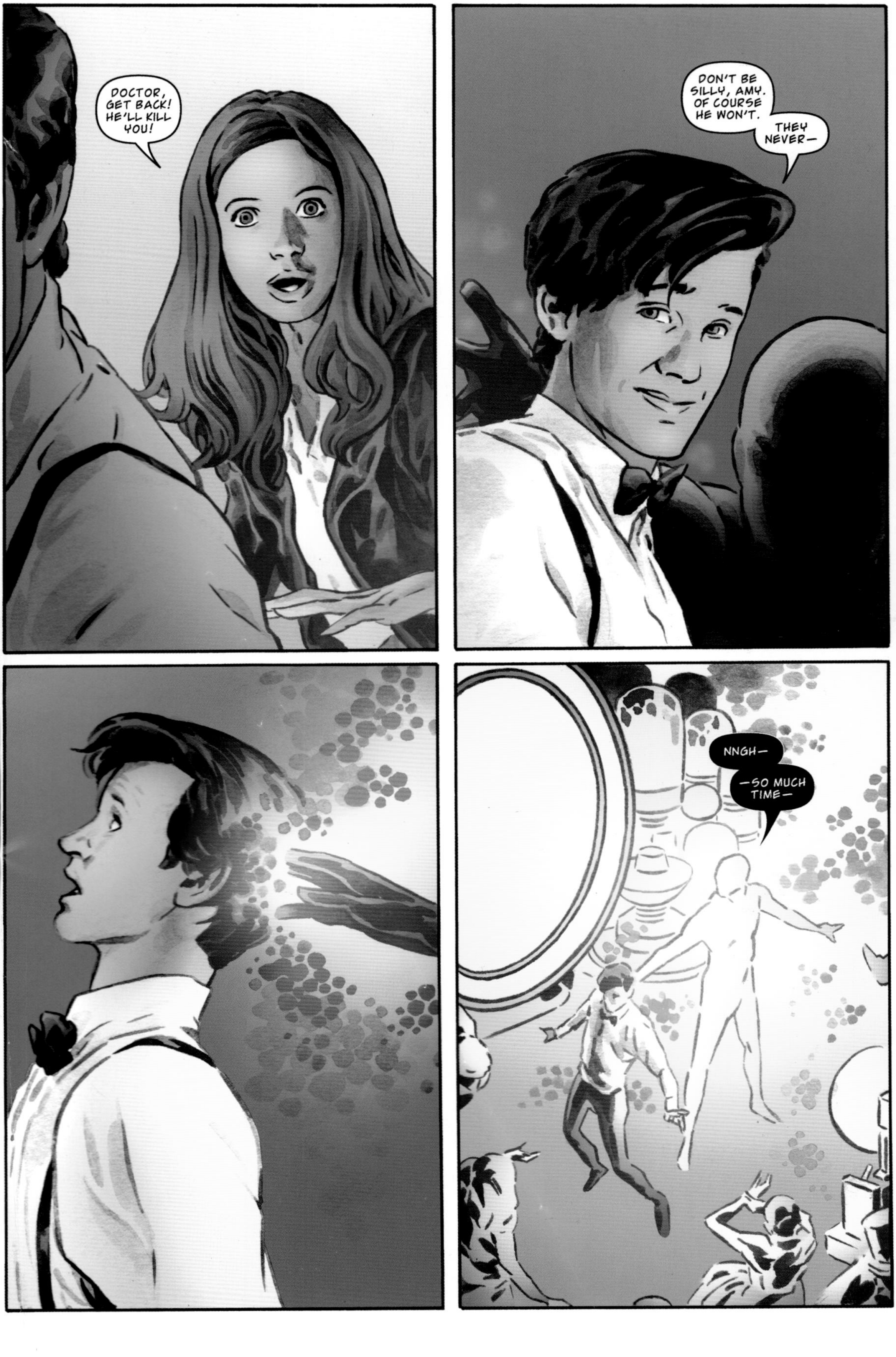
DOCTOR, GET BACK! HE'LL KILL YOU!
DON'T BE SILLY, AMY. OF COURSE HE WON'T.
THEY NEVER—
NNGH—
—SO MUCH TIME—

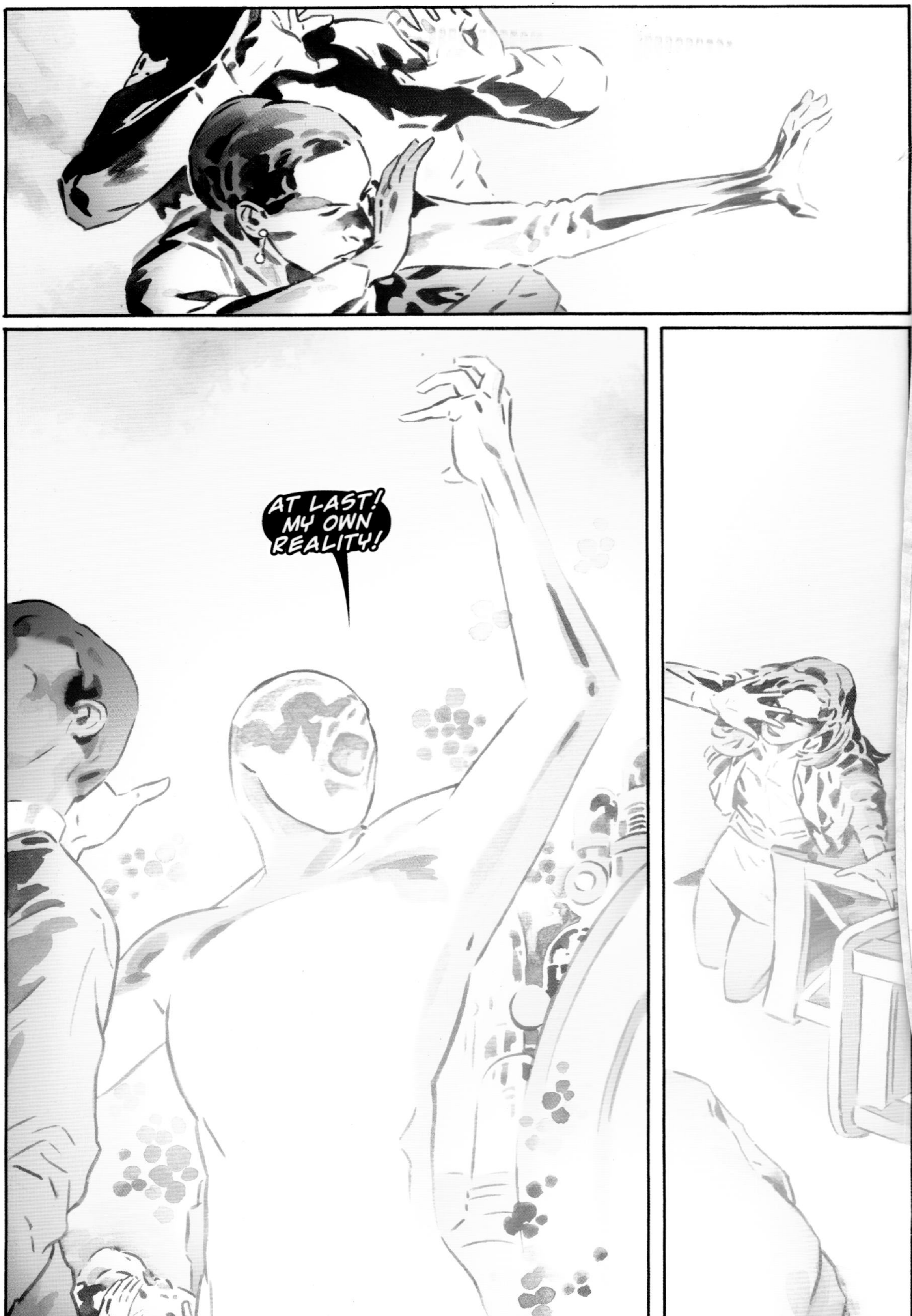
AT LAST! MY OWN REALITY!

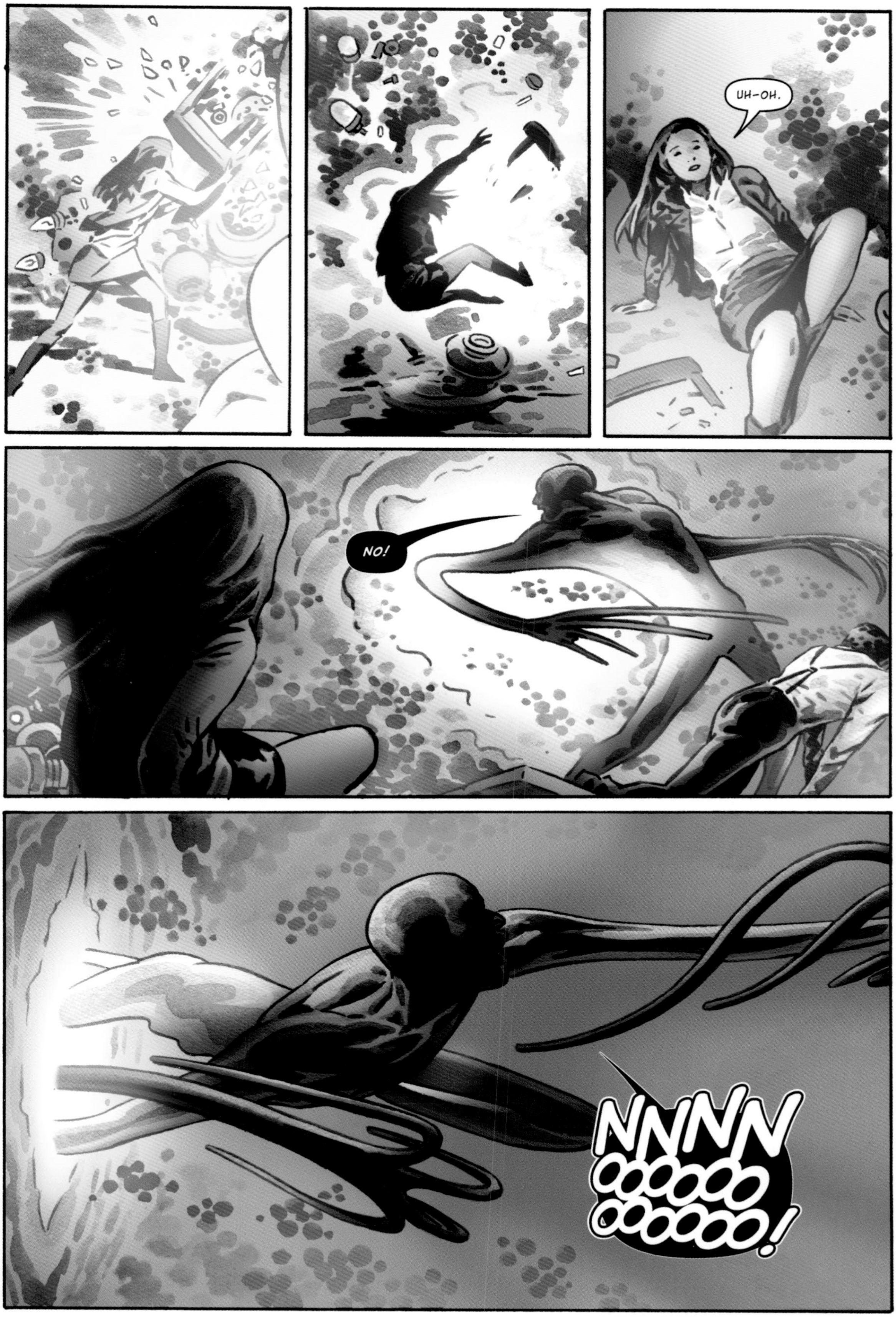
UH-OH.
NO!
NNNN OOOOOO OOOOOO!

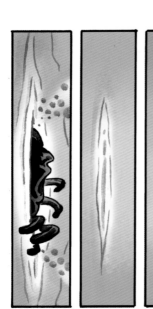

UNGH!

WH—WHAT?

AAAAH!

UHHF!

CAREFUL HOW YOU GO, SIR.

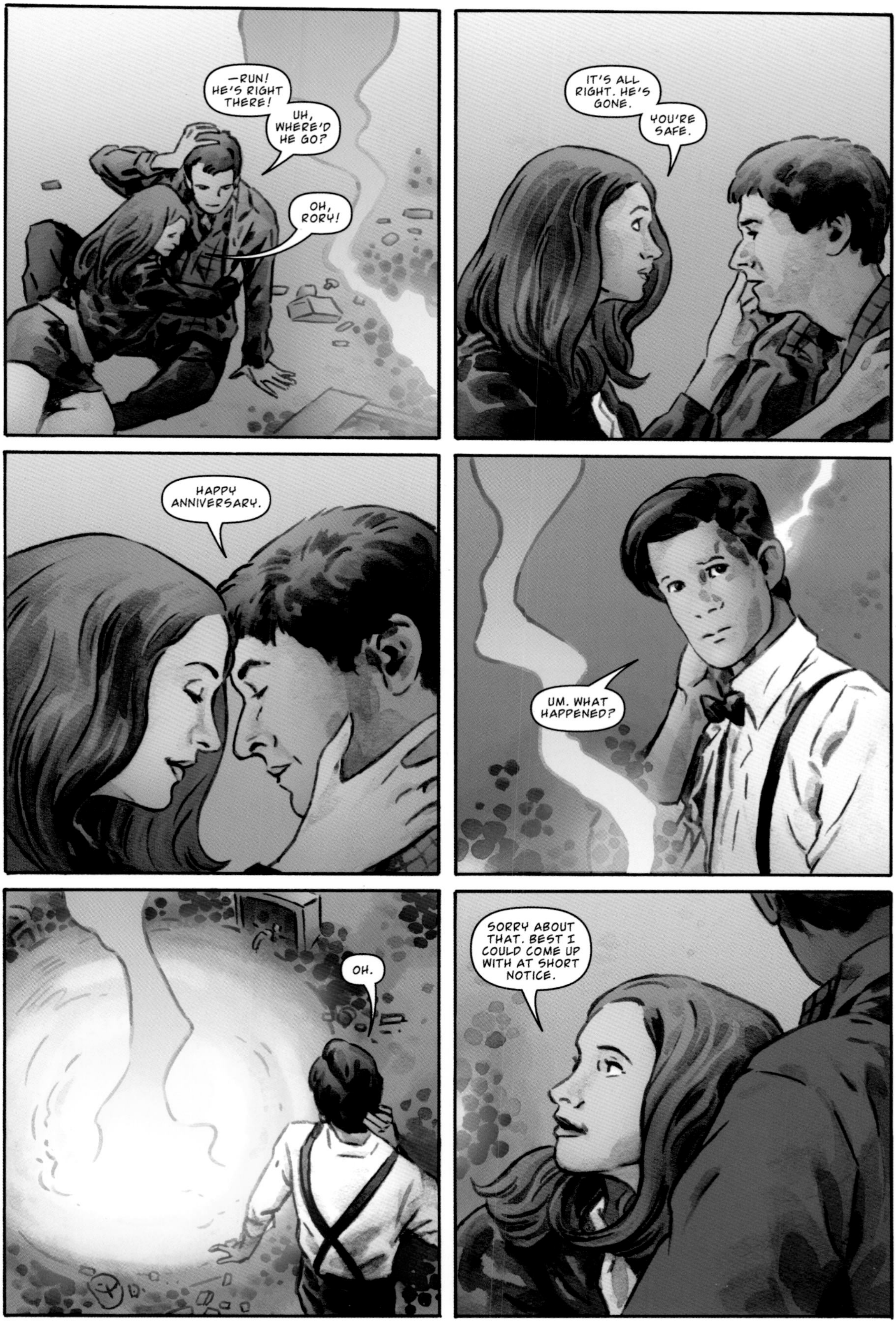
—RUN! HE'S RIGHT THERE!
UH, WHERE'D HE GO?
OH, RORY!
IT'S ALL RIGHT. HE'S GONE.
YOU'RE SAFE.
HAPPY ANNIVERSARY.
UM. WHAT HAPPENED?
OH.
SORRY ABOUT THAT. BEST I COULD COME UP WITH AT SHORT NOTICE.

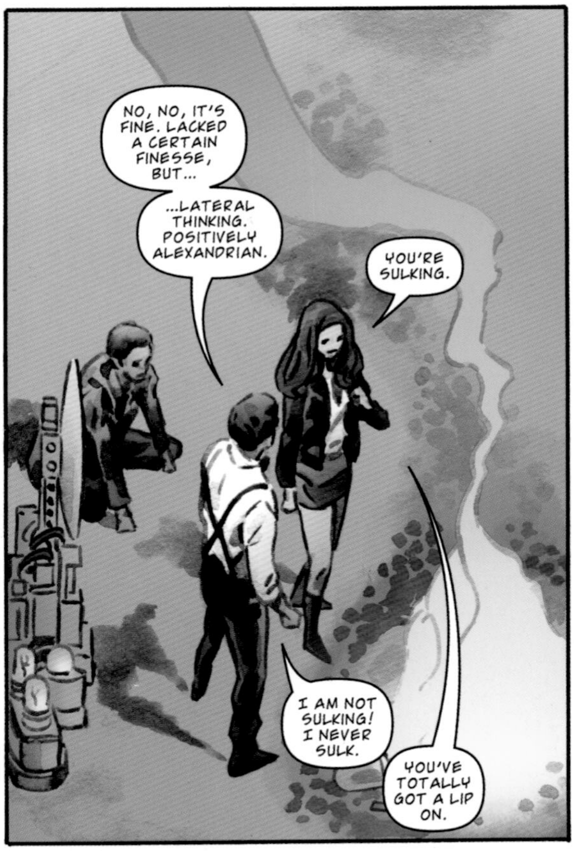
NO, NO, IT'S FINE. LACKED A CERTAIN FINESSE, BUT...
...LATERAL THINKING. POSITIVELY ALEXANDRIAN.
YOU'RE SULKING.
I AM NOT SULKING! I NEVER SULK.
YOU'VE TOTALLY GOT A LIP ON.

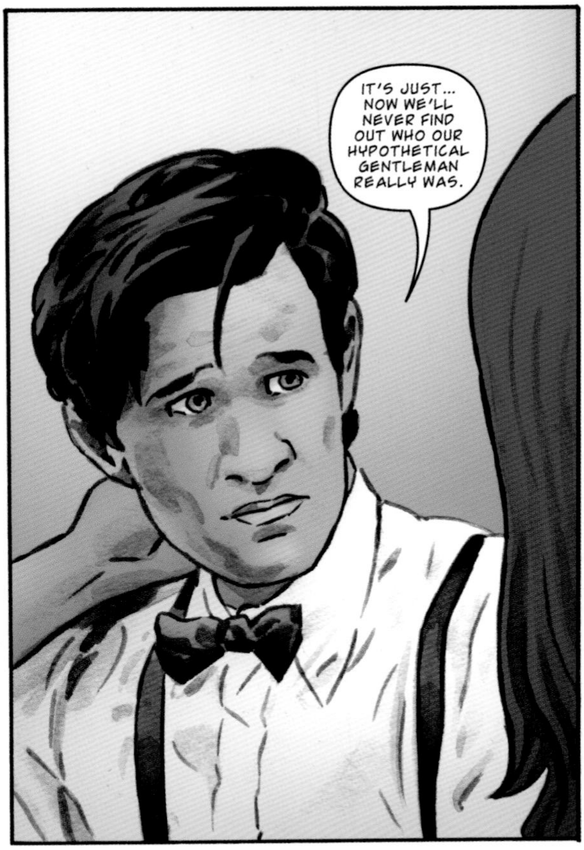
IT'S JUST... NOW WE'LL NEVER FIND OUT WHO OUR HYPOTHETICAL GENTLEMAN REALLY WAS.

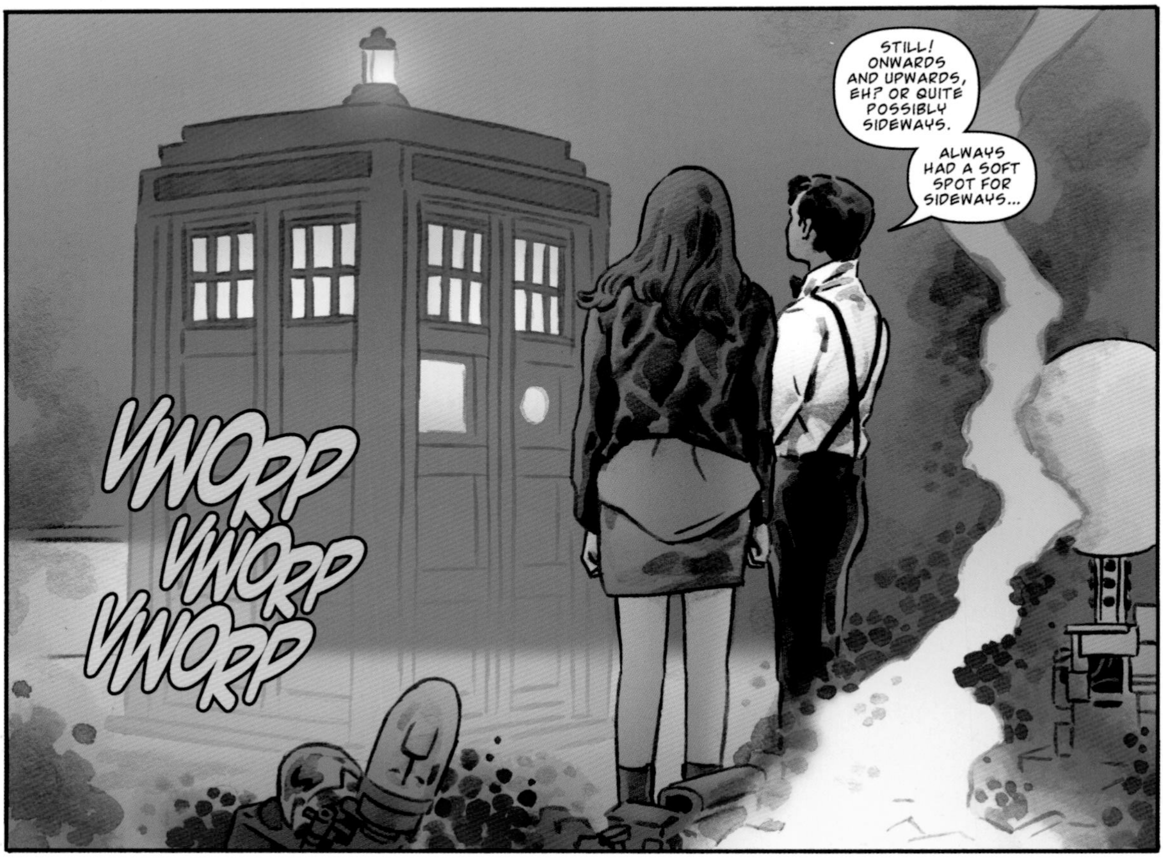
STILL! ONWARDS AND UPWARDS, EH? OR QUITE POSSIBLY SIDEWAYS.
ALWAYS HAD A SOFT SPOT FOR SIDEWAYS...
VWORP VWORP VWORP

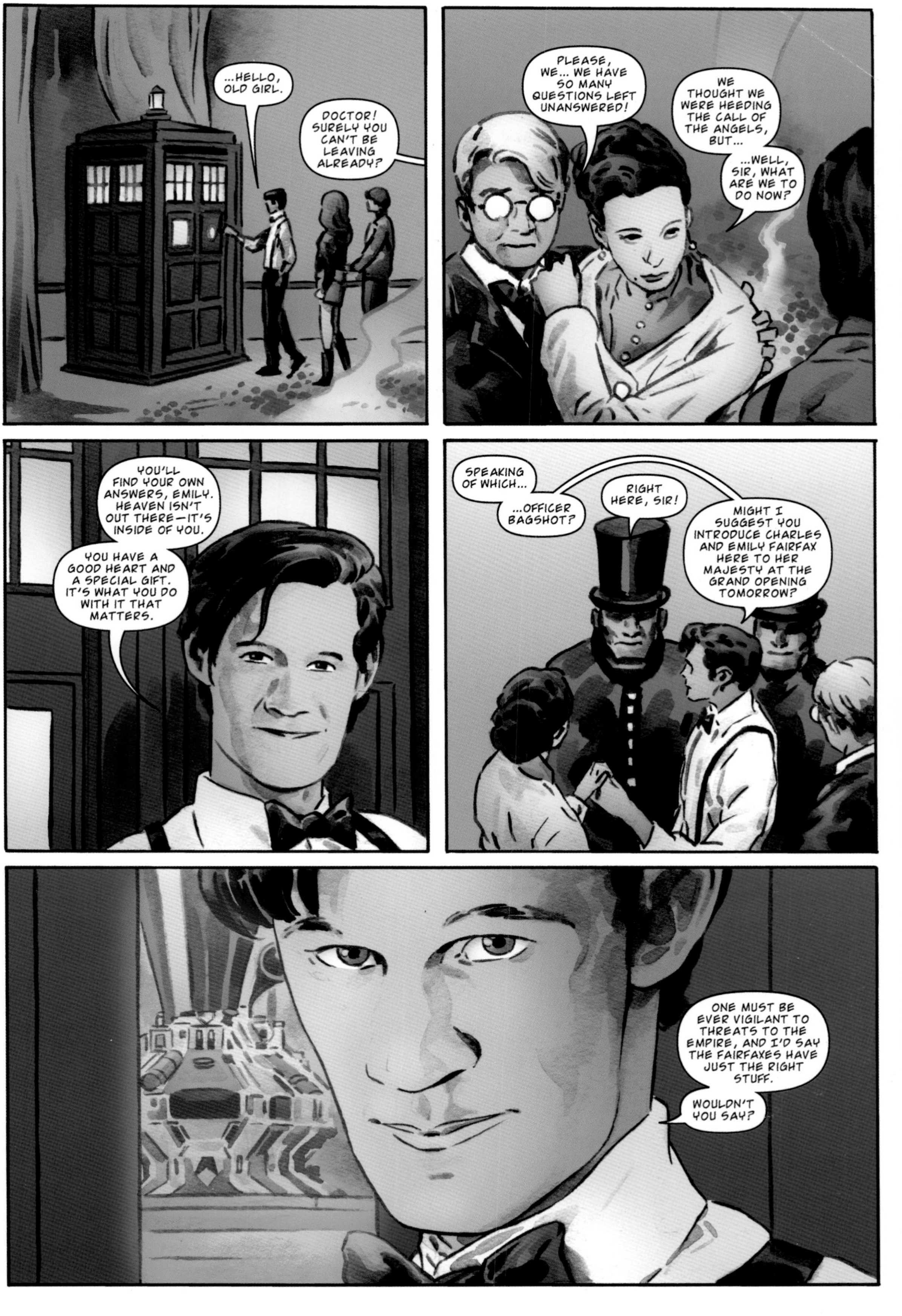
...HELLO, OLD GIRL.
DOCTOR! SURELY YOU CAN'T BE LEAVING ALREADY?
PLEASE, WE... WE HAVE SO MANY QUESTIONS LEFT UNANSWERED!
WE THOUGHT WE WERE HEEDING THE CALL OF THE ANGELS, BUT...
...WELL, SIR, WHAT ARE WE TO DO NOW?
YOU'LL FIND YOUR OWN ANSWERS, EMILY. HEAVEN ISN'T OUT THERE—IT'S INSIDE OF YOU.
YOU HAVE A GOOD HEART AND A SPECIAL GIFT. IT'S WHAT YOU DO WITH IT THAT MATTERS.
SPEAKING OF WHICH...
...OFFICER BAGSHOT?
RIGHT HERE, SIR!
MIGHT I SUGGEST YOU INTRODUCE CHARLES AND EMILY FAIRFAX HERE TO HER MAJESTY AT THE GRAND OPENING TOMORROW?
ONE MUST BE EVER VIGILANT TO THREATS TO THE EMPIRE, AND I'D SAY THE FAIRFAXES HAVE JUST THE RIGHT STUFF.
WOULDN'T YOU SAY?

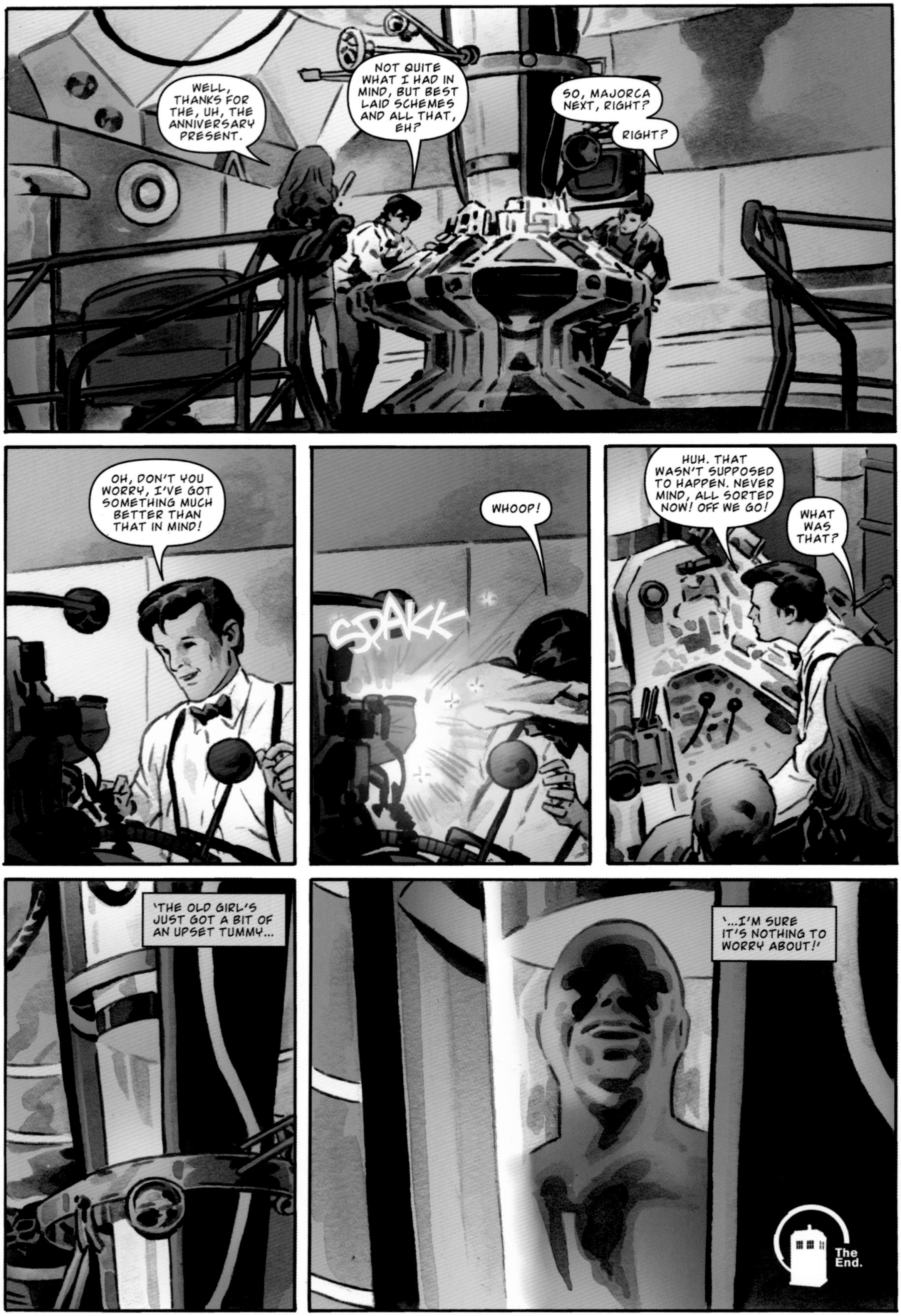
WELL, THANKS FOR THE, UH, THE ANNIVERSARY PRESENT.
NOT QUITE WHAT I HAD IN MIND, BUT BEST LAID SCHEMES AND ALL THAT, EH?
SO, MAJORCA NEXT, RIGHT?
RIGHT?
OH, DON'T YOU WORRY, I'VE GOT SOMETHING MUCH BETTER THAN THAT IN MIND!
WHOOP!
SPAKK
HUH. THAT WASN'T SUPPOSED TO HAPPEN. NEVER MIND, ALL SORTED NOW! OFF WE GO!
WHAT WAS THAT?
'THE OLD GIRL'S JUST GOT A BIT OF AN UPSET TUMMY...
'...I'M SURE IT'S NOTHING TO WORRY ABOUT!'
The End.

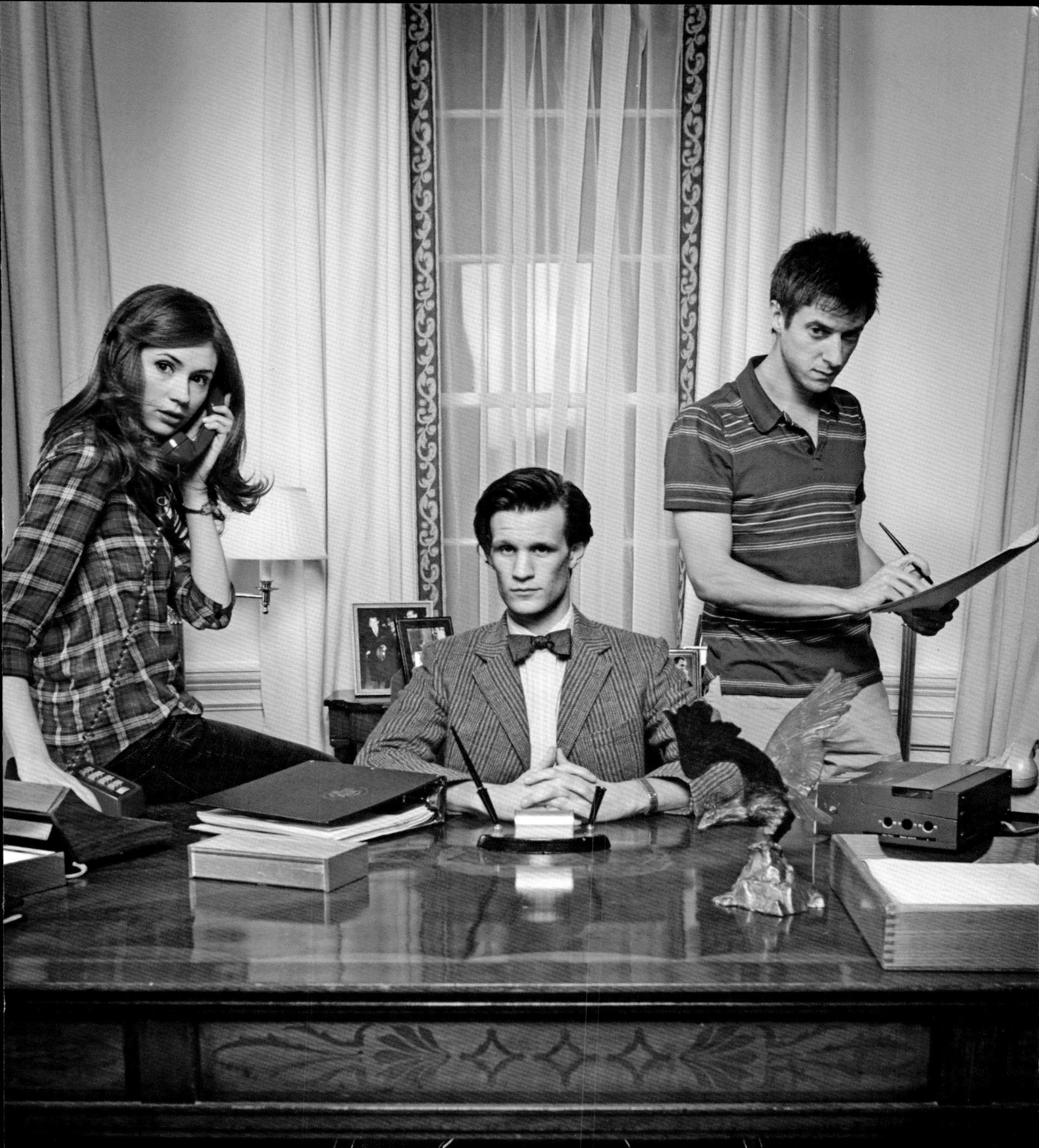

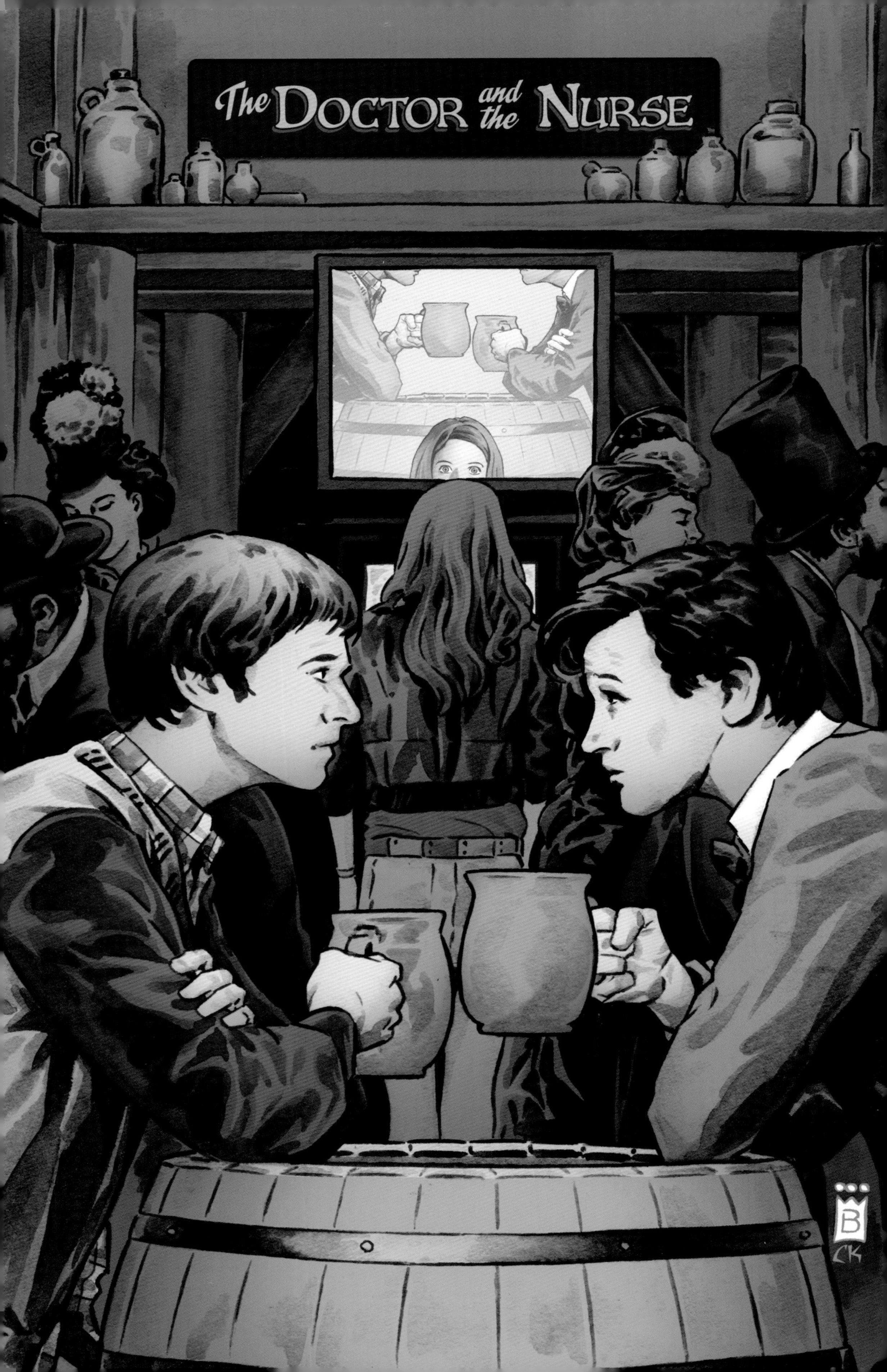
The Doctor and the Nurse

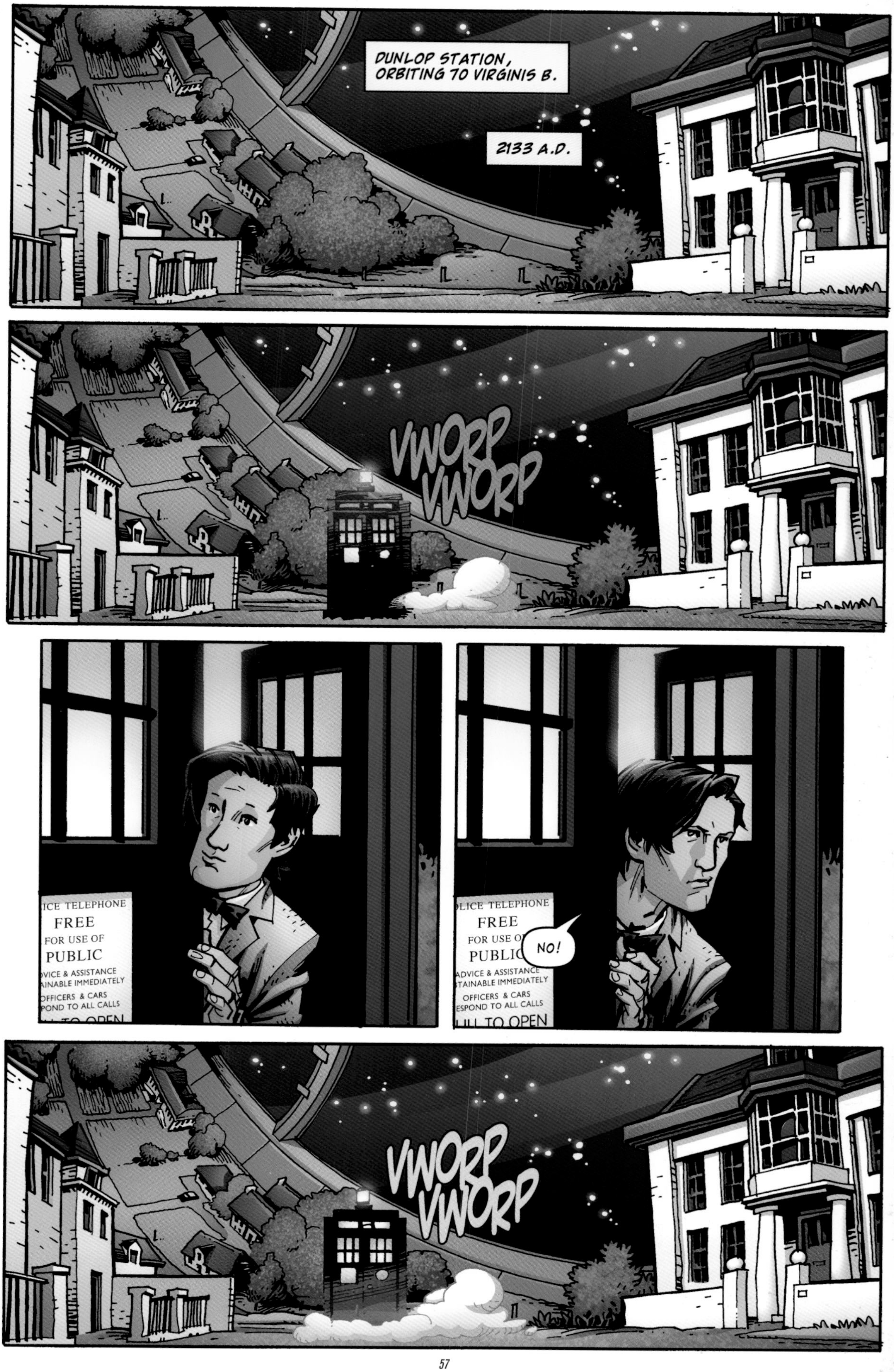
DUNLOP STATION, ORBITING 70 VIRGINIS B.
2133 A.D.
VWORP VWORP
ICE TELEPHONE
FREE
FOR USE OF
PUBLIC
DVICE & ASSISTANCE
TAINABLE IMMEDIATELY
OFFICERS & CARS
SPOND TO ALL CALLS
NO!
VWORP VWORP

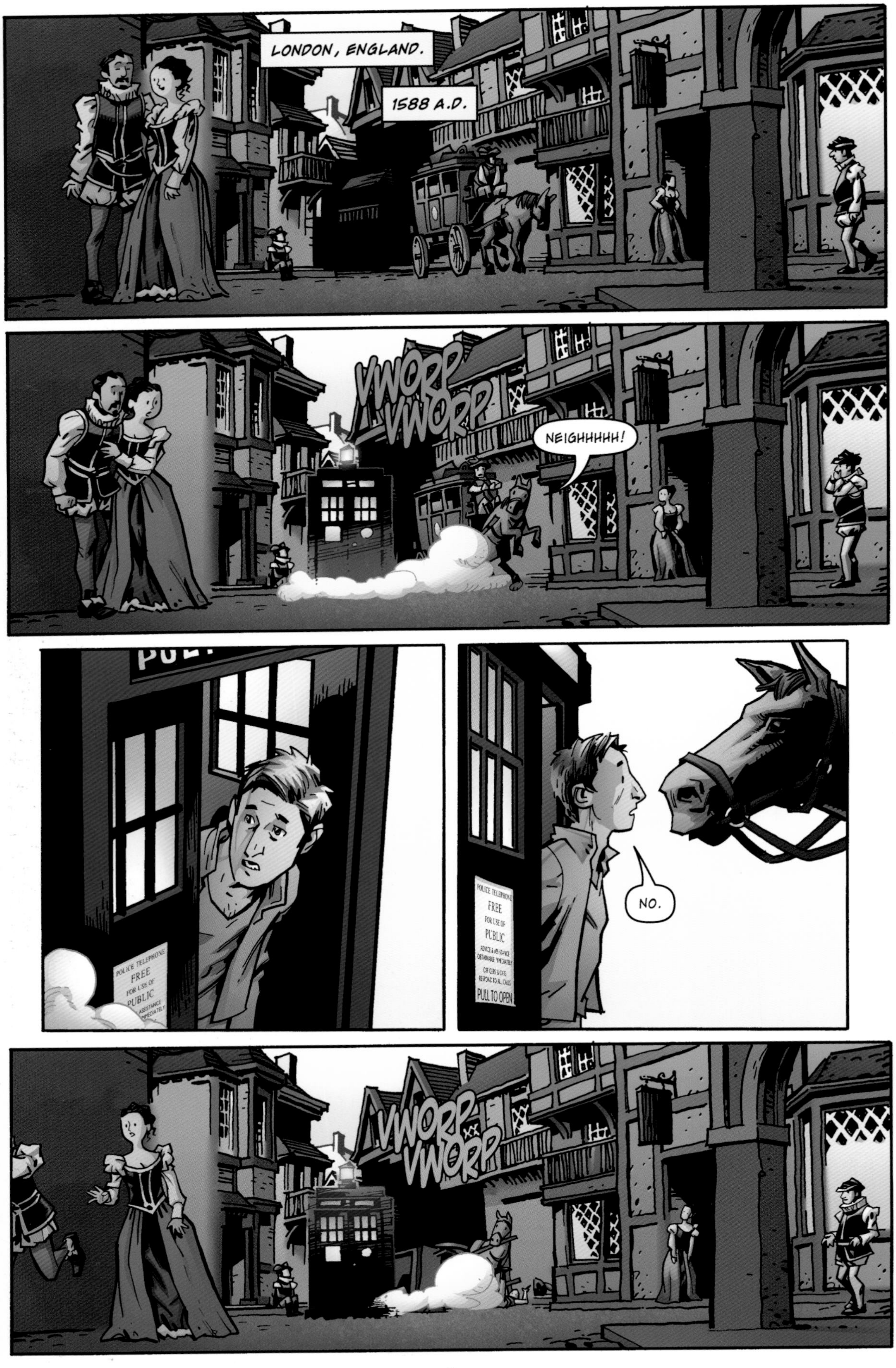
LONDON, ENGLAND.
1588 A.D.
VWORP VWORP
NEIGHHHHH!
POLICE TELEPHONE FREE FOR USE OF PUBLIC
POLICE TELEPHONE FREE FOR USE OF PUBLIC
PULL TO OPEN
NO.
VWORP VWORP

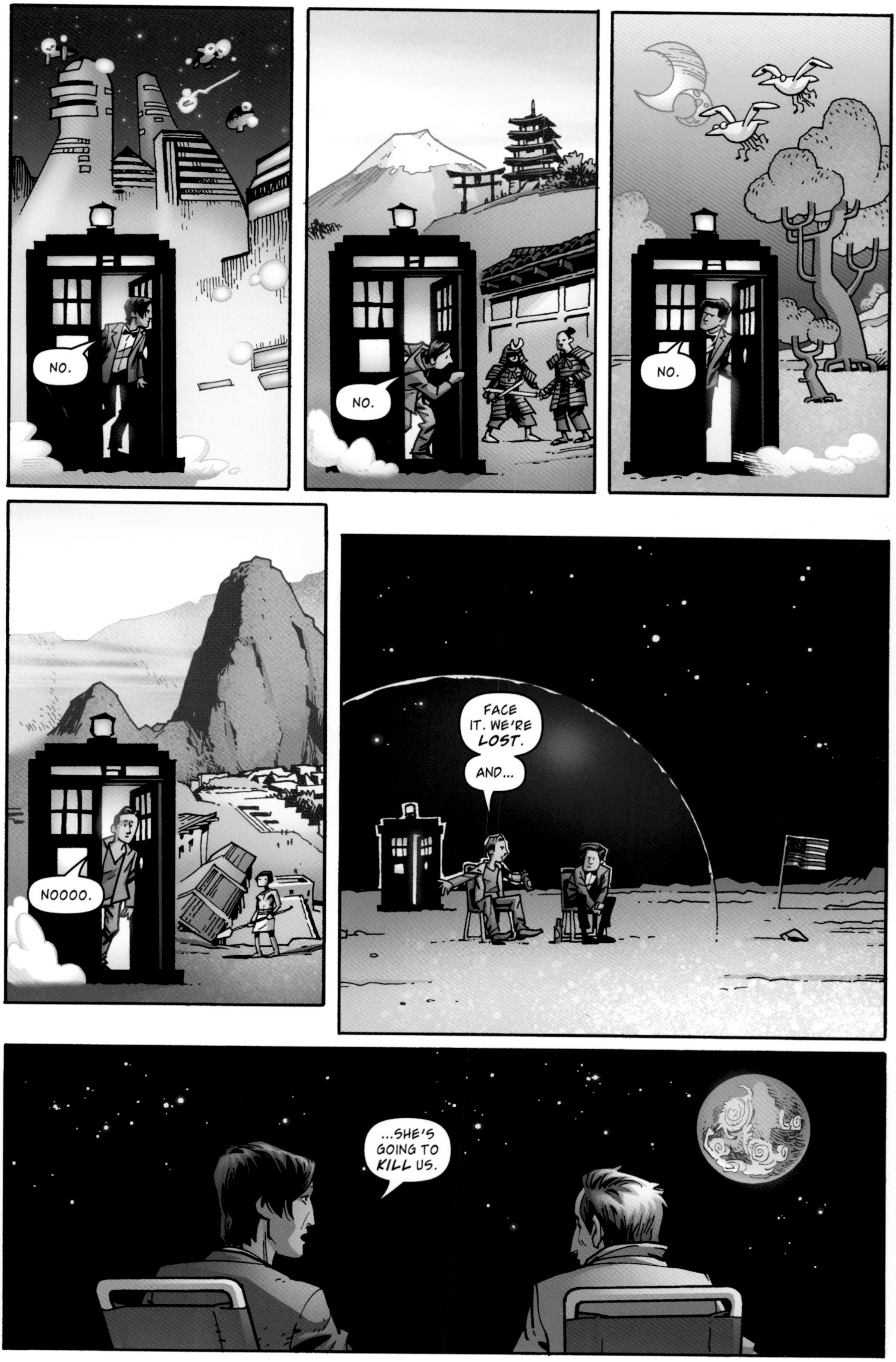
NO.
NO.
NO.
NOOOO.
FACE IT. WE'RE LOST.
AND...
...SHE'S GOING TO KILL US.

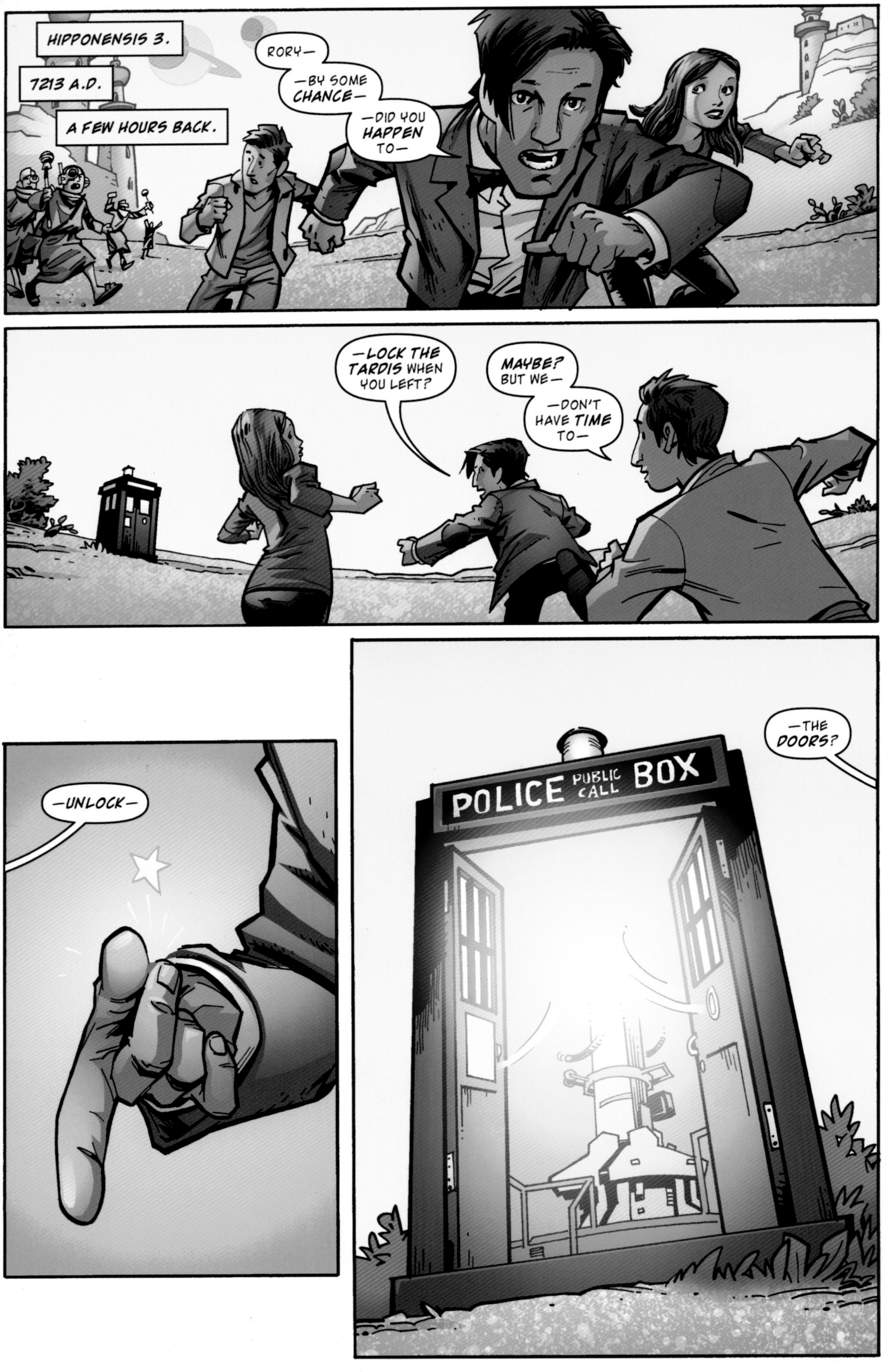
HIPPONENSIS 3.
7213 A.D.
A FEW HOURS BACK.
RORY—
—BY SOME CHANCE—
—DID YOU HAPPEN TO—
—LOCK THE TARDIS WHEN YOU LEFT?
MAYBE? BUT WE—
—DON'T HAVE TIME TO—
—UNLOCK—
—THE DOORS?
POLICE PUBLIC CALL BOX

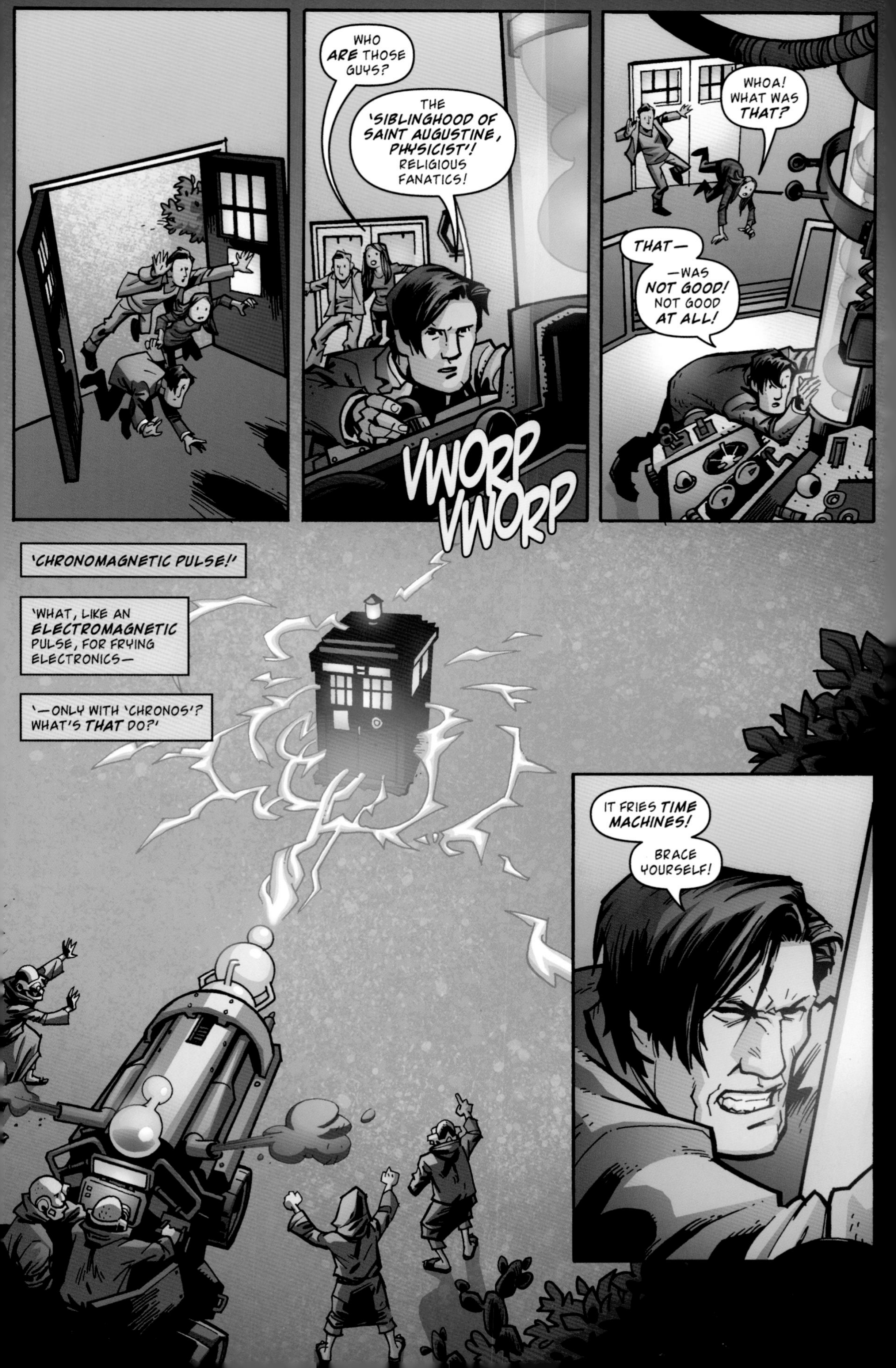

WHO ARE THOSE GUYS?
THE 'SIBLINGHOOD OF SAINT AUGUSTINE, PHYSICIST'! RELIGIOUS FANATICS!
VWORP VWORP
WHOA! WHAT WAS THAT?
THAT—
—WAS NOT GOOD! NOT GOOD AT ALL!
'CHRONOMAGNETIC PULSE!'
'WHAT, LIKE AN ELECTROMAGNETIC PULSE, FOR FRYING ELECTRONICS—
'—ONLY WITH 'CHRONOS'? WHAT'S THAT DO?'
IT FRIES TIME MACHINES!
BRACE YOURSELF!

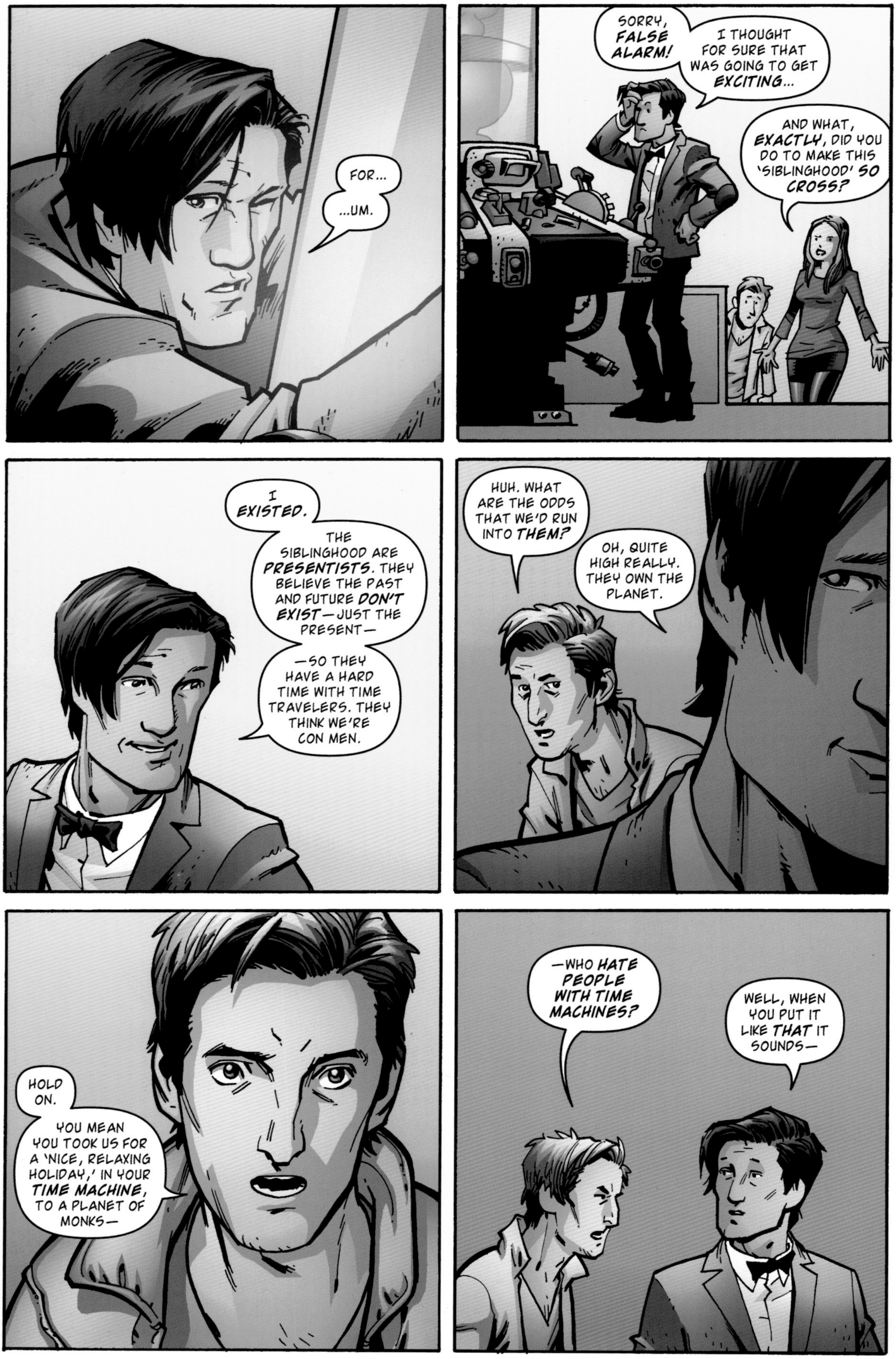
FOR...
...UM.
SORRY, FALSE ALARM!
I THOUGHT FOR SURE THAT WAS GOING TO GET EXCITING...
AND WHAT, EXACTLY, DID YOU DO TO MAKE THIS 'SIBLINGHOOD' SO CROSS?
I EXISTED.
THE SIBLINGHOOD ARE PRESENTISTS. THEY BELIEVE THE PAST AND FUTURE DON'T EXIST—JUST THE PRESENT—
—SO THEY HAVE A HARD TIME WITH TIME TRAVELERS. THEY THINK WE'RE CON MEN.
HUH. WHAT ARE THE ODDS THAT WE'D RUN INTO THEM?
OH, QUITE HIGH REALLY. THEY OWN THE PLANET.
HOLD ON.
YOU MEAN YOU TOOK US FOR A 'NICE, RELAXING HOLIDAY,' IN YOUR TIME MACHINE, TO A PLANET OF MONKS—
—WHO HATE PEOPLE WITH TIME MACHINES?
WELL, WHEN YOU PUT IT LIKE THAT IT SOUNDS—

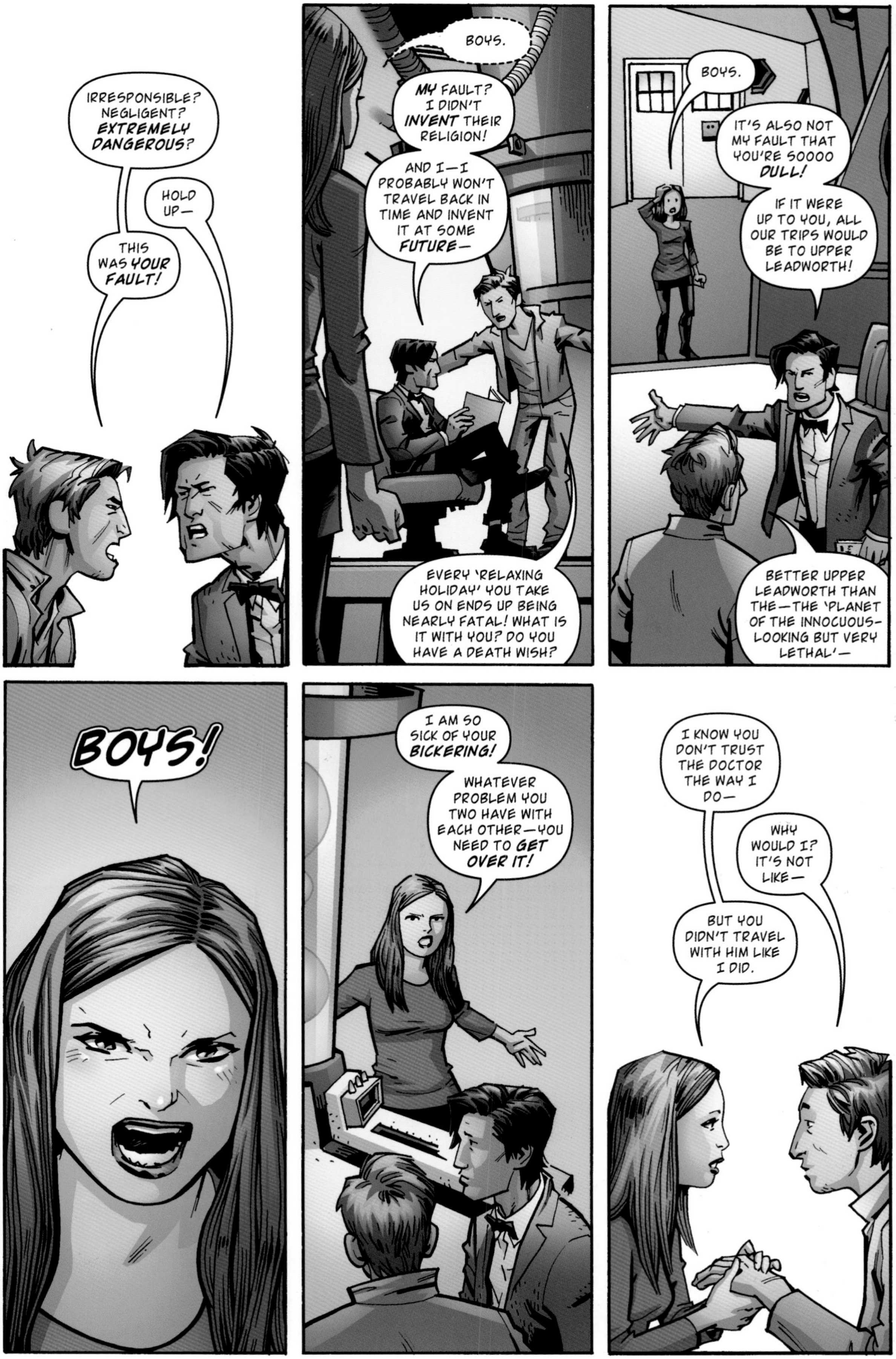
IRRESPONSIBLE? NEGLIGENT? EXTREMELY DANGEROUS?
HOLD UP—
THIS WAS YOUR FAULT!
BOYS.
MY FAULT? I DIDN'T INVENT THEIR RELIGION!
AND I—I PROBABLY WON'T TRAVEL BACK IN TIME AND INVENT IT AT SOME FUTURE—
EVERY 'RELAXING HOLIDAY' YOU TAKE US ON ENDS UP BEING NEARLY FATAL! WHAT IS IT WITH YOU? DO YOU HAVE A DEATH WISH?
BOYS.
IT'S ALSO NOT MY FAULT THAT YOU'RE SOOOO DULL!
IF IT WERE UP TO YOU, ALL OUR TRIPS WOULD BE TO UPPER LEADWORTH!
BETTER UPPER LEADWORTH THAN THE—THE 'PLANET OF THE INNOCUOUS-LOOKING BUT VERY LETHAL'—
BOYS!
I AM SO SICK OF YOUR BICKERING!
WHATEVER PROBLEM YOU TWO HAVE WITH EACH OTHER—YOU NEED TO GET OVER IT!
I KNOW YOU DON'T TRUST THE DOCTOR THE WAY I DO—
WHY WOULD I? IT'S NOT LIKE—
BUT YOU DIDN'T TRAVEL WITH HIM LIKE I DID.

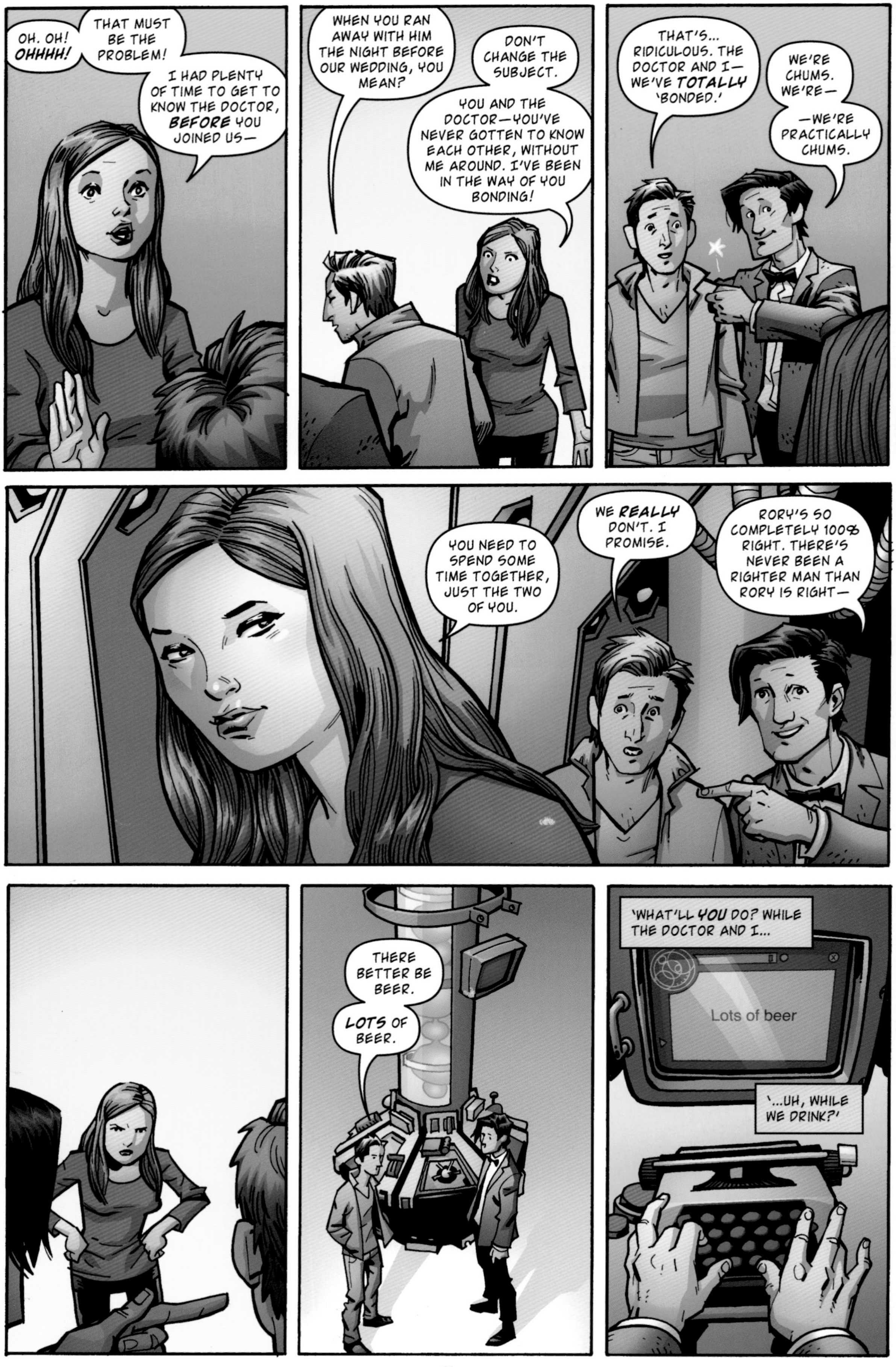
OH. OH! OHHHH!
THAT MUST BE THE PROBLEM!
I HAD PLENTY OF TIME TO GET TO KNOW THE DOCTOR, BEFORE YOU JOINED US—
WHEN YOU RAN AWAY WITH HIM THE NIGHT BEFORE OUR WEDDING, YOU MEAN?
DON'T CHANGE THE SUBJECT.
YOU AND THE DOCTOR—YOU'VE NEVER GOTTEN TO KNOW EACH OTHER, WITHOUT ME AROUND. I'VE BEEN IN THE WAY OF YOU BONDING!
THAT'S... RIDICULOUS. THE DOCTOR AND I— WE'VE TOTALLY 'BONDED.'
WE'RE CHUMS. WE'RE—
—WE'RE PRACTICALLY CHUMS.
YOU NEED TO SPEND SOME TIME TOGETHER, JUST THE TWO OF YOU.
WE REALLY DON'T. I PROMISE.
RORY'S SO COMPLETELY 100% RIGHT. THERE'S NEVER BEEN A RIGHTER MAN THAN RORY IS RIGHT—
THERE BETTER BE BEER.
LOTS OF BEER.
'WHAT'LL YOU DO? WHILE THE DOCTOR AND I...
Lots of beer
'...UH, WHILE WE DRINK?'

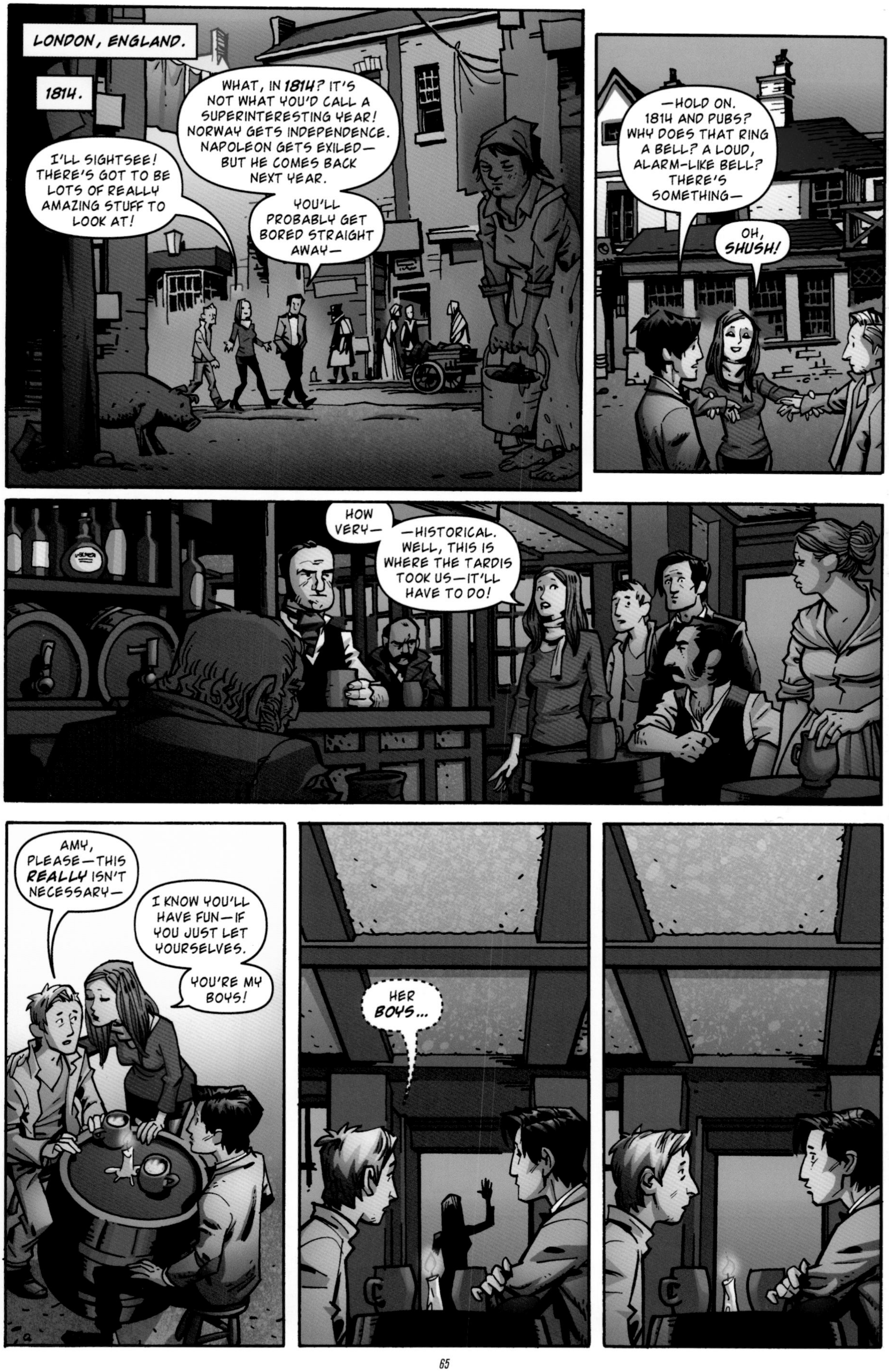
LONDON, ENGLAND.
1814.
I'LL SIGHTSEE! THERE'S GOT TO BE LOTS OF REALLY AMAZING STUFF TO LOOK AT!
WHAT, IN 1814? IT'S NOT WHAT YOU'D CALL A SUPERINTERESTING YEAR! NORWAY GETS INDEPENDENCE. NAPOLEON GETS EXILED— BUT HE COMES BACK NEXT YEAR.
YOU'LL PROBABLY GET BORED STRAIGHT AWAY—
—HOLD ON. 1814 AND PUBS? WHY DOES THAT RING A BELL? A LOUD, ALARM-LIKE BELL? THERE'S SOMETHING—
OH, SHUSH!
HOW VERY—
—HISTORICAL. WELL, THIS IS WHERE THE TARDIS TOOK US—IT'LL HAVE TO DO!
AMY, PLEASE—THIS REALLY ISN'T NECESSARY—
I KNOW YOU'LL HAVE FUN—IF YOU JUST LET YOURSELVES.
YOU'RE MY BOYS!
HER BOYS...

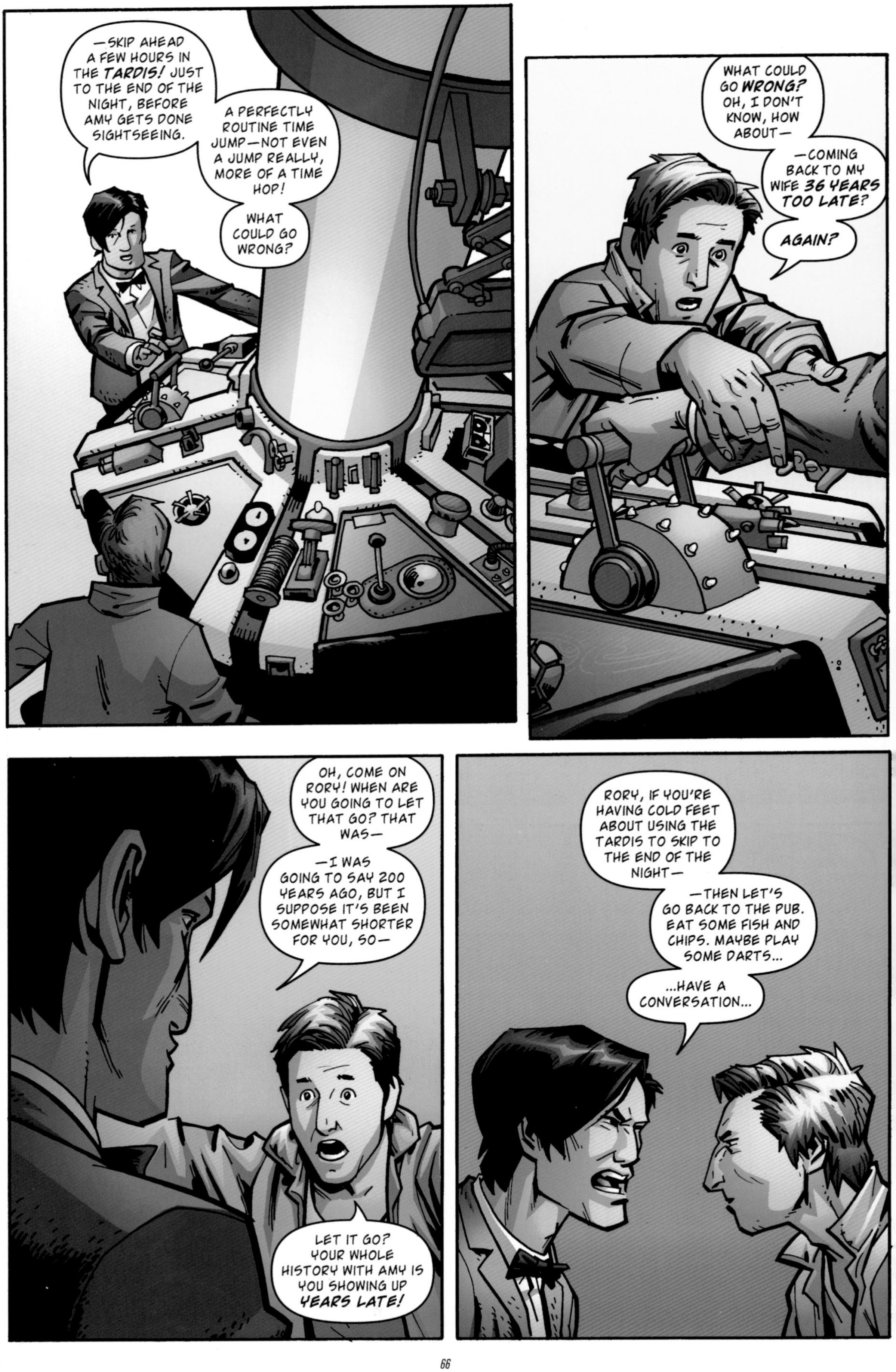
—SKIP AHEAD A FEW HOURS IN THE TARDIS! JUST TO THE END OF THE NIGHT, BEFORE AMY GETS DONE SIGHTSEEING.
A PERFECTLY ROUTINE TIME JUMP—NOT EVEN A JUMP REALLY, MORE OF A TIME HOP!
WHAT COULD GO WRONG?
WHAT COULD GO WRONG? OH, I DON'T KNOW, HOW ABOUT—
—COMING BACK TO MY WIFE 36 YEARS TOO LATE?
AGAIN?
OH, COME ON RORY! WHEN ARE YOU GOING TO LET THAT GO? THAT WAS—
—I WAS GOING TO SAY 200 YEARS AGO, BUT I SUPPOSE IT'S BEEN SOMEWHAT SHORTER FOR YOU, SO—
LET IT GO? YOUR WHOLE HISTORY WITH AMY IS YOU SHOWING UP YEARS LATE!
RORY, IF YOU'RE HAVING COLD FEET ABOUT USING THE TARDIS TO SKIP TO THE END OF THE NIGHT—
—THEN LET'S GO BACK TO THE PUB. EAT SOME FISH AND CHIPS. MAYBE PLAY SOME DARTS...
...HAVE A CONVERSATION...

...ABOUT...

VWORP VWORP

...YES, THAT'S IT! JUST LIKE THAT! YOU'VE GOT TO KEEP THE NEUTRON FLOW STEADY—

—YOU DON'T WANT IT REVERSING UNLESS YOU TELL IT TO!

IT JUST LOOKS LIKE A PINBALL MACHINE TO ME...

SEE? THE SAME ALLEYWAY! THERE'S ST. GILES IN THE FIELDS, RIGHT WHERE WE LEFT IT. THE TOTTENHAM COURT ROAD TUBE STATION'S RIGHT AROUND THE CORNER—

—OR IT, YOU KNOW, WILL BE, IN APPROXIMATELY—

THE FIRST THING WE DO IS FIND A NEWSPAPER, AND CHECK THE DATE. THEN—

—THEN WE ASK SOMEONE FOR THE TIME OF DAY, AND—

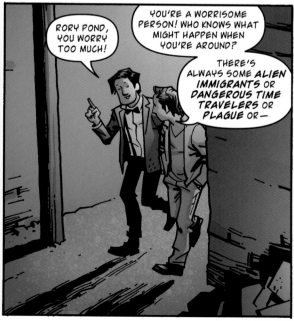

RORY POND, YOU WORRY TOO MUCH!

YOU'RE A WORRISOME PERSON! WHO KNOWS WHAT MIGHT HAPPEN WHEN YOU'RE AROUND?

THERE'S ALWAYS SOME ALIEN IMMIGRANTS OR DANGEROUS TIME TRAVELERS OR PLAGUE OR—

—OR—

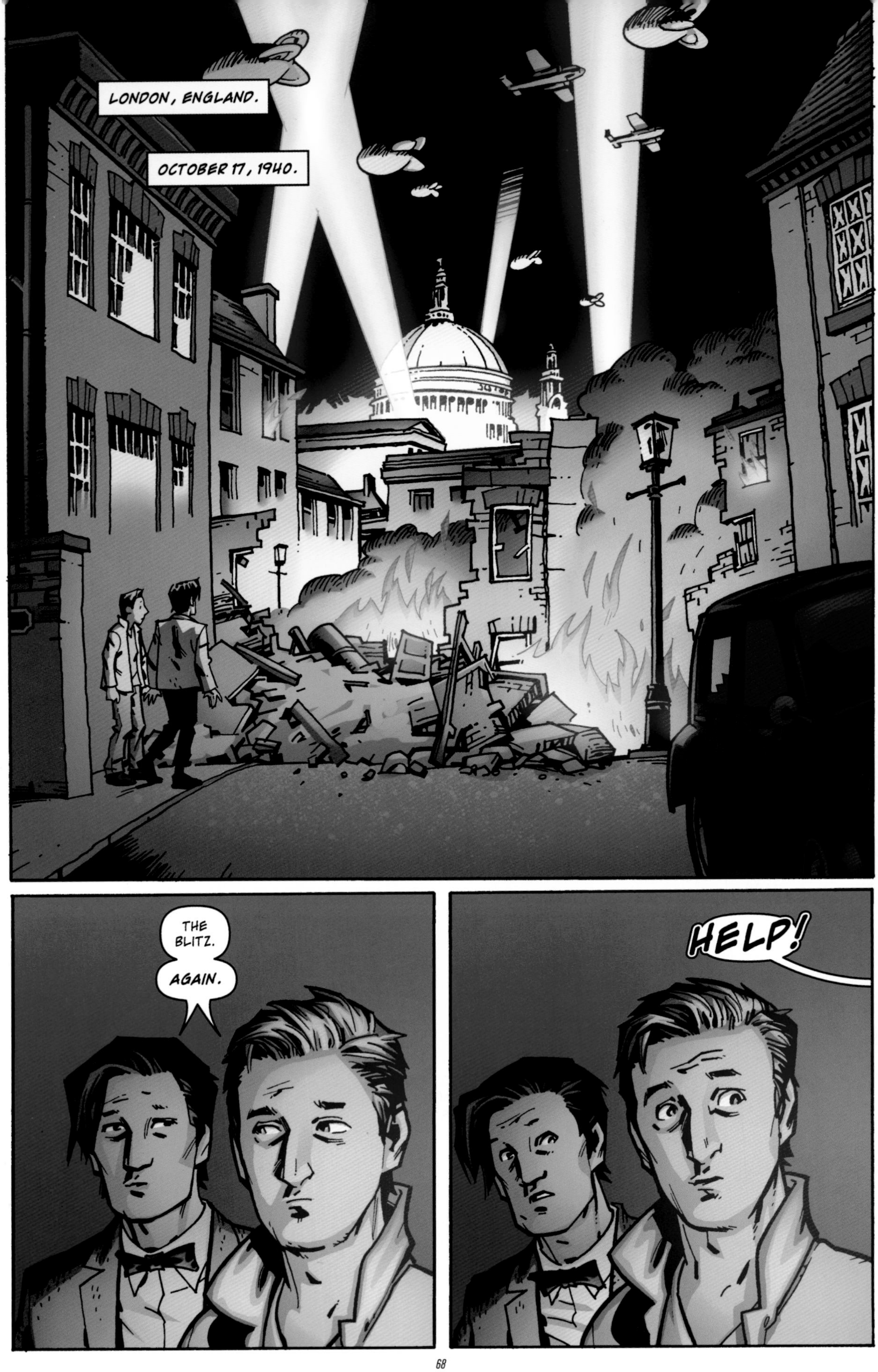
LONDON, ENGLAND.
OCTOBER 17, 1940.
THE BLITZ.
AGAIN.
HELP!

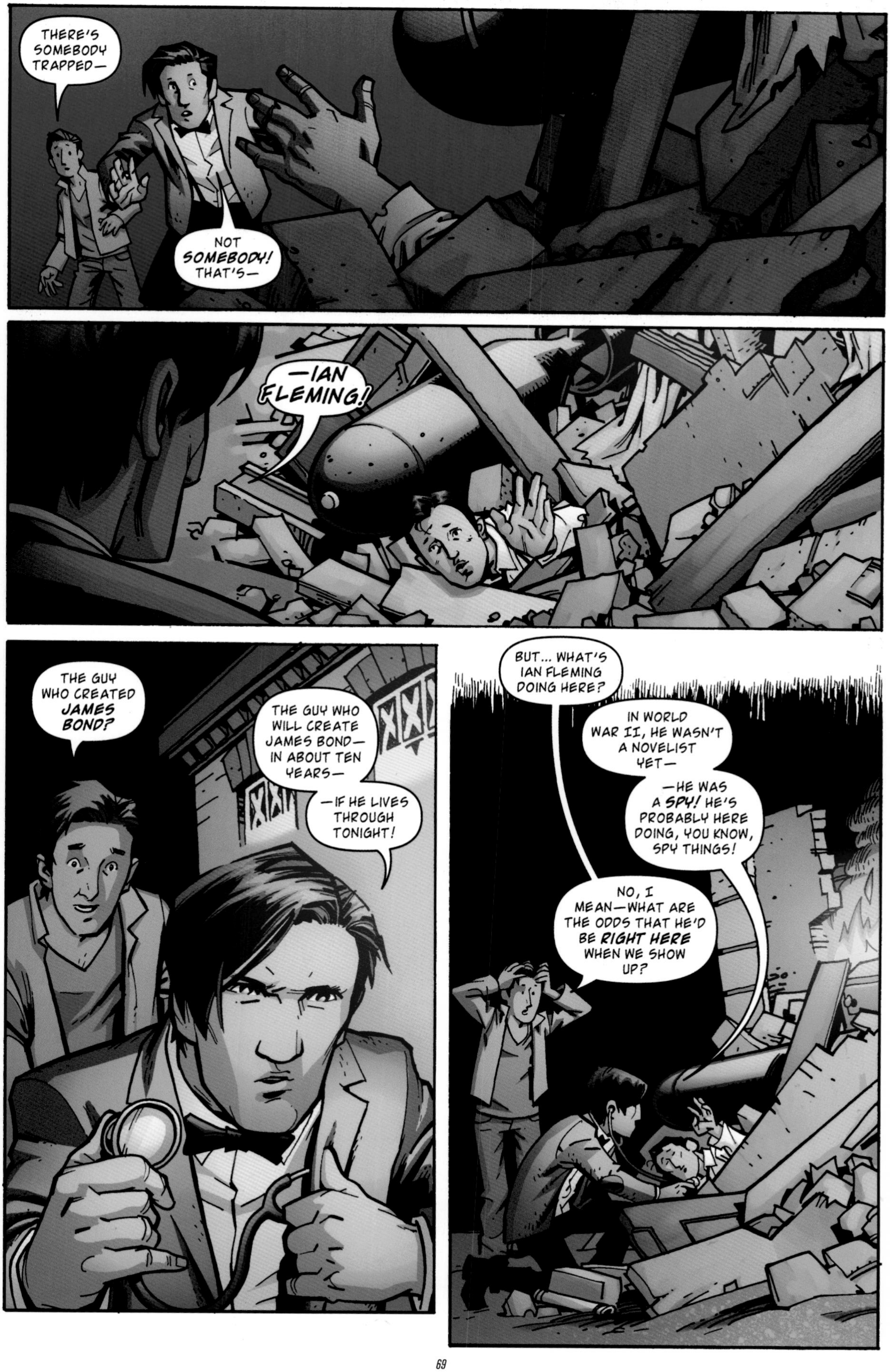
THERE'S SOMEBODY TRAPPED—
NOT SOMEBODY! THAT'S—
—IAN FLEMING!
THE GUY WHO CREATED JAMES BOND?
THE GUY WHO WILL CREATE JAMES BOND—IN ABOUT TEN YEARS—
—IF HE LIVES THROUGH TONIGHT!
BUT... WHAT'S IAN FLEMING DOING HERE?
IN WORLD WAR II, HE WASN'T A NOVELIST YET—
—HE WAS A SPY! HE'S PROBABLY HERE DOING, YOU KNOW, SPY THINGS!
NO, I MEAN—WHAT ARE THE ODDS THAT HE'D BE RIGHT HERE WHEN WE SHOW UP?

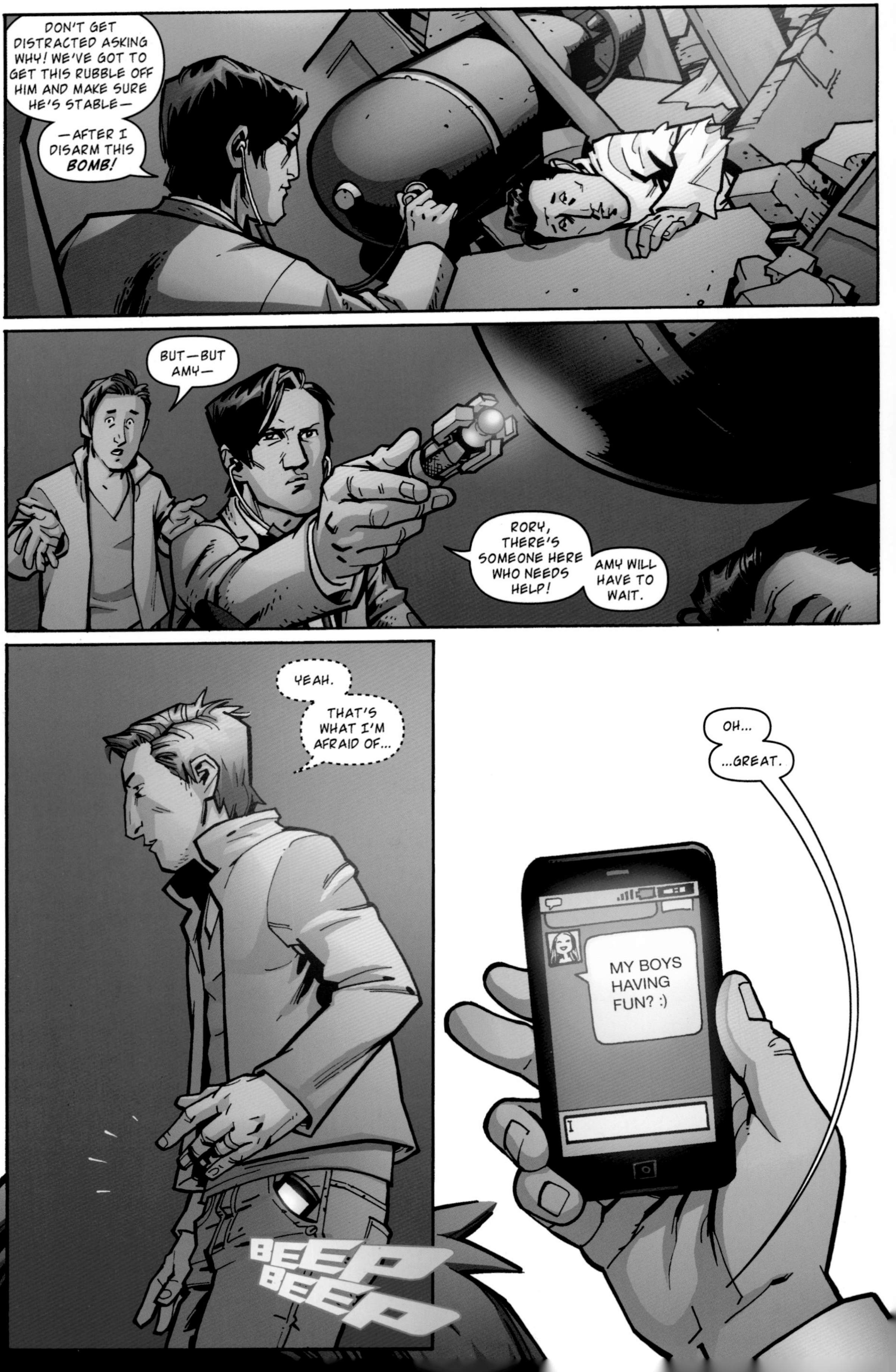
DON'T GET DISTRACTED ASKING WHY! WE'VE GOT TO GET THIS RUBBLE OFF HIM AND MAKE SURE HE'S STABLE—
—AFTER I DISARM THIS BOMB!
BUT—BUT AMY—
RORY, THERE'S SOMEONE HERE WHO NEEDS HELP!
AMY WILL HAVE TO WAIT.
YEAH.
THAT'S WHAT I'M AFRAID OF...
BEEP BEEP
MY BOYS HAVING FUN? :)
OH...
...GREAT.

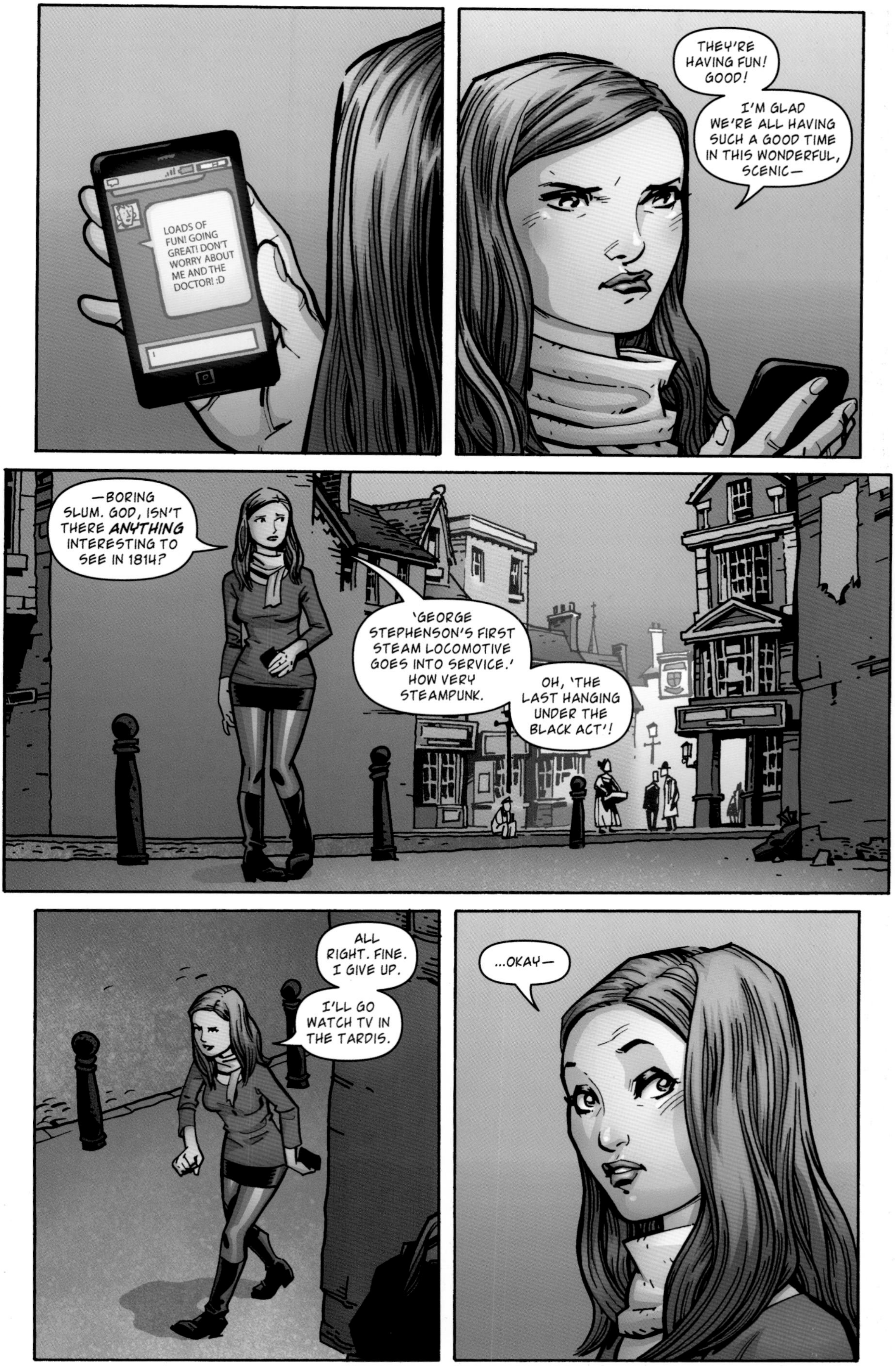
LOADS OF FUN! GOING GREAT! DON'T WORRY ABOUT ME AND THE DOCTOR! :D
THEY'RE HAVING FUN! GOOD!
I'M GLAD WE'RE ALL HAVING SUCH A GOOD TIME IN THIS WONDERFUL, SCENIC—
—BORING SLUM. GOD, ISN'T THERE ANYTHING INTERESTING TO SEE IN 1814?
'GEORGE STEPHENSON'S FIRST STEAM LOCOMOTIVE GOES INTO SERVICE.' HOW VERY STEAMPUNK.
OH, 'THE LAST HANGING UNDER THE BLACK ACT'!
ALL RIGHT. FINE. I GIVE UP.
I'LL GO WATCH TV IN THE TARDIS.
...OKAY—

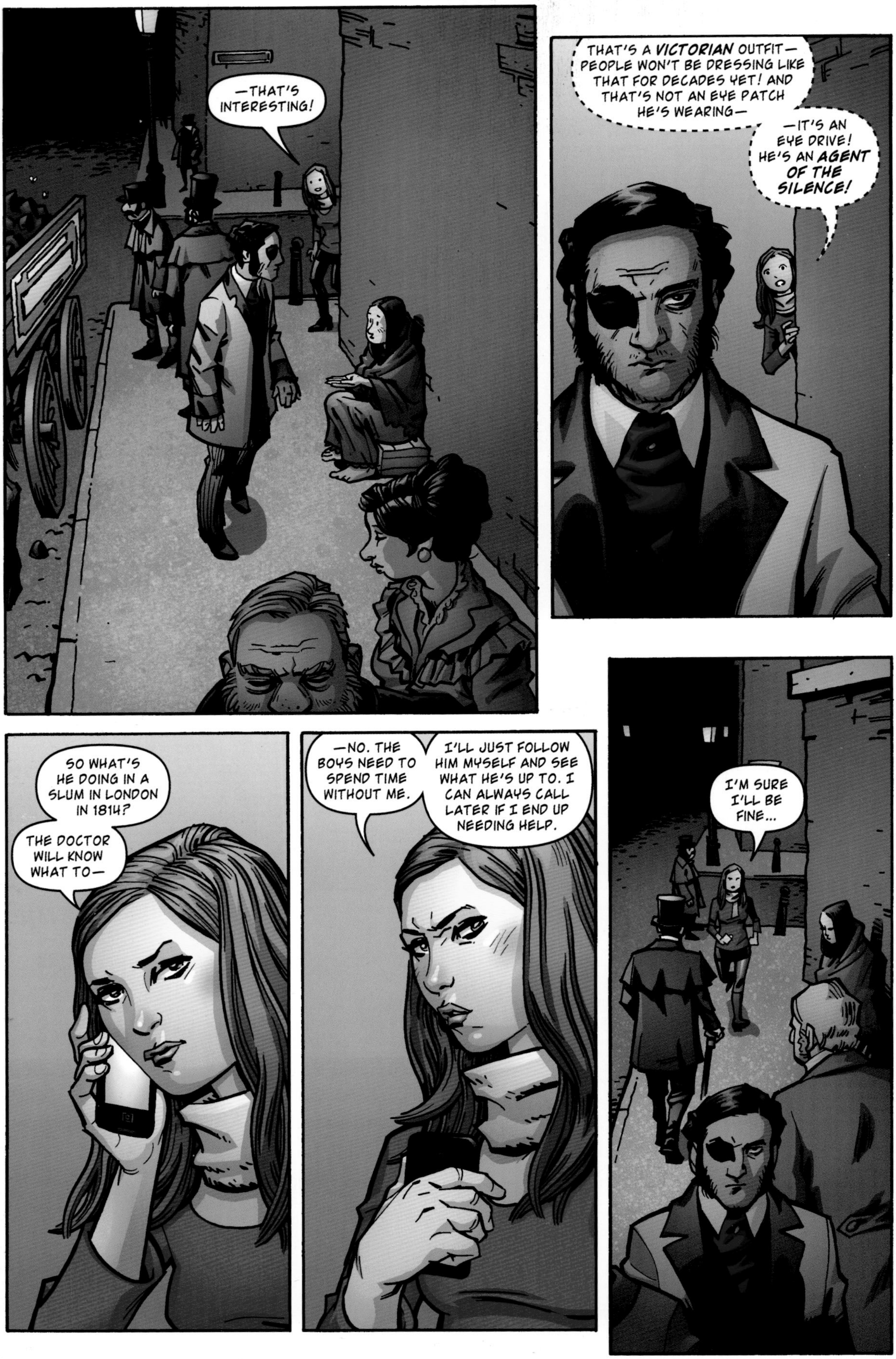
—THAT'S INTERESTING!
THAT'S A VICTORIAN OUTFIT— PEOPLE WON'T BE DRESSING LIKE THAT FOR DECADES YET! AND THAT'S NOT AN EYE PATCH HE'S WEARING—
—IT'S AN EYE DRIVE! HE'S AN AGENT OF THE SILENCE!
SO WHAT'S HE DOING IN A SLUM IN LONDON IN 1814?
THE DOCTOR WILL KNOW WHAT TO—
—NO. THE BOYS NEED TO SPEND TIME WITHOUT ME.
I'LL JUST FOLLOW HIM MYSELF AND SEE WHAT HE'S UP TO. I CAN ALWAYS CALL LATER IF I END UP NEEDING HELP.
I'M SURE I'LL BE FINE...

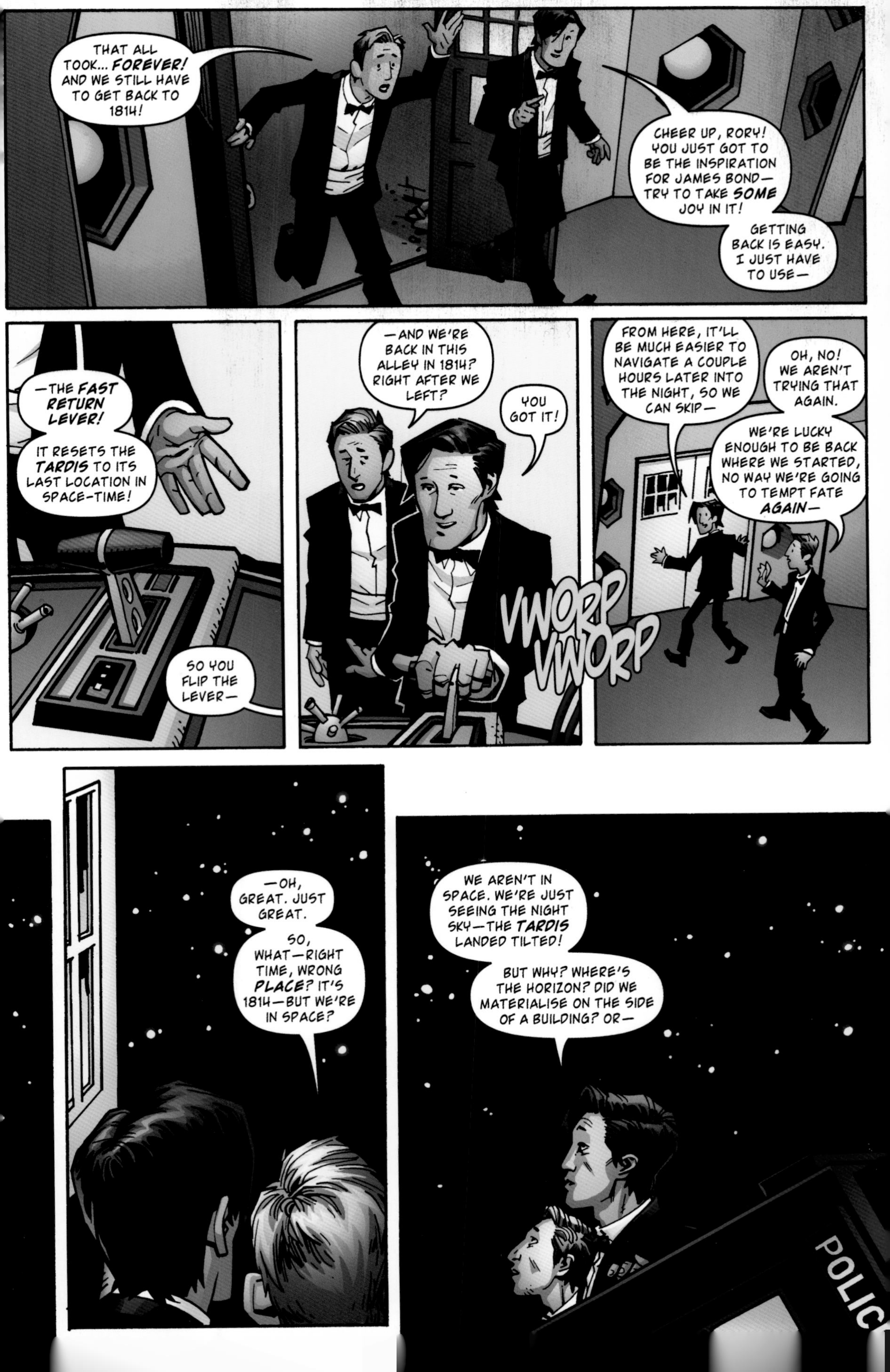
THAT ALL TOOK... FOREVER! AND WE STILL HAVE TO GET BACK TO 1814!
CHEER UP, RORY! YOU JUST GOT TO BE THE INSPIRATION FOR JAMES BOND—TRY TO TAKE SOME JOY IN IT!
GETTING BACK IS EASY. I JUST HAVE TO USE—
—THE FAST RETURN LEVER!
IT RESETS THE TARDIS TO ITS LAST LOCATION IN SPACE-TIME!
SO YOU FLIP THE LEVER—
—AND WE'RE BACK IN THIS ALLEY IN 1814? RIGHT AFTER WE LEFT?
YOU GOT IT!
VWORP VWORP
FROM HERE, IT'LL BE MUCH EASIER TO NAVIGATE A COUPLE HOURS LATER INTO THE NIGHT, SO WE CAN SKIP—
OH, NO! WE AREN'T TRYING THAT AGAIN.
WE'RE LUCKY ENOUGH TO BE BACK WHERE WE STARTED, NO WAY WE'RE GOING TO TEMPT FATE AGAIN—
—OH, GREAT. JUST GREAT.
SO, WHAT—RIGHT TIME, WRONG PLACE? IT'S 1814—BUT WE'RE IN SPACE?
WE AREN'T IN SPACE. WE'RE JUST SEEING THE NIGHT SKY—THE TARDIS LANDED TILTED!
BUT WHY? WHERE'S THE HORIZON? DID WE MATERIALISE ON THE SIDE OF A BUILDING? OR—
POLIC

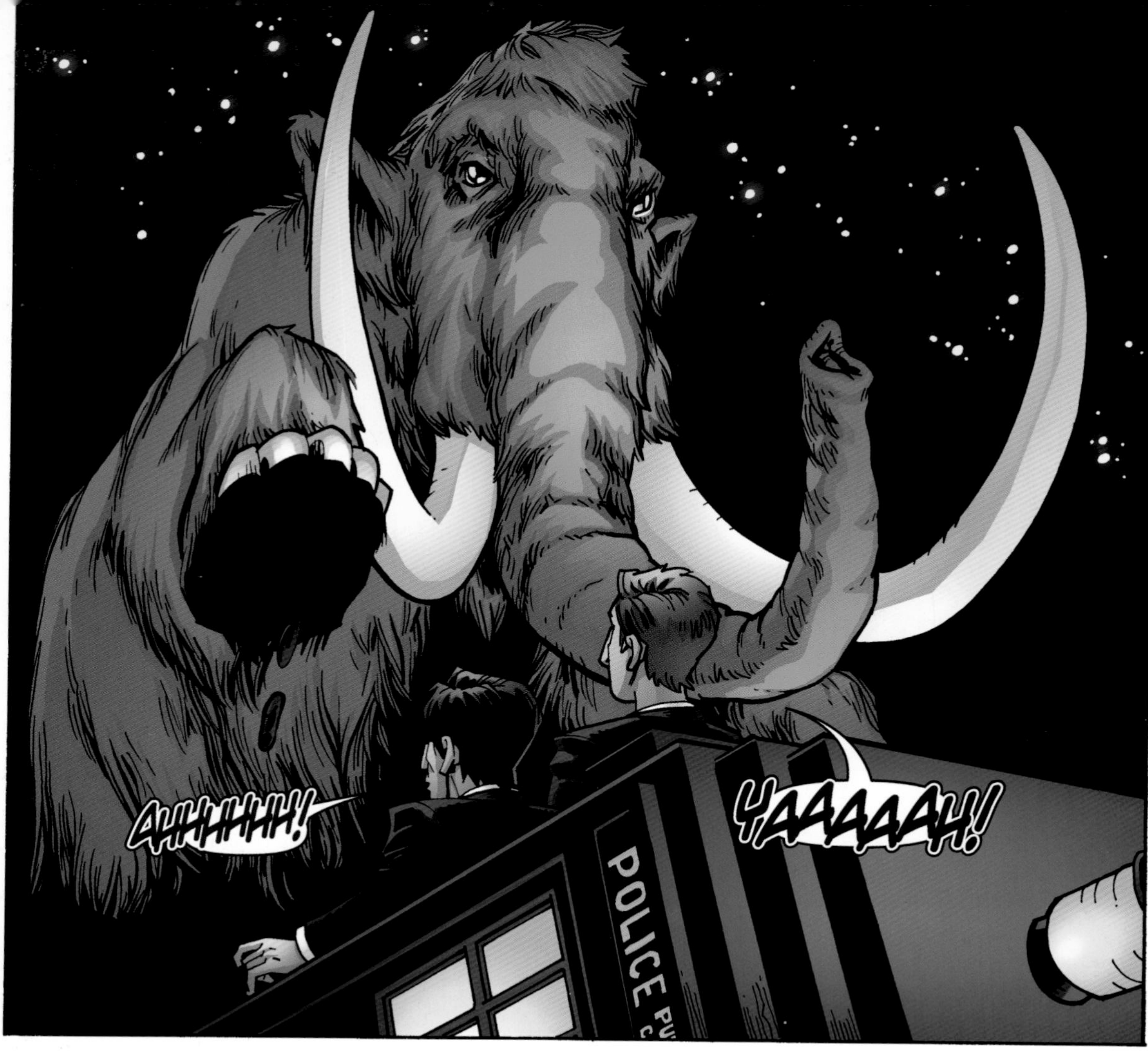
AHHHHHH!
YAAAAAH!
POLICE

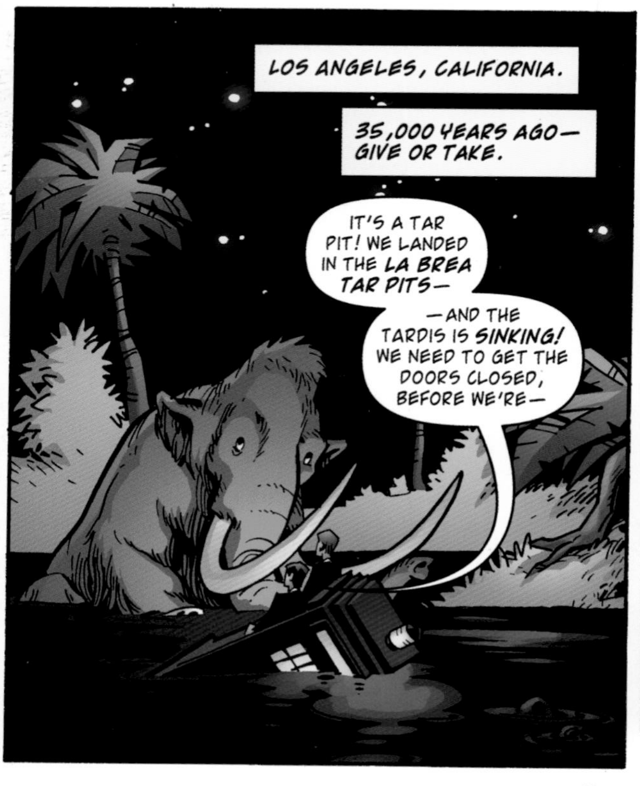
LOS ANGELES, CALIFORNIA.
35,000 YEARS AGO—GIVE OR TAKE.
IT'S A TAR PIT! WE LANDED IN THE LA BREA TAR PITS—
—AND THE TARDIS IS SINKING! WE NEED TO GET THE DOORS CLOSED, BEFORE WE'RE—

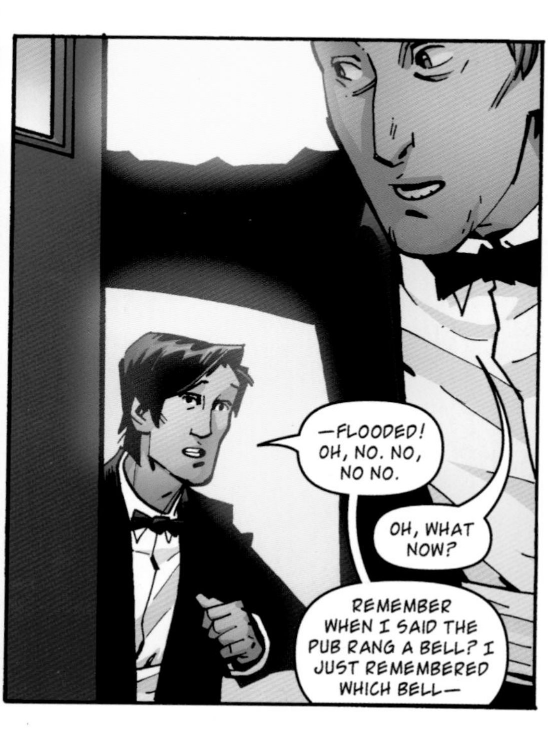
—FLOODED! OH, NO. NO, NO NO.
OH, WHAT NOW?
REMEMBER WHEN I SAID THE PUB RANG A BELL? I JUST REMEMBERED WHICH BELL—

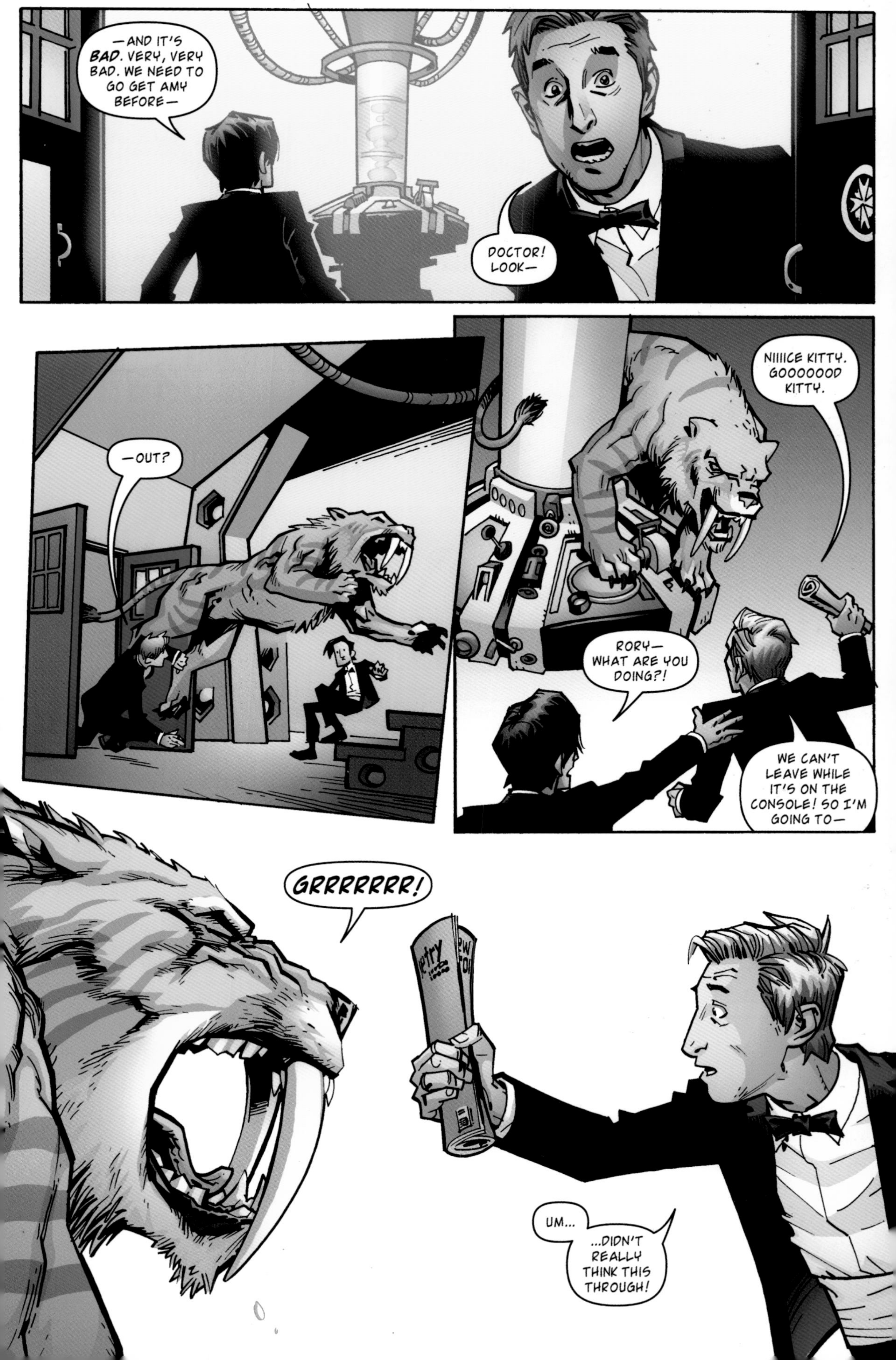
—AND IT'S BAD. VERY, VERY BAD. WE NEED TO GO GET AMY BEFORE—
DOCTOR! LOOK—
—OUT?
NIIIICE KITTY. GOOOOOOD KITTY.
RORY— WHAT ARE YOU DOING?!
WE CAN'T LEAVE WHILE IT'S ON THE CONSOLE! SO I'M GOING TO—
GRRRRRRR!
UM...
...DIDN'T REALLY THINK THIS THROUGH!

WHAP

MEW?

RORY—

—YOU JUST HIT A SABERTOOTH WITH A MAGAZINE!

I THOUGHT IT WAS GOING TO—UH—*SABERBITE* ME!

IT'S OFF THE CONSOLE—COULD YOU GET US OUT OF THE TAR PIT AND BACK TO AMY? I'LL GO—UH, CATCH IT OR SOMETHING?

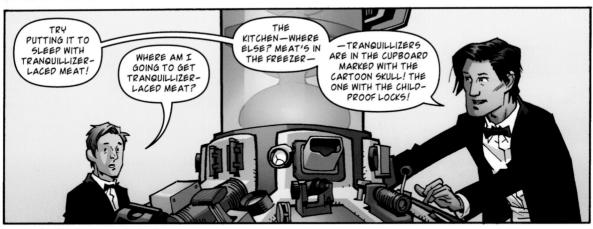

TRY PUTTING IT TO SLEEP WITH TRANQUILLIZER-LACED MEAT!

WHERE AM I GOING TO GET TRANQUILLIZER-LACED MEAT?

THE KITCHEN—WHERE ELSE? MEAT'S IN THE FREEZER—

—TRANQUILLIZERS ARE IN THE CUPBOARD MARKED WITH THE CARTOON SKULL! THE ONE WITH THE CHILD-PROOF LOCKS!

'PERFECTLY ROUTINE'— I SHOULD'VE FIGURED THAT'S *DOCTOR-ESE* FOR 'EXCEEDINGLY DANGEROUS'...

...I HOPE AMY'S OKAY.

AND TRY NOT TO DIE FOR ONCE!

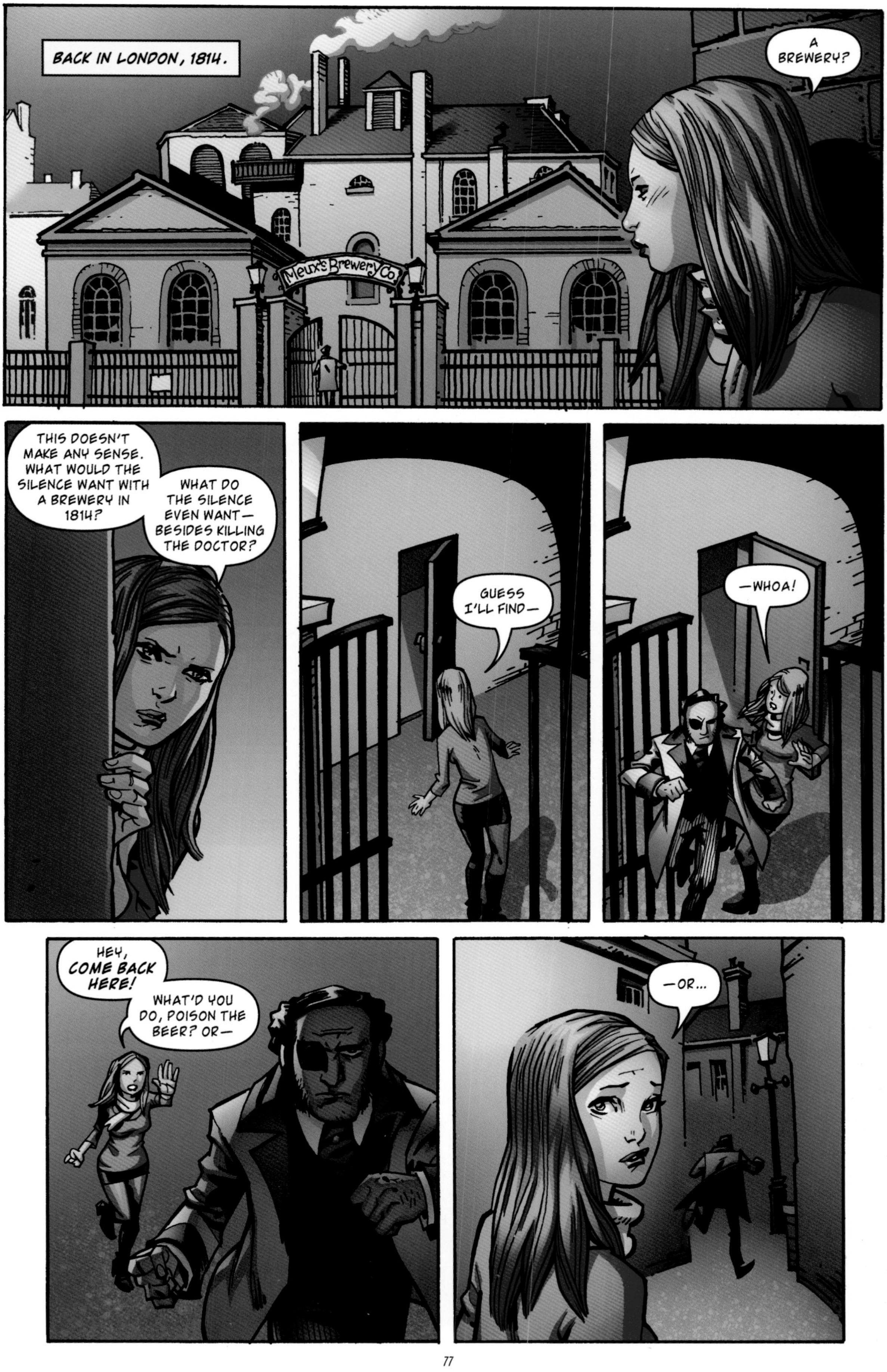
BACK IN LONDON, 1814.
A BREWERY?
Meux's Brewery Co.
THIS DOESN'T MAKE ANY SENSE. WHAT WOULD THE SILENCE WANT WITH A BREWERY IN 1814?
WHAT DO THE SILENCE EVEN WANT— BESIDES KILLING THE DOCTOR?
GUESS I'LL FIND—
—WHOA!
HEY, COME BACK HERE!
WHAT'D YOU DO, POISON THE BEER? OR—
—OR...

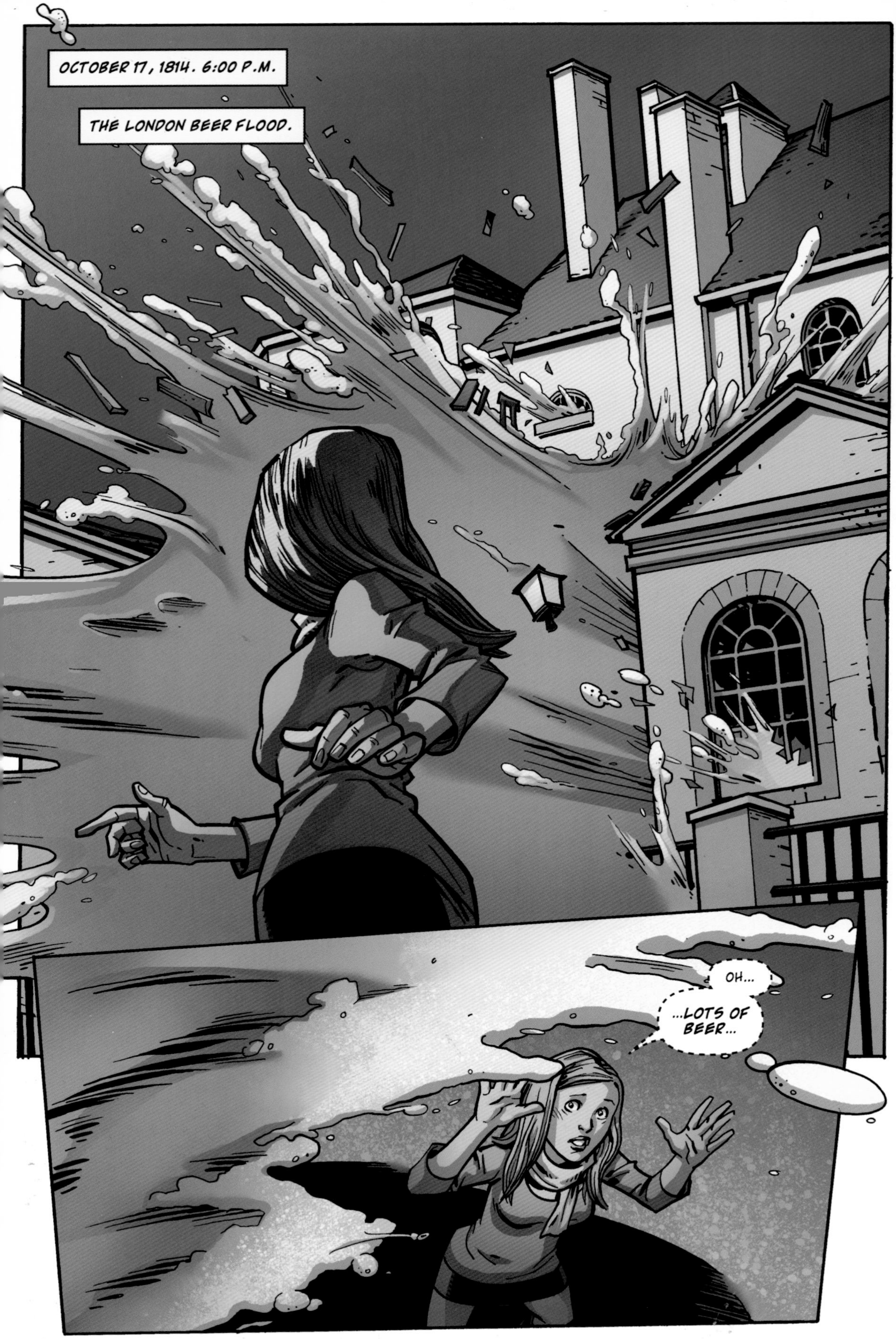
OCTOBER 17, 1814. 6:00 P.M.
THE LONDON BEER FLOOD.
OH...
...LOTS OF BEER...

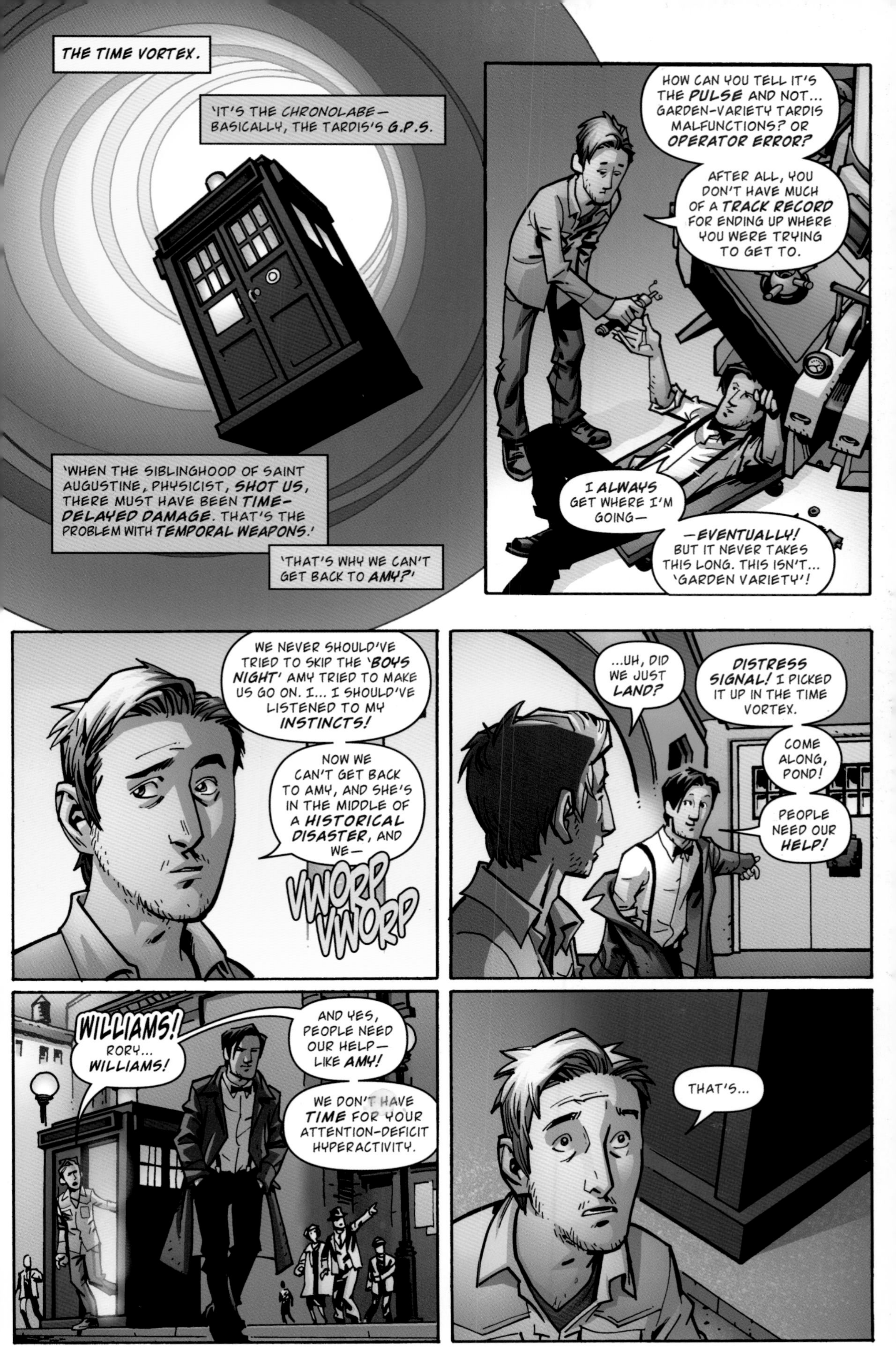

THE TIME VORTEX.
'IT'S THE CHRONOLABE— BASICALLY, THE TARDIS'S G.P.S.
'WHEN THE SIBLINGHOOD OF SAINT AUGUSTINE, PHYSICIST, SHOT US, THERE MUST HAVE BEEN TIME-DELAYED DAMAGE. THAT'S THE PROBLEM WITH TEMPORAL WEAPONS.'
'THAT'S WHY WE CAN'T GET BACK TO AMY?'
HOW CAN YOU TELL IT'S THE PULSE AND NOT... GARDEN-VARIETY TARDIS MALFUNCTIONS? OR OPERATOR ERROR?
AFTER ALL, YOU DON'T HAVE MUCH OF A TRACK RECORD FOR ENDING UP WHERE YOU WERE TRYING TO GET TO.
I ALWAYS GET WHERE I'M GOING—
—EVENTUALLY! BUT IT NEVER TAKES THIS LONG. THIS ISN'T... 'GARDEN VARIETY'!
WE NEVER SHOULD'VE TRIED TO SKIP THE 'BOYS NIGHT' AMY TRIED TO MAKE US GO ON. I... I SHOULD'VE LISTENED TO MY INSTINCTS!
NOW WE CAN'T GET BACK TO AMY, AND SHE'S IN THE MIDDLE OF A HISTORICAL DISASTER, AND WE—
VWORP VWORP
...UH, DID WE JUST LAND?
DISTRESS SIGNAL! I PICKED IT UP IN THE TIME VORTEX.
COME ALONG, POND!
PEOPLE NEED OUR HELP!
WILLIAMS! RORY... WILLIAMS!
AND YES, PEOPLE NEED OUR HELP— LIKE AMY!
WE DON'T HAVE TIME FOR YOUR ATTENTION-DEFICIT HYPERACTIVITY.
THAT'S...

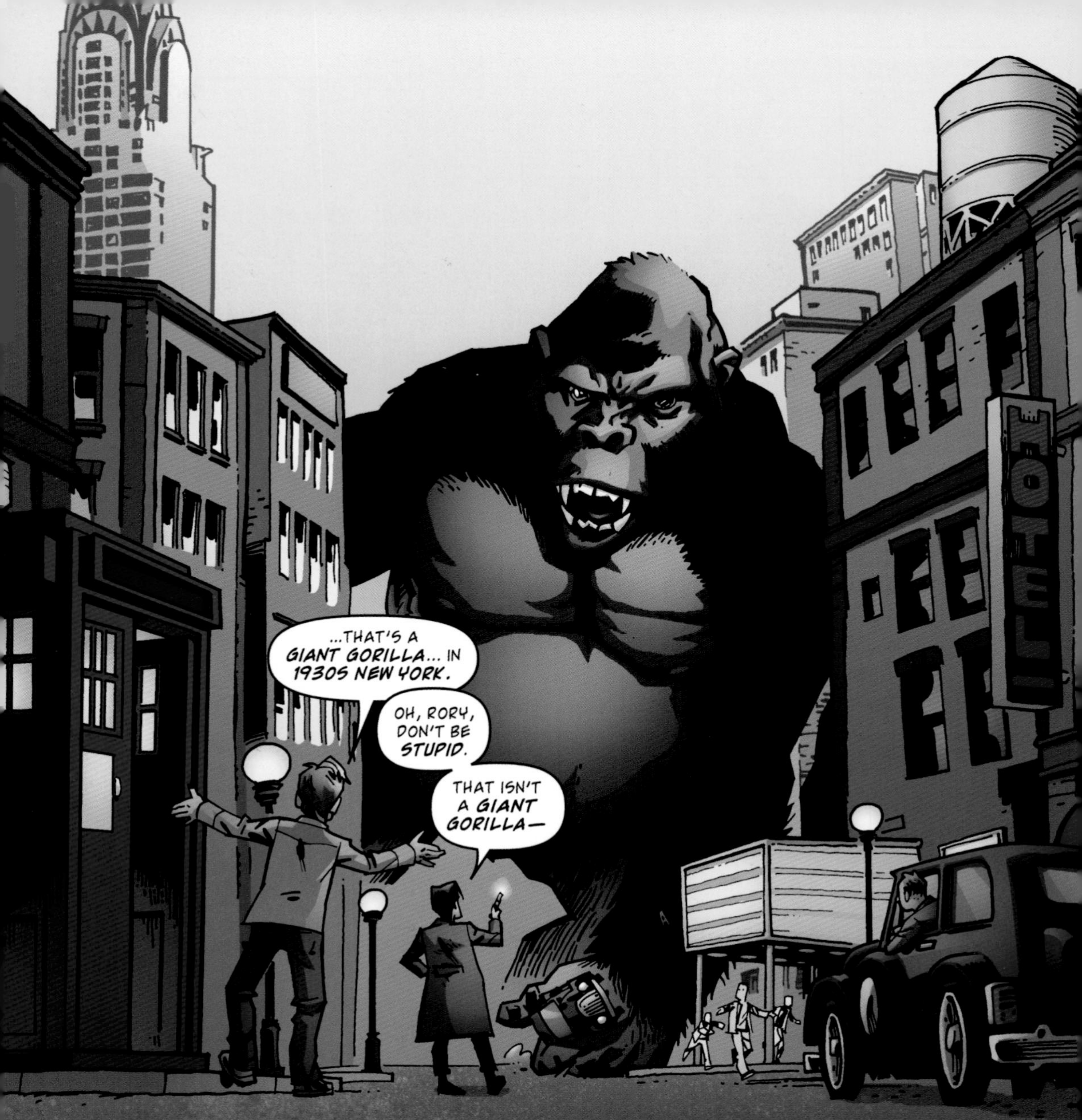
...THAT'S A GIANT GORILLA... IN 1930S NEW YORK.
OH, RORY, DON'T BE STUPID.
THAT ISN'T A GIANT GORILLA—
HOTEL

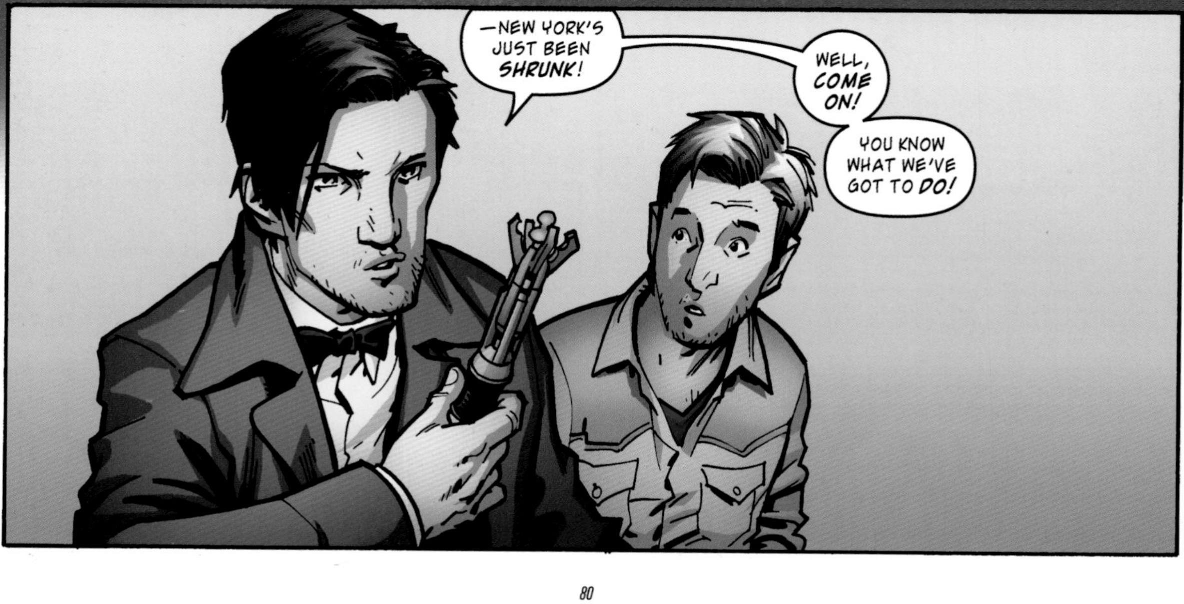
—NEW YORK'S JUST BEEN SHRUNK!
WELL, COME ON!
YOU KNOW WHAT WE'VE GOT TO DO!

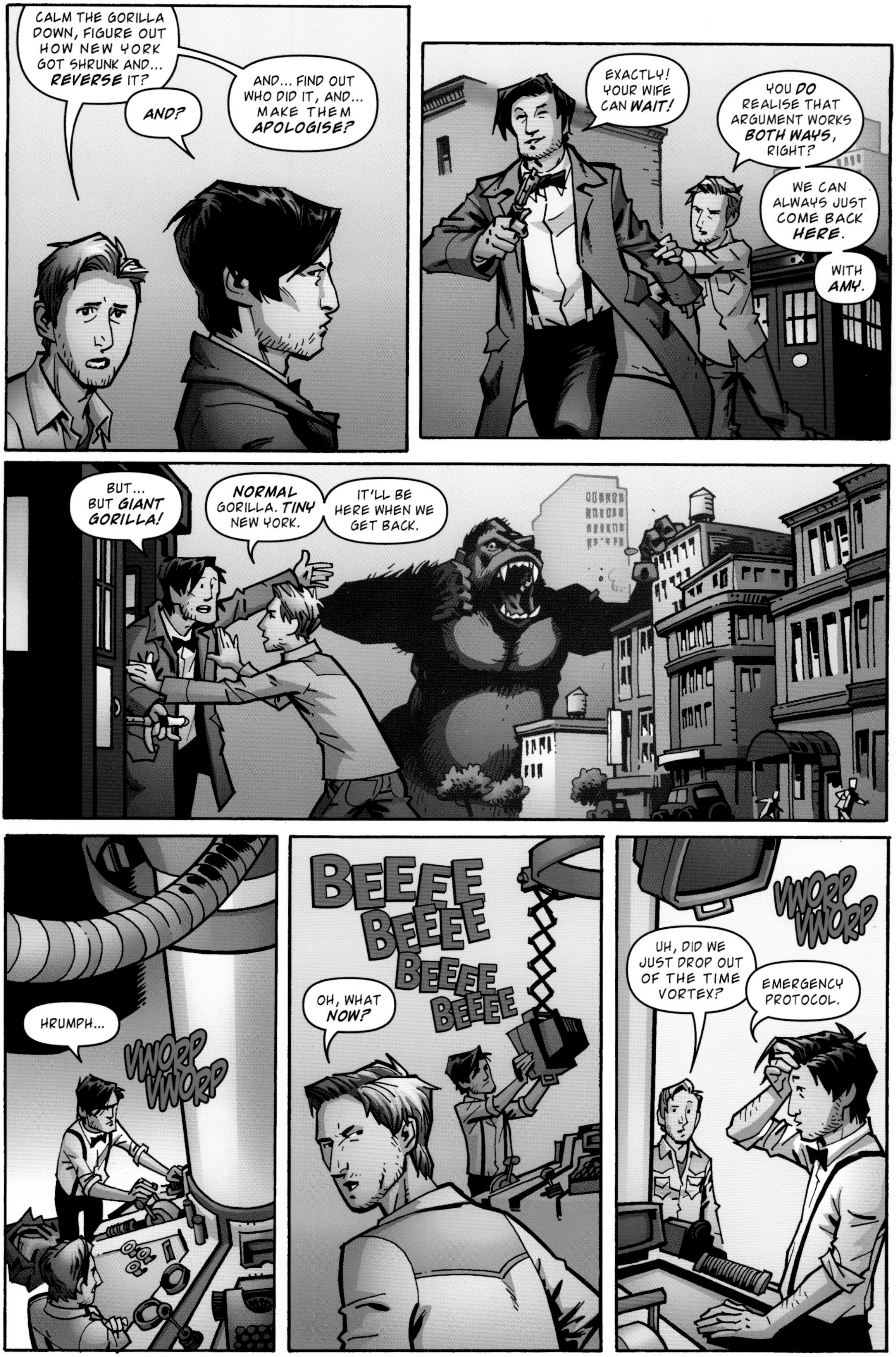
CALM THE GORILLA DOWN, FIGURE OUT HOW NEW YORK GOT SHRUNK AND... *REVERSE* IT?
AND?
AND... FIND OUT WHO DID IT, AND... MAKE THEM *APOLOGISE?*
EXACTLY! YOUR WIFE CAN *WAIT!*
YOU *DO* REALISE THAT ARGUMENT WORKS *BOTH WAYS*, RIGHT?
WE CAN ALWAYS JUST COME BACK *HERE*.
WITH *AMY*.
BUT... BUT *GIANT GORILLA!*
NORMAL GORILLA. *TINY* NEW YORK.
IT'LL BE HERE WHEN WE GET BACK.
HRUMPH...
VWORP VWORP
BEEEE BEEEE BEEEE BEEEE
OH, WHAT *NOW?*
VWORP VWORP
UH, DID WE JUST DROP OUT OF THE TIME VORTEX?
EMERGENCY PROTOCOL.

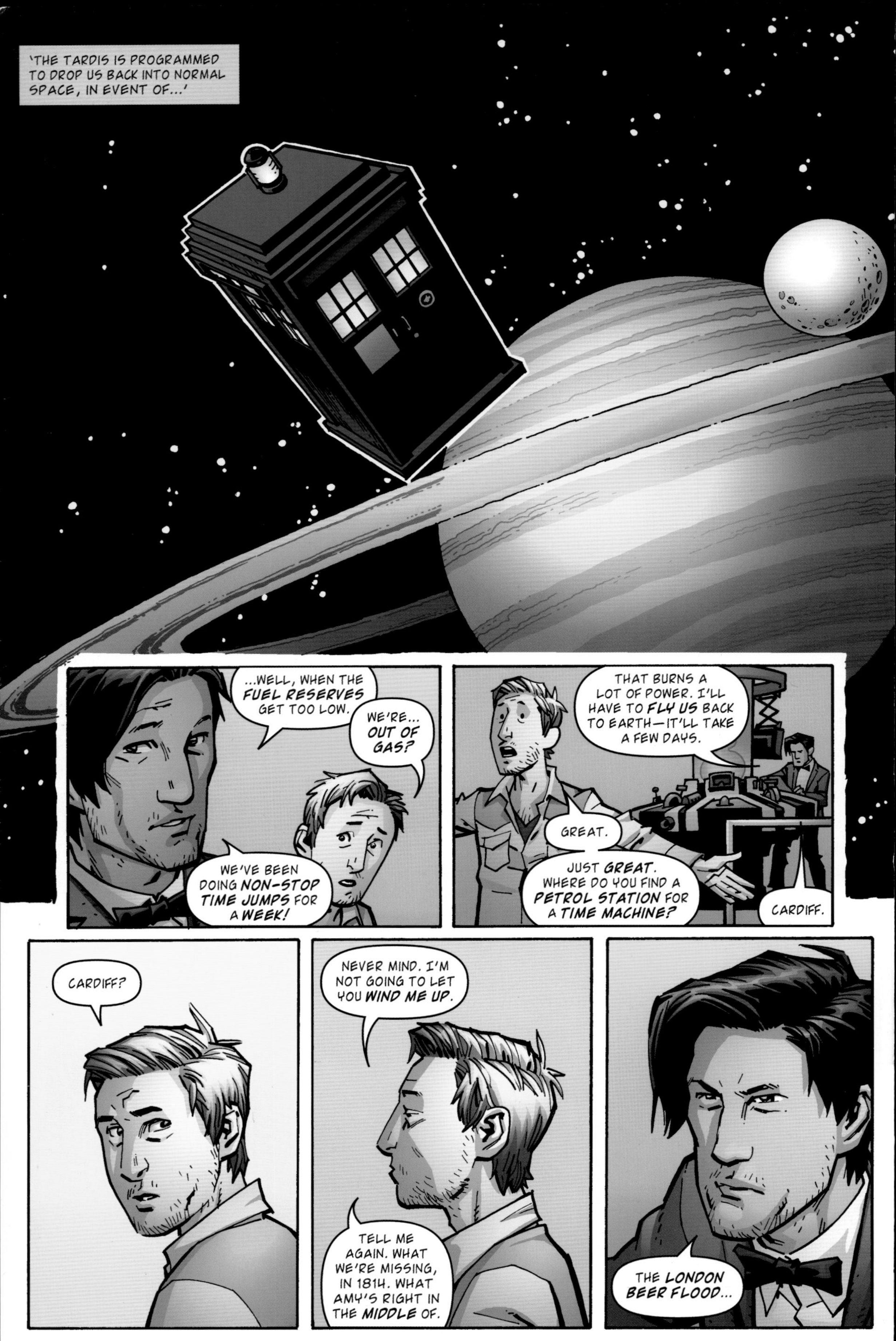
'THE TARDIS IS PROGRAMMED TO DROP US BACK INTO NORMAL SPACE, IN EVENT OF...'
...WELL, WHEN THE FUEL RESERVES GET TOO LOW.
WE'RE... OUT OF GAS?
WE'VE BEEN DOING NON-STOP TIME JUMPS FOR A WEEK!
THAT BURNS A LOT OF POWER. I'LL HAVE TO FLY US BACK TO EARTH—IT'LL TAKE A FEW DAYS.
GREAT.
JUST GREAT. WHERE DO YOU FIND A PETROL STATION FOR A TIME MACHINE?
CARDIFF.
CARDIFF?
NEVER MIND. I'M NOT GOING TO LET YOU WIND ME UP.
TELL ME AGAIN. WHAT WE'RE MISSING, IN 1814. WHAT AMY'S RIGHT IN THE MIDDLE OF.
THE LONDON BEER FLOOD...

'ONE OF THE *ODDEST* TRAGEDIES IN HUMAN HISTORY—UP THERE WITH THE *GREAT BOSTON MOLASSES DISASTER.*

'ON 17 OCTOBER, 1814, THE HORSE SHOE BREWERY BURST OPEN, FLOODING THE ST. GILES NEIGHBORHOOD WITH *323,000 GALLONS* OF BEER!

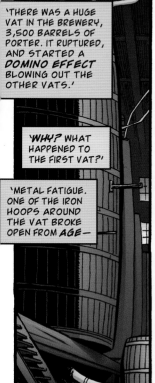

'THERE WAS A HUGE VAT IN THE BREWERY, 3,500 BARRELS OF PORTER. IT RUPTURED, AND STARTED A *DOMINO EFFECT* BLOWING OUT THE OTHER VATS.'

'*WHY?* WHAT HAPPENED TO THE FIRST VAT?'

'METAL FATIGUE. ONE OF THE IRON HOOPS AROUND THE VAT BROKE OPEN FROM *AGE*—

'—IF YOU TRUST WHAT'S IN THE *HISTORY BOOKS,* ANYWAY—WHICH I *RARELY* RECOMMEND.

'THE *BEER TSUNAMI* DESTROYED TWO HOUSES—

'—AND THE *PUB* WE WERE IN EARLIER! SO, LUCKY BREAK WE *SKIPPED OUT!*'

'LUCKY—FOR *US!* BUT—

'—WHAT ABOUT *AMY?*'

GHHUUUU!

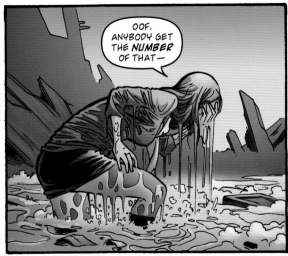

OOF. ANYBODY GET THE **NUMBER** OF THAT—

—UH... **TSUNAMI OF BEER?**

I CAN'T BELIEVE THIS THING STILL **WORKS!**

'17 OCTOBER, 1814— THE LONDON BEER FLOOD'. OKAY, THAT EXPLAINS **THIS**. NOW, WHAT ABOUT—

—OH!

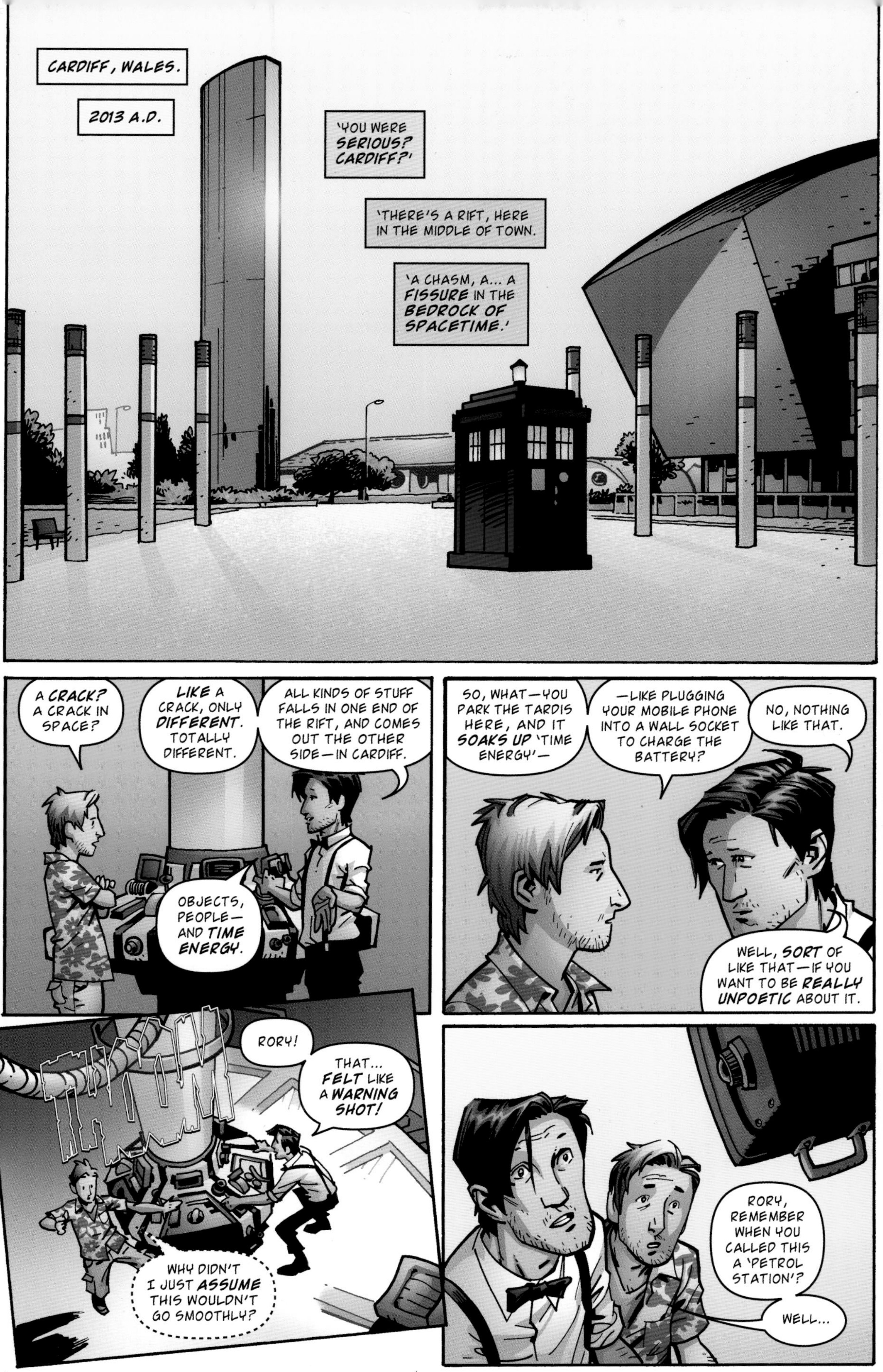
CARDIFF, WALES.
2013 A.D.
'YOU WERE SERIOUS? CARDIFF?'
'THERE'S A RIFT, HERE IN THE MIDDLE OF TOWN.
'A CHASM, A... A FISSURE IN THE BEDROCK OF SPACETIME.'
A CRACK? A CRACK IN SPACE?
LIKE A CRACK, ONLY DIFFERENT. TOTALLY DIFFERENT.
ALL KINDS OF STUFF FALLS IN ONE END OF THE RIFT, AND COMES OUT THE OTHER SIDE—IN CARDIFF.
OBJECTS, PEOPLE—AND TIME ENERGY.
SO, WHAT—YOU PARK THE TARDIS HERE, AND IT SOAKS UP 'TIME ENERGY'—
—LIKE PLUGGING YOUR MOBILE PHONE INTO A WALL SOCKET TO CHARGE THE BATTERY?
NO, NOTHING LIKE THAT.
WELL, SORT OF LIKE THAT—IF YOU WANT TO BE REALLY UNPOETIC ABOUT IT.
RORY!
THAT... FELT LIKE A WARNING SHOT!
WHY DIDN'T I JUST ASSUME THIS WOULDN'T GO SMOOTHLY?
RORY, REMEMBER WHEN YOU CALLED THIS A 'PETROL STATION'?
WELL...

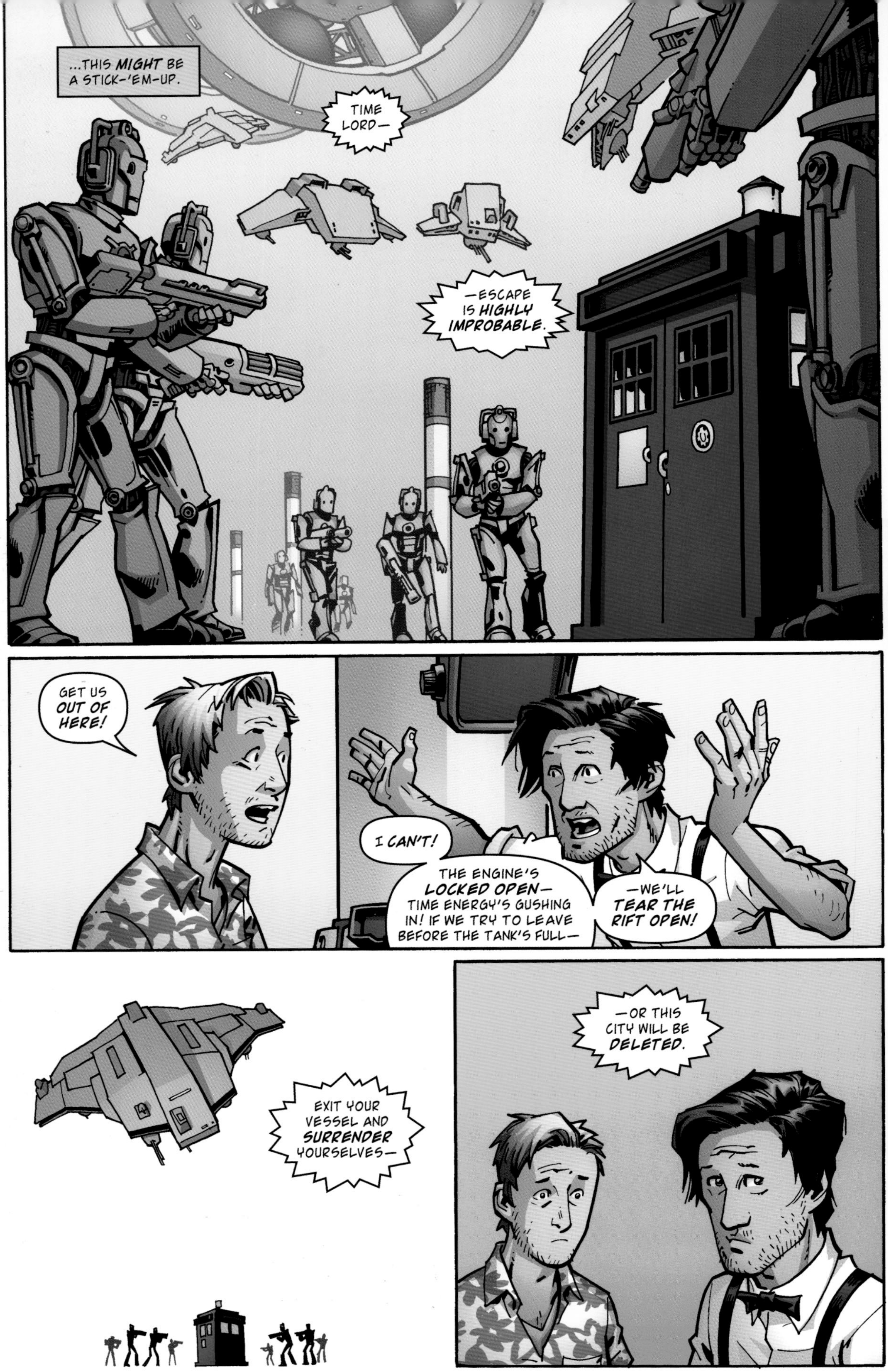
...THIS MIGHT BE A STICK-'EM-UP.
TIME LORD—
—ESCAPE IS HIGHLY IMPROBABLE.
GET US OUT OF HERE!
I CAN'T!
THE ENGINE'S LOCKED OPEN— TIME ENERGY'S GUSHING IN! IF WE TRY TO LEAVE BEFORE THE TANK'S FULL—
—WE'LL TEAR THE RIFT OPEN!
EXIT YOUR VESSEL AND SURRENDER YOURSELVES—
—OR THIS CITY WILL BE DELETED.

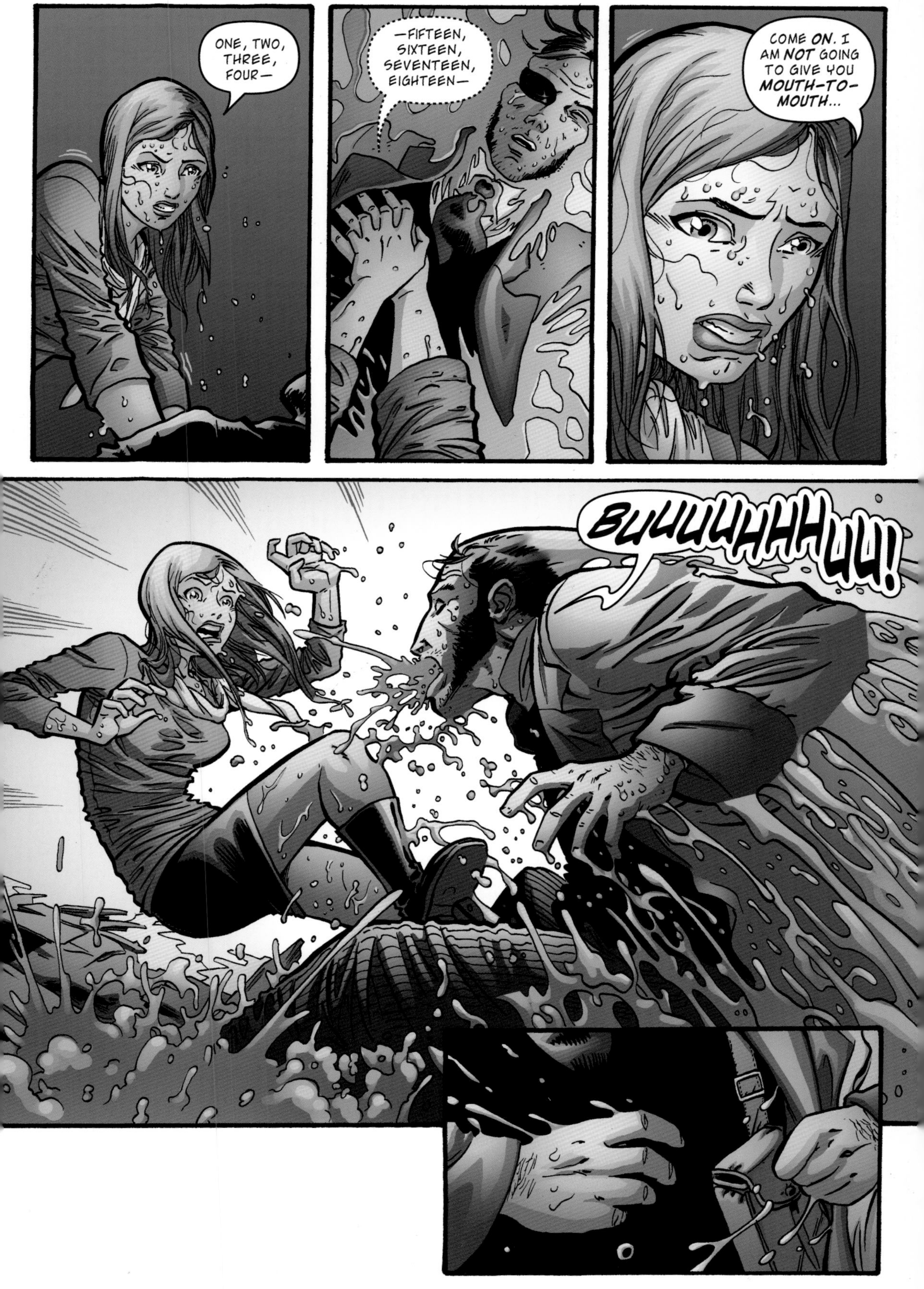
ONE, TWO, THREE, FOUR—
—FIFTEEN, SIXTEEN, SEVENTEEN, EIGHTEEN—
COME ON. I AM NOT GOING TO GIVE YOU MOUTH-TO-MOUTH...
BUUUUHHHUU!

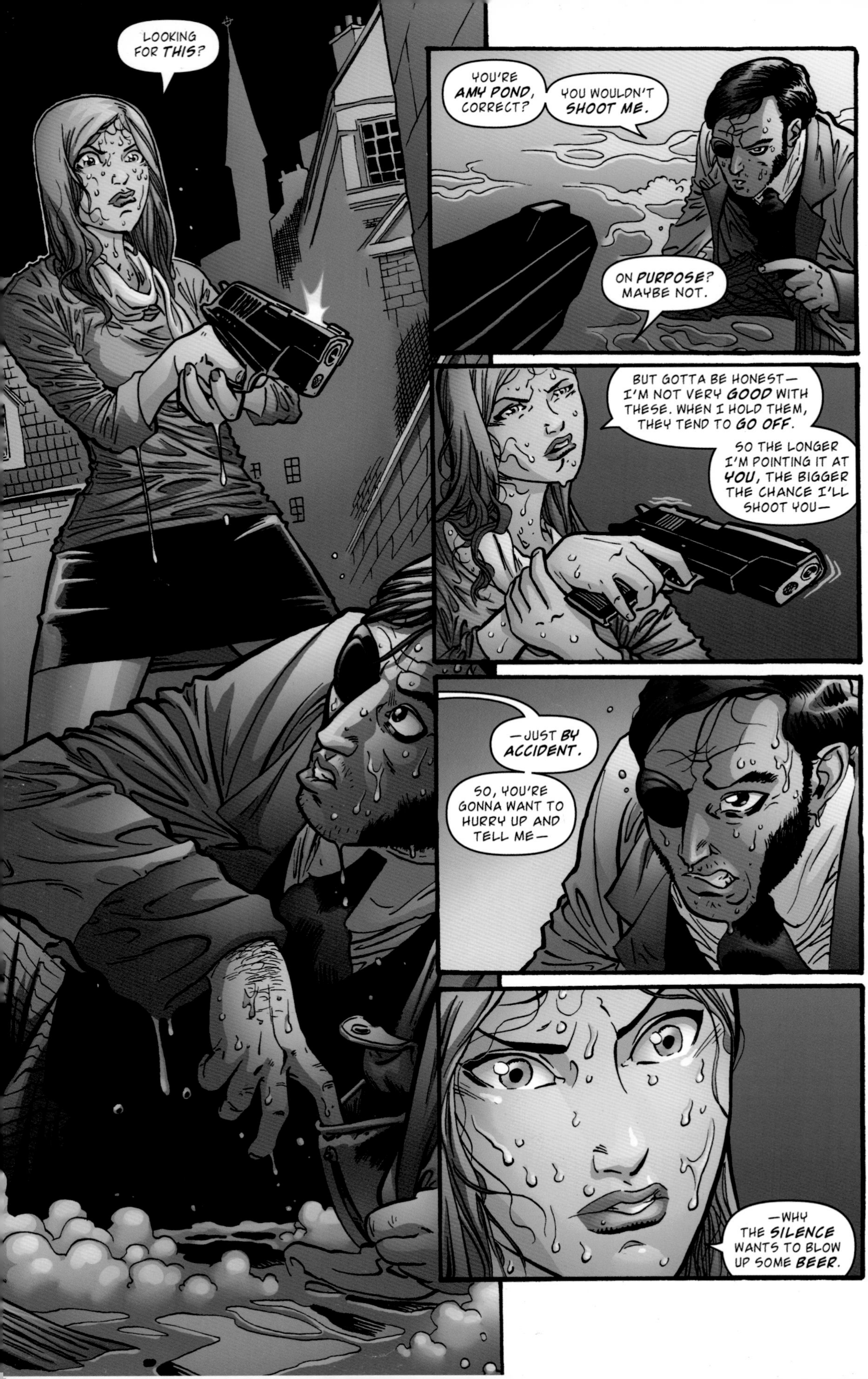
LOOKING FOR THIS?
YOU'RE AMY POND, CORRECT?
YOU WOULDN'T SHOOT ME.
ON PURPOSE? MAYBE NOT.
BUT GOTTA BE HONEST— I'M NOT VERY GOOD WITH THESE. WHEN I HOLD THEM, THEY TEND TO GO OFF.
SO THE LONGER I'M POINTING IT AT YOU, THE BIGGER THE CHANCE I'LL SHOOT YOU—
—JUST BY ACCIDENT.
SO, YOU'RE GONNA WANT TO HURRY UP AND TELL ME—
—WHY THE SILENCE WANTS TO BLOW UP SOME BEER.

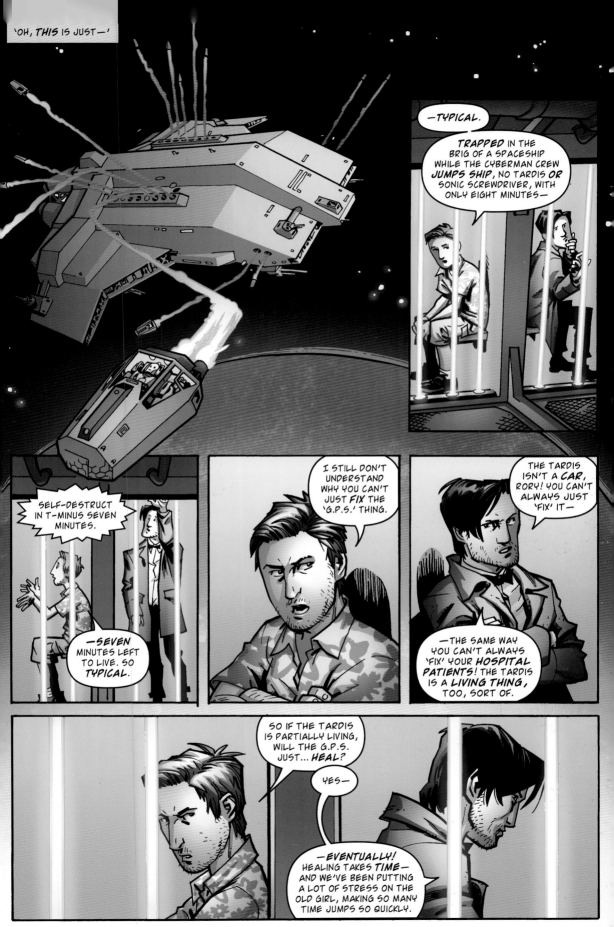

'OH, *THIS* IS JUST—'

—*TYPICAL.*

TRAPPED IN THE BRIG OF A SPACESHIP WHILE THE CYBERMAN CREW *JUMPS SHIP*, NO TARDIS *OR* SONIC SCREWDRIVER, WITH ONLY EIGHT MINUTES—

SELF-DESTRUCT IN T-MINUS SEVEN MINUTES.

—*SEVEN* MINUTES LEFT TO LIVE. SO *TYPICAL.*

I STILL DON'T UNDERSTAND WHY YOU CAN'T JUST *FIX* THE 'G.P.S.' THING.

THE TARDIS ISN'T A *CAR,* RORY! YOU CAN'T ALWAYS JUST 'FIX' IT—

—THE SAME WAY YOU CAN'T ALWAYS 'FIX' YOUR *HOSPITAL PATIENTS!* THE TARDIS IS A *LIVING THING,* TOO, SORT OF.

SO IF THE TARDIS IS PARTIALLY LIVING, WILL THE G.P.S. JUST... *HEAL?*

YES—

—*EVENTUALLY!* HEALING TAKES *TIME*— AND WE'VE BEEN PUTTING A LOT OF STRESS ON THE OLD GIRL, MAKING SO MANY TIME JUMPS SO QUICKLY.

WELL, IS THERE ANYTHING WE CAN DO TO *SPEED UP* THE TARDIS'S HEALING?

YOU KNOW, GIVE THE TARDIS...

...'BED REST'?

YES!

NURSE POND, I COULD *KISS YOU!* BED REST! YES! LET'S *TRY* IT!

HOW? THE TARDIS ISN'T HERE, IT'S IN *WALES.* AND THIS SHIP IS GOING TO BLOW UP IN... UM...

SELF-DESTRUCT IN T-MINUS SIX MINUTES.

...SIX MINUTES.

DON'T WEIGH ME DOWN WITH *TRIVIA!* HOW DO YOU EAT A WOOLLY MAMMOTH, RORY?

HOW DO I—?

YOU EAT IT *ONE BITE AT A TIME!*

AND PREFERABLY IN A GOOD YELLOW CURRY!

MMMM, I HAVEN'T HAD MAMMOTH CURRY IN *DECADES!*

RIGHT NOW, THE *FIRST* 'BITE'—

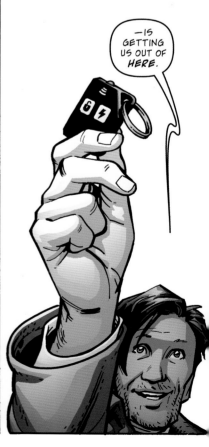

—IS GETTING US OUT OF *HERE.*

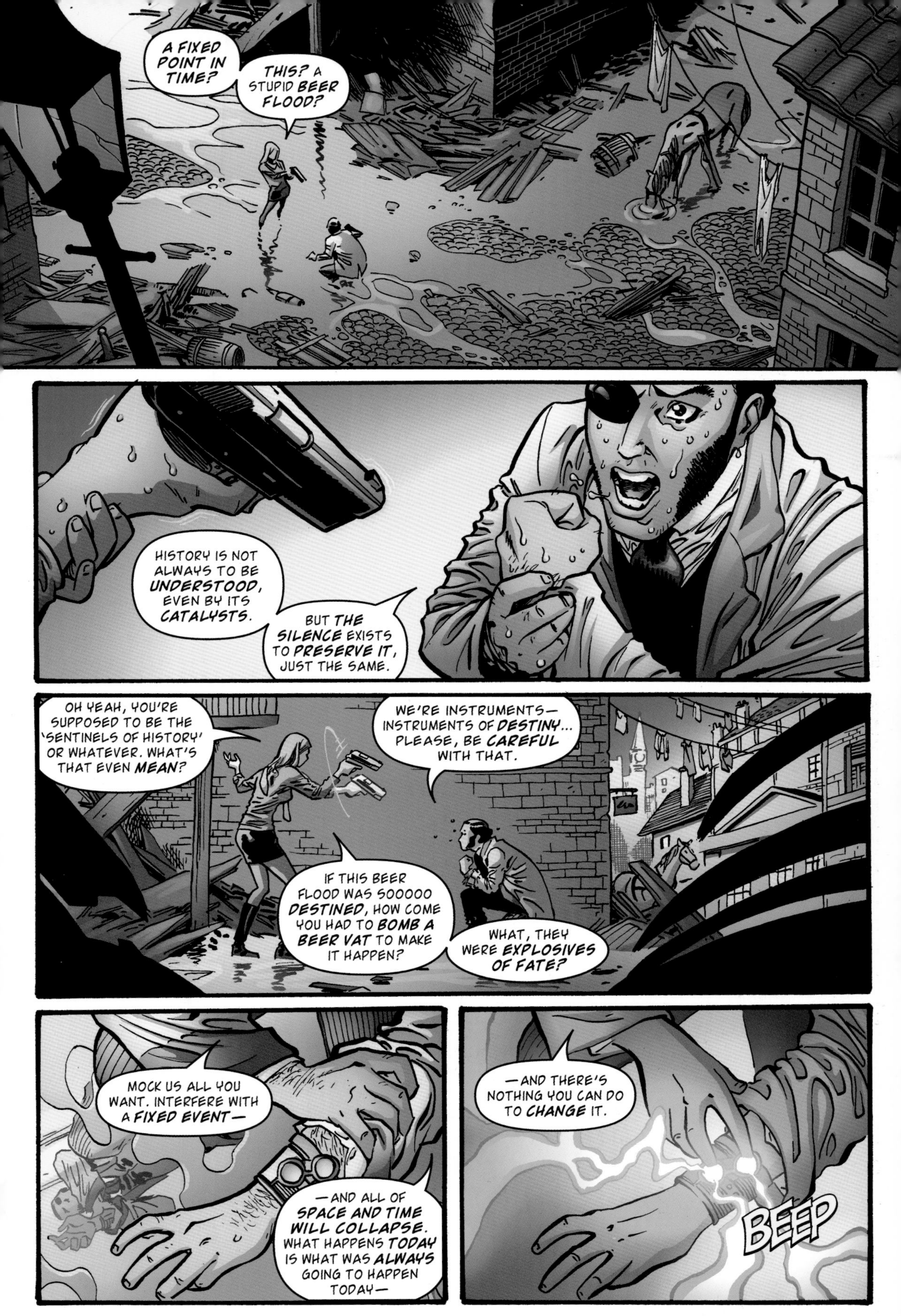

A FIXED POINT IN TIME?
THIS? A STUPID BEER FLOOD?
HISTORY IS NOT ALWAYS TO BE UNDERSTOOD, EVEN BY ITS CATALYSTS.
BUT THE SILENCE EXISTS TO PRESERVE IT, JUST THE SAME.
OH YEAH, YOU'RE SUPPOSED TO BE THE 'SENTINELS OF HISTORY' OR WHATEVER. WHAT'S THAT EVEN MEAN?
WE'RE INSTRUMENTS— INSTRUMENTS OF DESTINY... PLEASE, BE CAREFUL WITH THAT.
IF THIS BEER FLOOD WAS SOOOOO DESTINED, HOW COME YOU HAD TO BOMB A BEER VAT TO MAKE IT HAPPEN?
WHAT, THEY WERE EXPLOSIVES OF FATE?
MOCK US ALL YOU WANT. INTERFERE WITH A FIXED EVENT—
—AND ALL OF SPACE AND TIME WILL COLLAPSE. WHAT HAPPENS TODAY IS WHAT WAS ALWAYS GOING TO HAPPEN TODAY—
—AND THERE'S NOTHING YOU CAN DO TO CHANGE IT.
BEEP

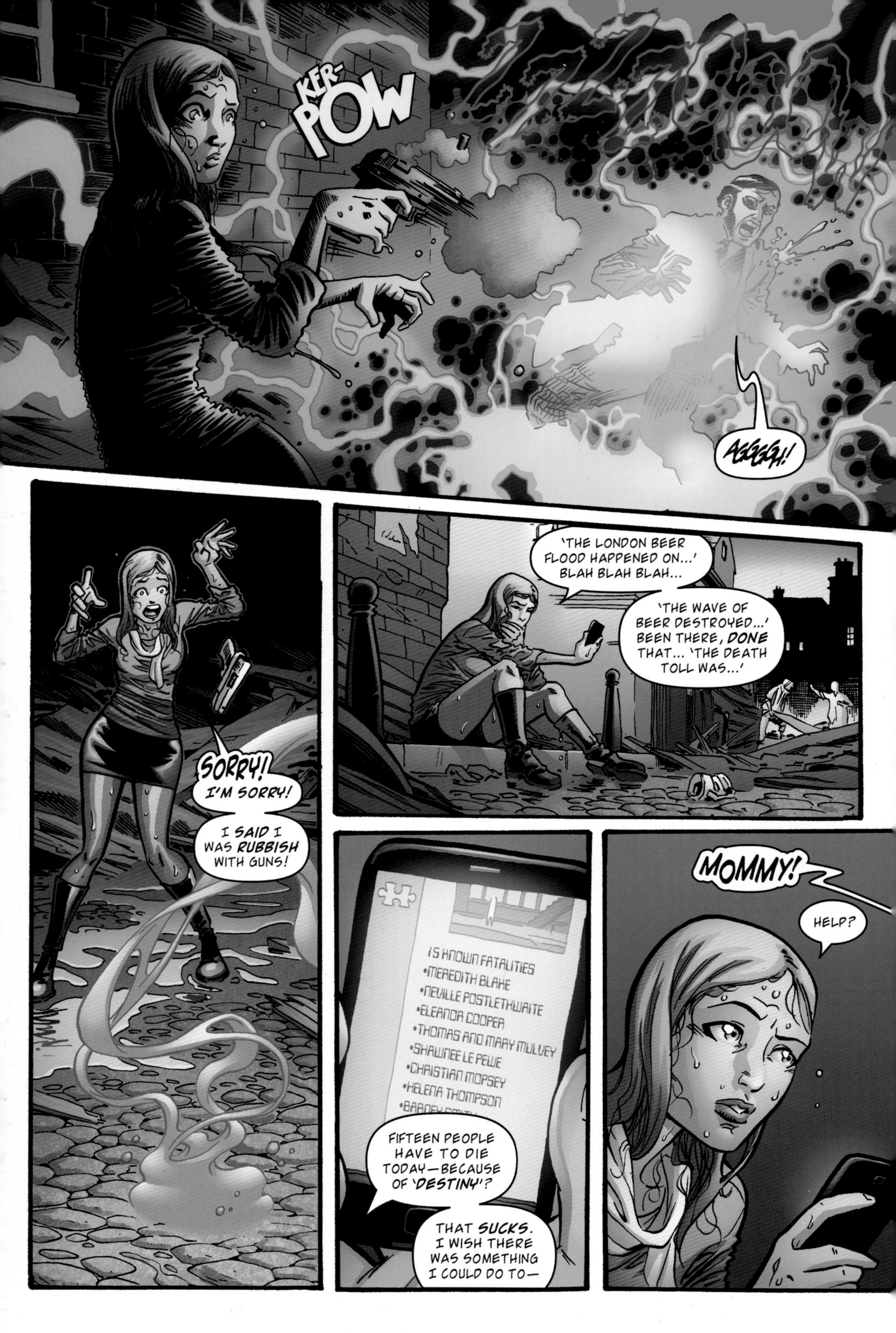

KER-POW
AGGGGH!
SORRY! I'M SORRY!
I SAID I WAS RUBBISH WITH GUNS!
'THE LONDON BEER FLOOD HAPPENED ON...' BLAH BLAH BLAH...
'THE WAVE OF BEER DESTROYED...' BEEN THERE, DONE THAT... 'THE DEATH TOLL WAS...'
15 KNOWN FATALITIES
•MEREDITH BLAKE
•NEVILLE POSTLETHWAITE
•ELEANOR COOPER
•THOMAS AND MARY MULVEY
•SHAWNEE LE PEWE
•CHRISTIAN MOPSEY
•HELENA THOMPSON
FIFTEEN PEOPLE HAVE TO DIE TODAY—BECAUSE OF 'DESTINY'?
THAT SUCKS. I WISH THERE WAS SOMETHING I COULD DO TO—
MOMMY!
HELP?

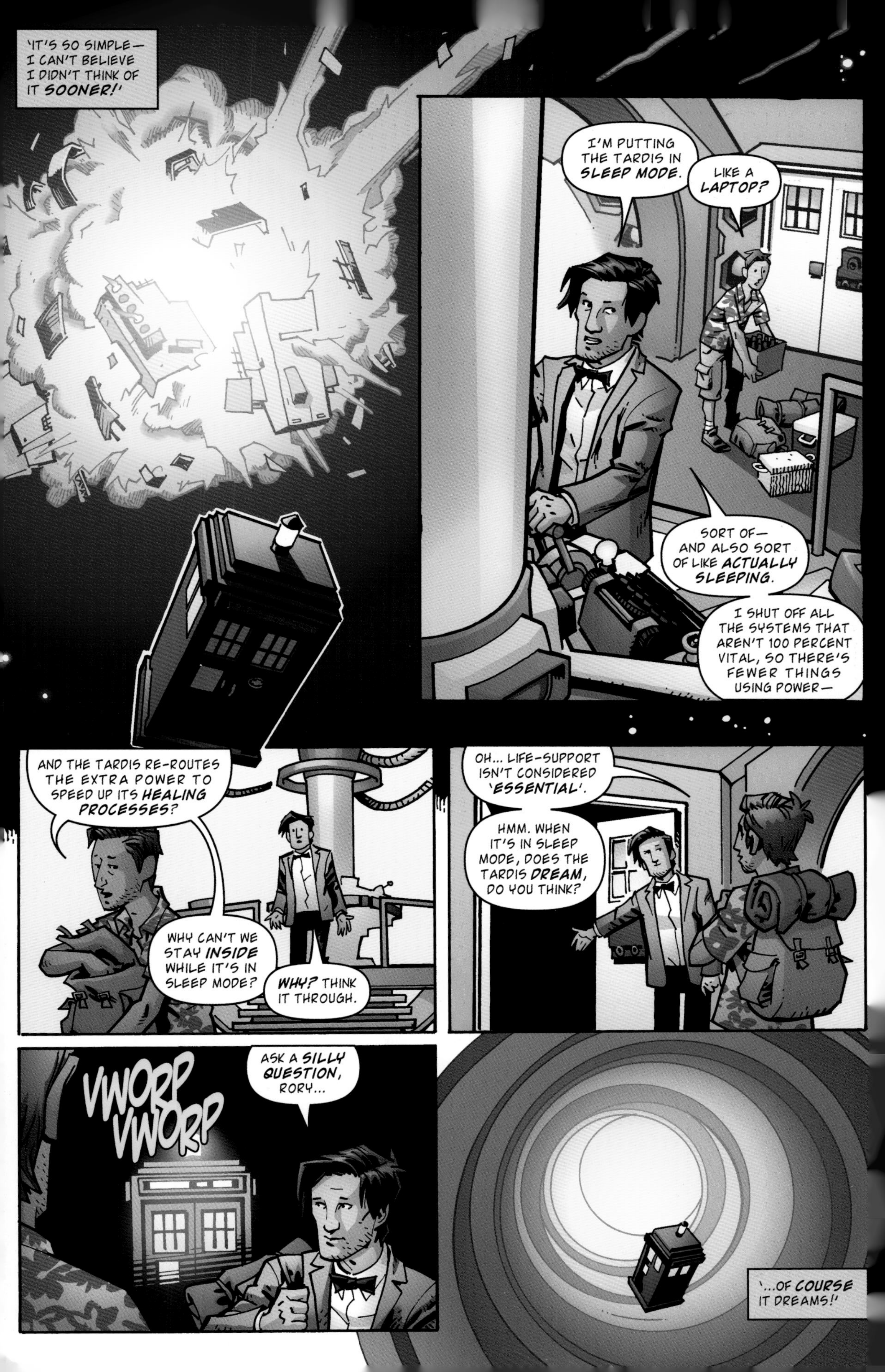
'IT'S SO SIMPLE— I CAN'T BELIEVE I DIDN'T THINK OF IT SOONER!'
I'M PUTTING THE TARDIS IN SLEEP MODE.
LIKE A LAPTOP?
SORT OF— AND ALSO SORT OF LIKE ACTUALLY SLEEPING.
I SHUT OFF ALL THE SYSTEMS THAT AREN'T 100 PERCENT VITAL, SO THERE'S FEWER THINGS USING POWER—
AND THE TARDIS RE-ROUTES THE EXTRA POWER TO SPEED UP ITS HEALING PROCESSES?
WHY CAN'T WE STAY INSIDE WHILE IT'S IN SLEEP MODE?
WHY? THINK IT THROUGH.
OH... LIFE-SUPPORT ISN'T CONSIDERED 'ESSENTIAL'.
HMM. WHEN IT'S IN SLEEP MODE, DOES THE TARDIS DREAM, DO YOU THINK?
VWORP VWORP
ASK A SILLY QUESTION, RORY...
'...OF COURSE IT DREAMS!'

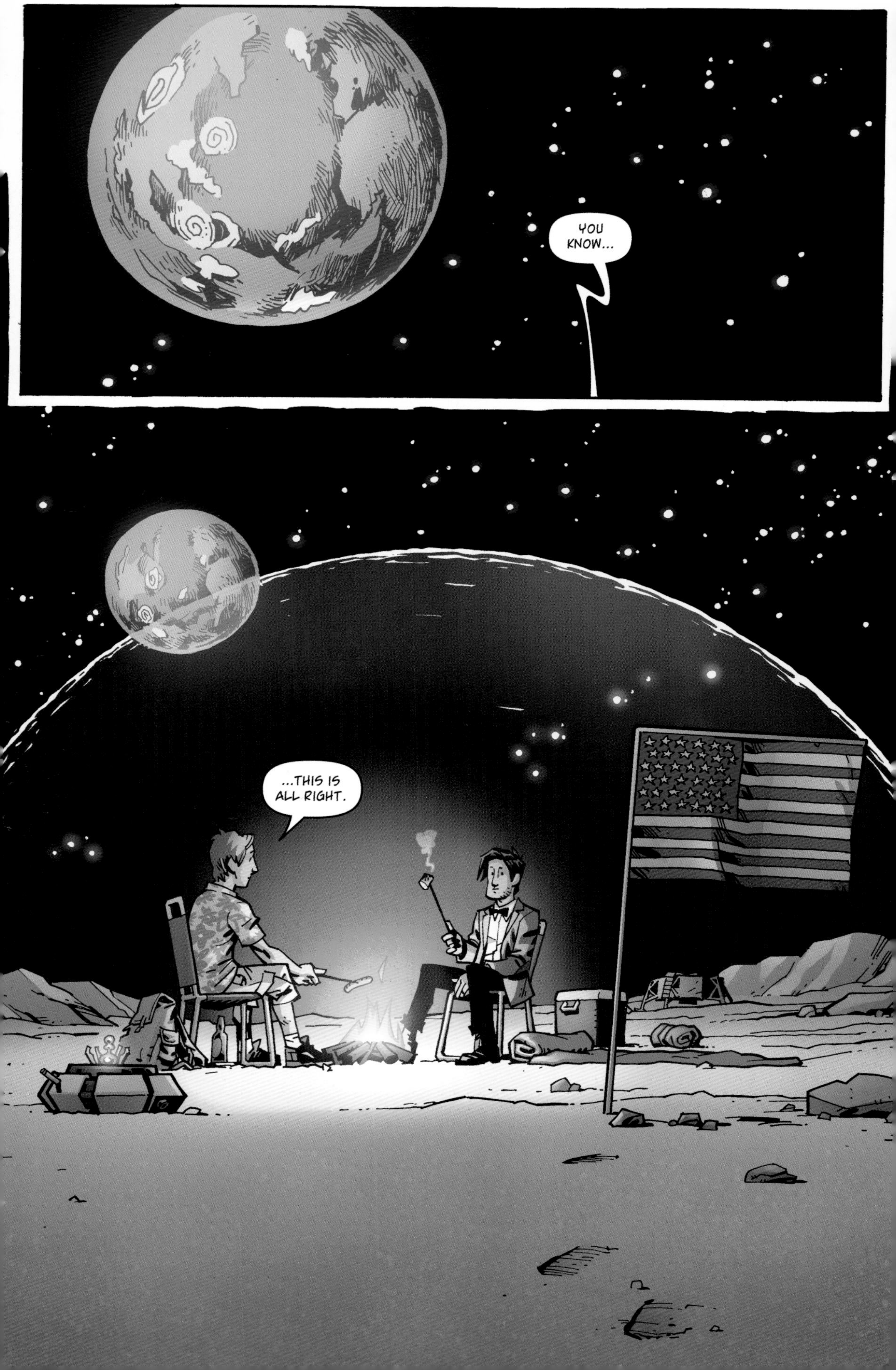
YOU KNOW...
...THIS IS ALL RIGHT.

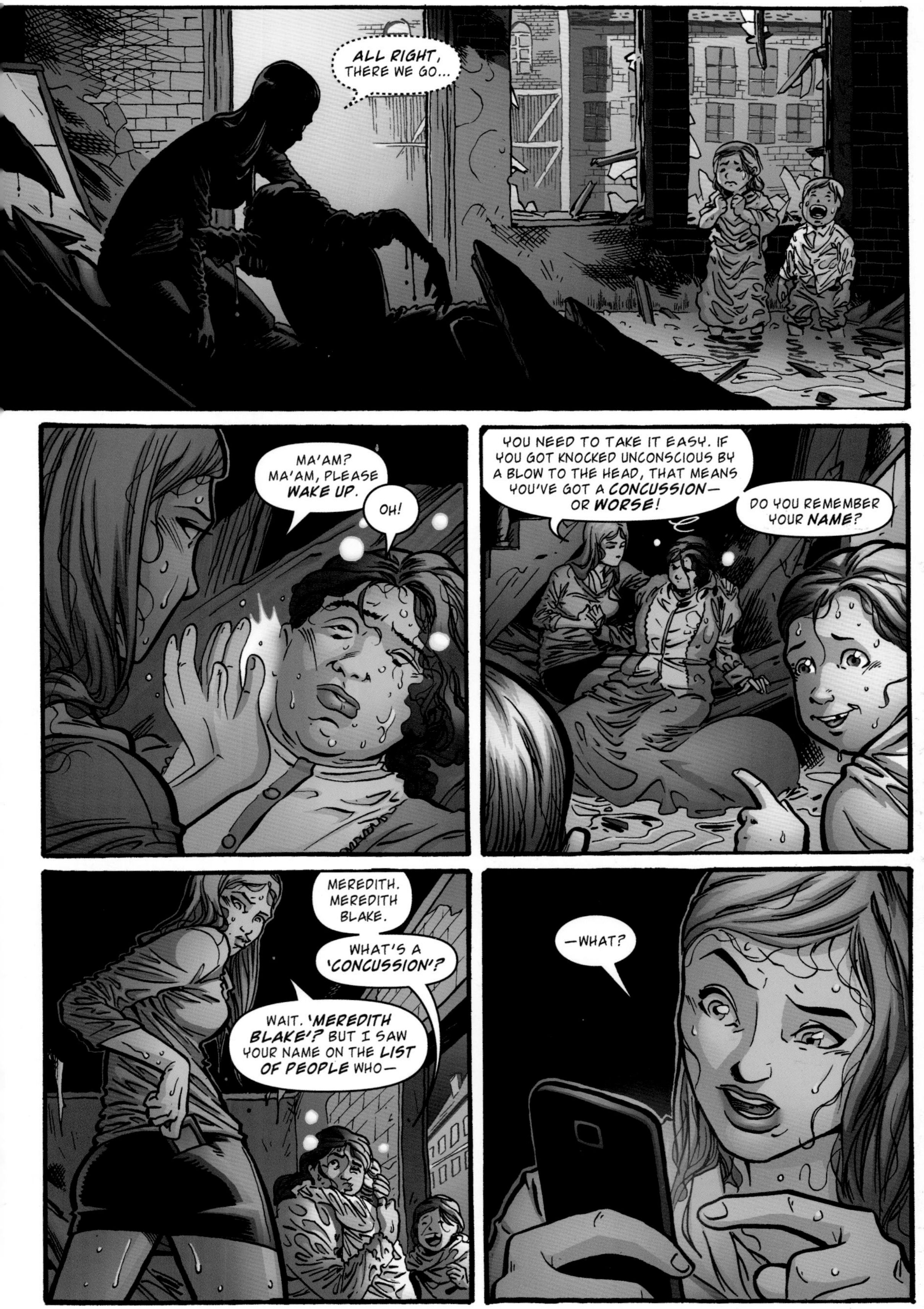
ALL RIGHT, THERE WE GO...
MA'AM? MA'AM, PLEASE WAKE UP.
OH!
YOU NEED TO TAKE IT EASY. IF YOU GOT KNOCKED UNCONSCIOUS BY A BLOW TO THE HEAD, THAT MEANS YOU'VE GOT A CONCUSSION— OR WORSE!
DO YOU REMEMBER YOUR NAME?
MEREDITH. MEREDITH BLAKE.
WHAT'S A 'CONCUSSION'?
WAIT. 'MEREDITH BLAKE'? BUT I SAW YOUR NAME ON THE LIST OF PEOPLE WHO—
—WHAT?

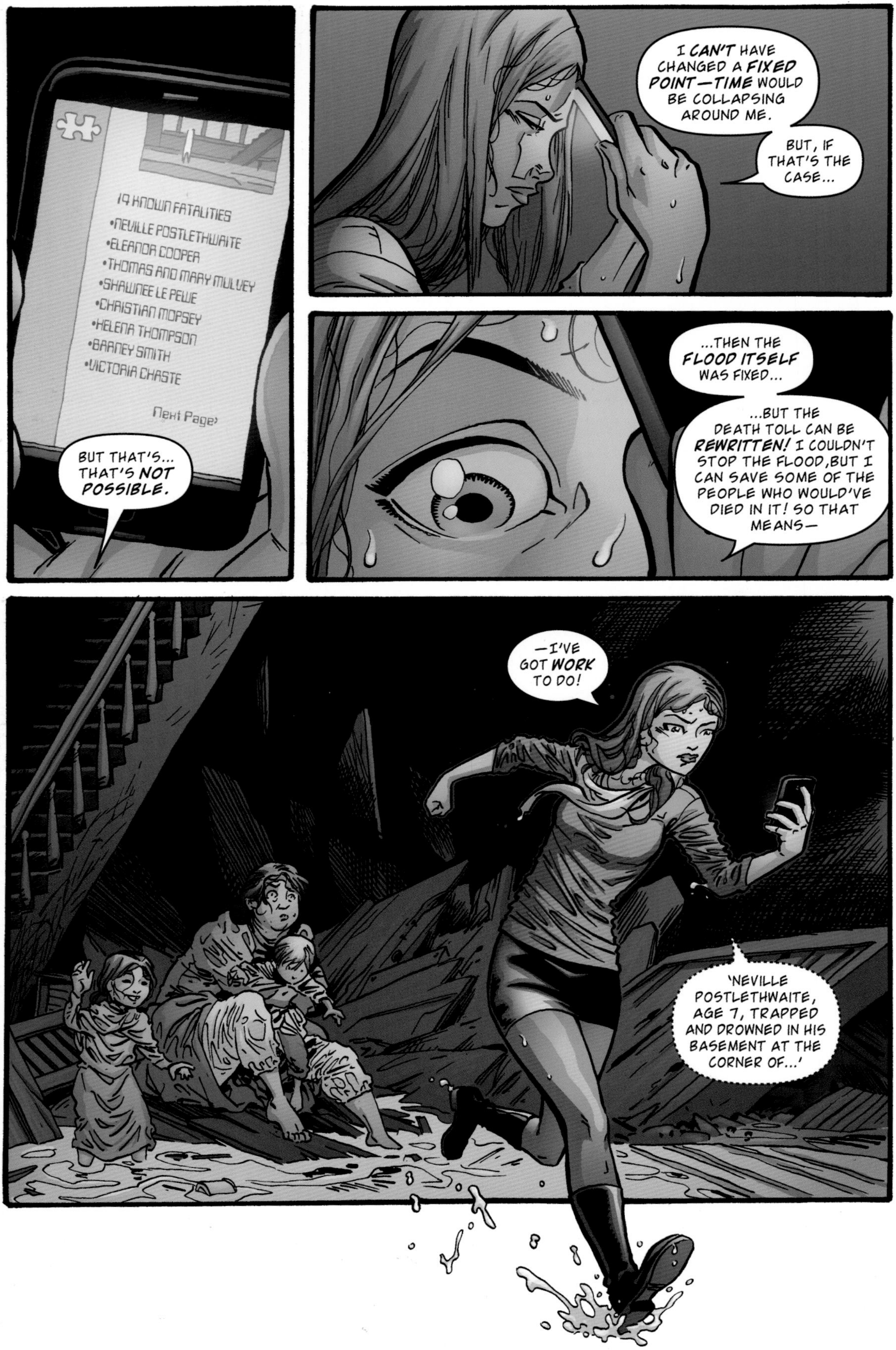
19 KNOWN FATALITIES
•NEVILLE POSTLETHWAITE
•ELEANOR COOPER
•THOMAS AND MARY MULVEY
•SHAWNEE LE PEWE
•CHRISTIAN MOPSEY
•HELENA THOMPSON
•BARNEY SMITH
•VICTORIA CHASTE
Next Page›
BUT THAT'S... THAT'S NOT POSSIBLE.
I CAN'T HAVE CHANGED A FIXED POINT—TIME WOULD BE COLLAPSING AROUND ME.
BUT, IF THAT'S THE CASE...
...THEN THE FLOOD ITSELF WAS FIXED...
...BUT THE DEATH TOLL CAN BE REWRITTEN! I COULDN'T STOP THE FLOOD, BUT I CAN SAVE SOME OF THE PEOPLE WHO WOULD'VE DIED IN IT! SO THAT MEANS—
—I'VE GOT WORK TO DO!
'NEVILLE POSTLETHWAITE, AGE 7, TRAPPED AND DROWNED IN HIS BASEMENT AT THE CORNER OF...'

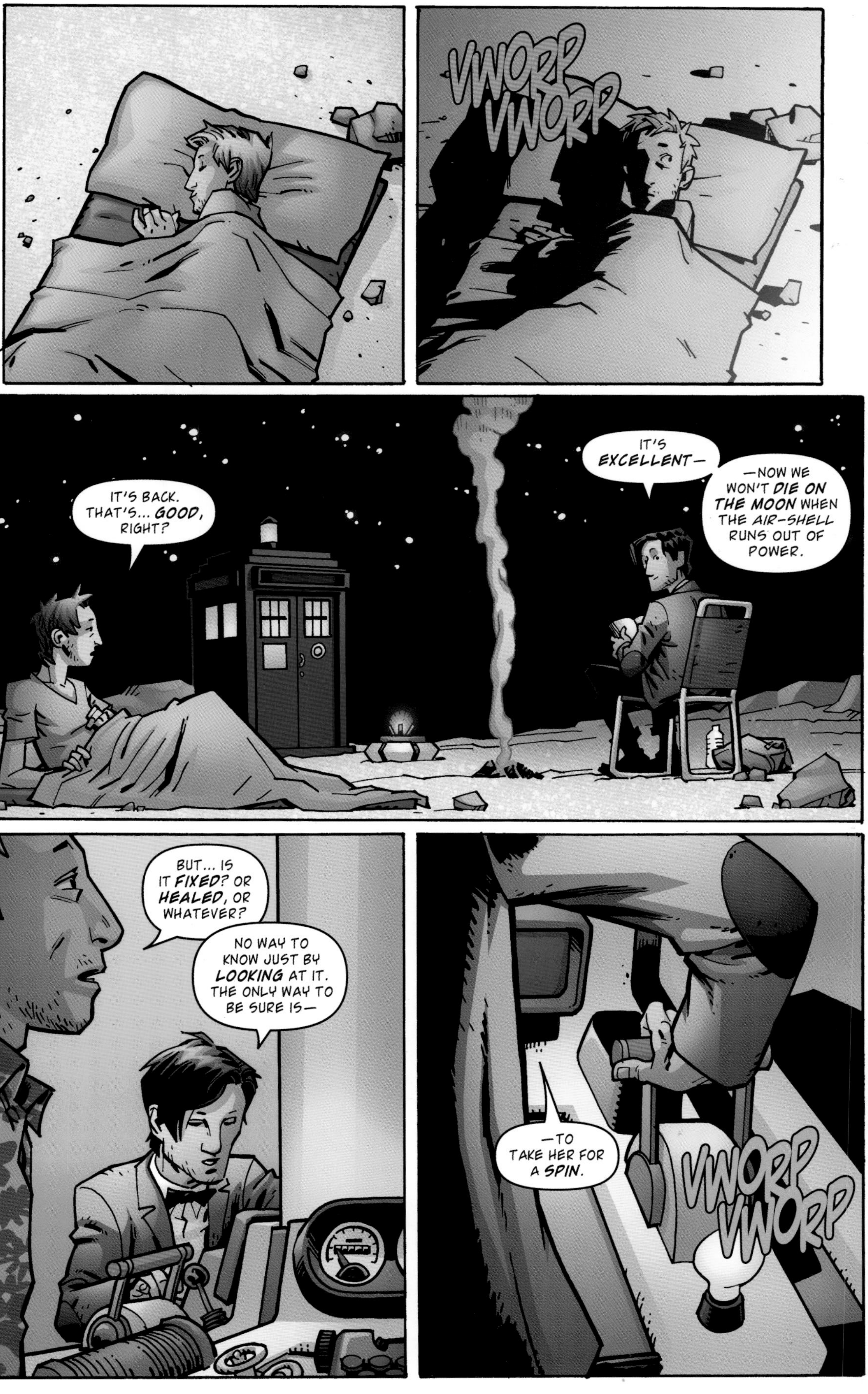
VWORP VWORP
IT'S BACK. THAT'S... GOOD, RIGHT?
IT'S EXCELLENT—
—NOW WE WON'T DIE ON THE MOON WHEN THE AIR-SHELL RUNS OUT OF POWER.
BUT... IS IT FIXED? OR HEALED, OR WHATEVER?
NO WAY TO KNOW JUST BY LOOKING AT IT. THE ONLY WAY TO BE SURE IS—
—TO TAKE HER FOR A SPIN.
VWORP VWORP

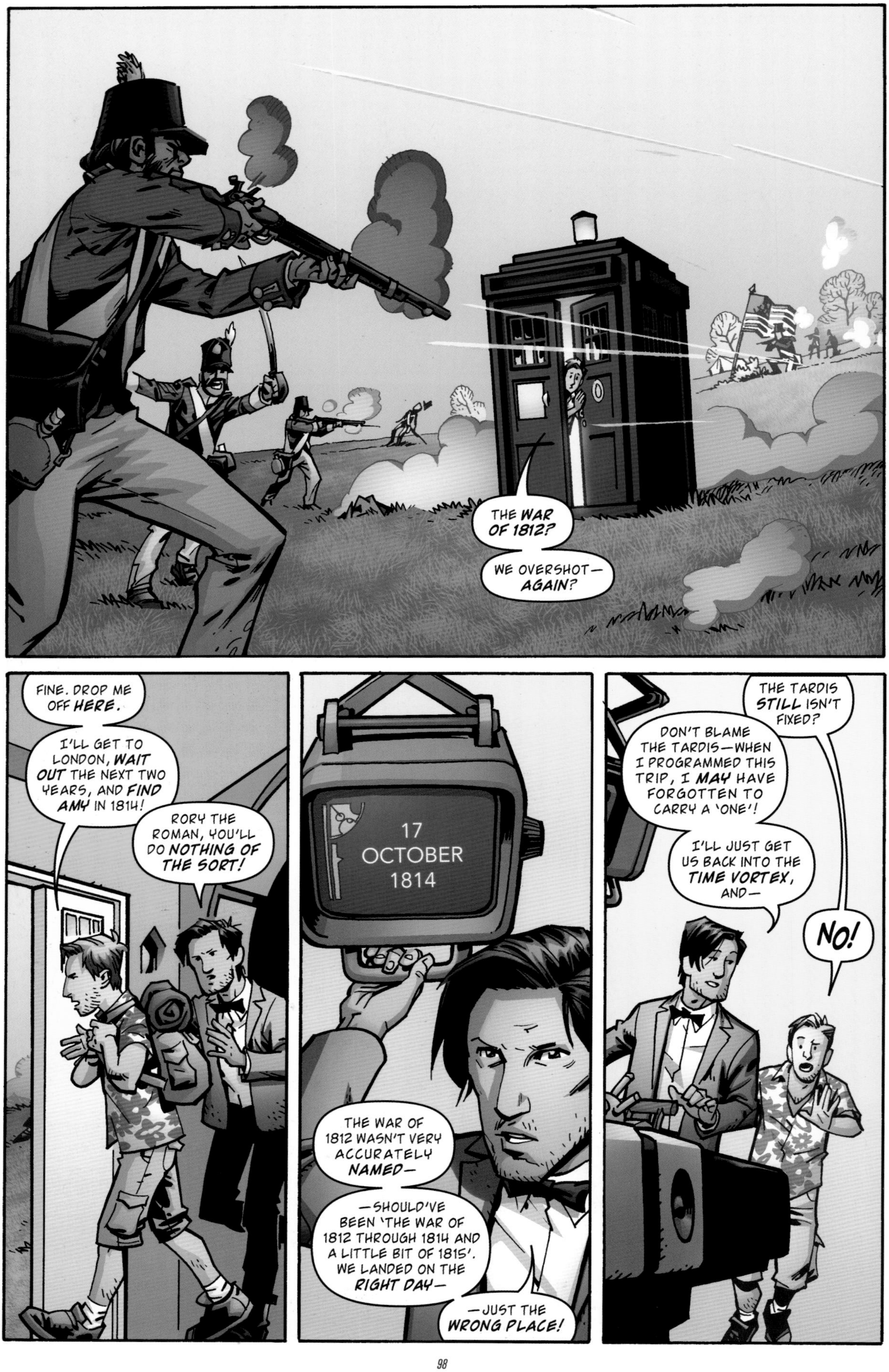
THE WAR OF 1812?
WE OVERSHOT— AGAIN?
FINE. DROP ME OFF HERE.
I'LL GET TO LONDON, WAIT OUT THE NEXT TWO YEARS, AND FIND AMY IN 1814!
RORY THE ROMAN, YOU'LL DO NOTHING OF THE SORT!
17 OCTOBER 1814
THE WAR OF 1812 WASN'T VERY ACCURATELY NAMED—
—SHOULD'VE BEEN 'THE WAR OF 1812 THROUGH 1814 AND A LITTLE BIT OF 1815'. WE LANDED ON THE RIGHT DAY—
—JUST THE WRONG PLACE!
THE TARDIS STILL ISN'T FIXED?
DON'T BLAME THE TARDIS—WHEN I PROGRAMMED THIS TRIP, I MAY HAVE FORGOTTEN TO CARRY A 'ONE'!
I'LL JUST GET US BACK INTO THE TIME VORTEX, AND—
NO!

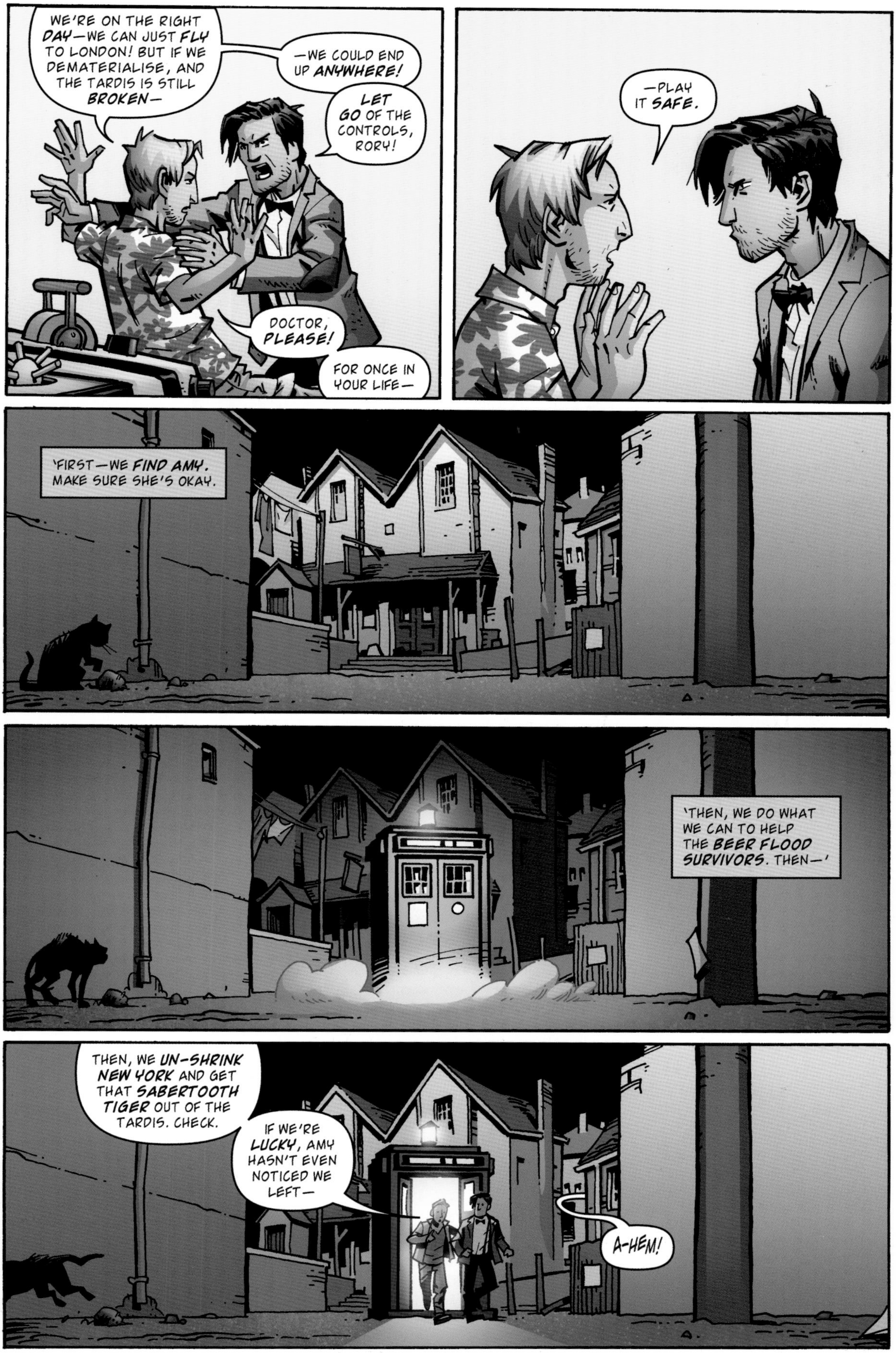
WE'RE ON THE RIGHT DAY—WE CAN JUST FLY TO LONDON! BUT IF WE DEMATERIALISE, AND THE TARDIS IS STILL BROKEN—
—WE COULD END UP ANYWHERE!
LET GO OF THE CONTROLS, RORY!
DOCTOR, PLEASE!
FOR ONCE IN YOUR LIFE—
—PLAY IT SAFE.
'FIRST—WE FIND AMY. MAKE SURE SHE'S OKAY.
'THEN, WE DO WHAT WE CAN TO HELP THE BEER FLOOD SURVIVORS. THEN—'
THEN, WE UN-SHRINK NEW YORK AND GET THAT SABERTOOTH TIGER OUT OF THE TARDIS. CHECK.
IF WE'RE LUCKY, AMY HASN'T EVEN NOTICED WE LEFT—
A-HEM!

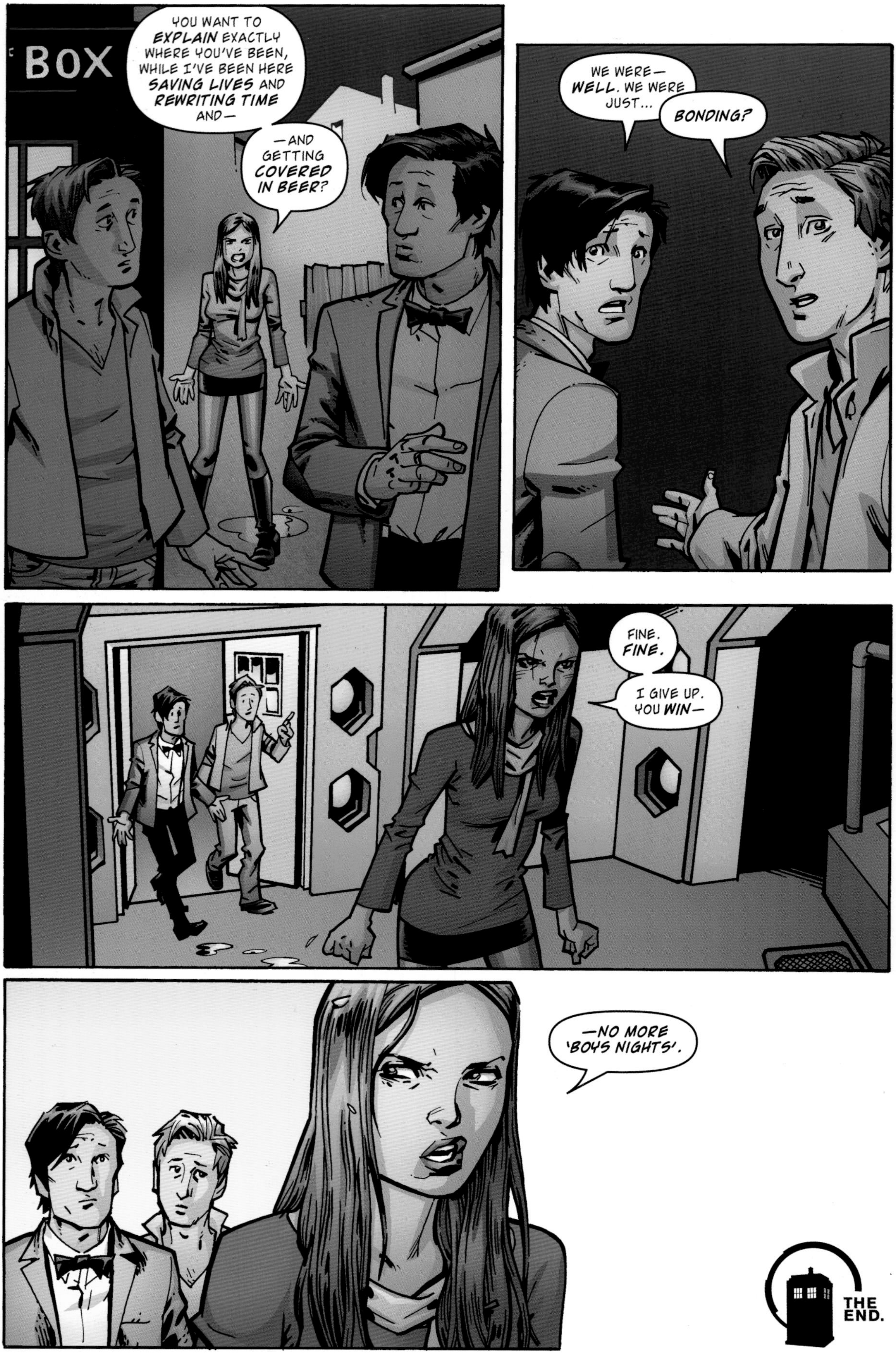
BOX
YOU WANT TO EXPLAIN EXACTLY WHERE YOU'VE BEEN, WHILE I'VE BEEN HERE SAVING LIVES AND REWRITING TIME AND—
—AND GETTING COVERED IN BEER?
WE WERE— WELL. WE WERE JUST...
BONDING?
FINE. FINE.
I GIVE UP. YOU WIN—
—NO MORE 'BOYS NIGHTS'.
THE END.

ART GALLERY

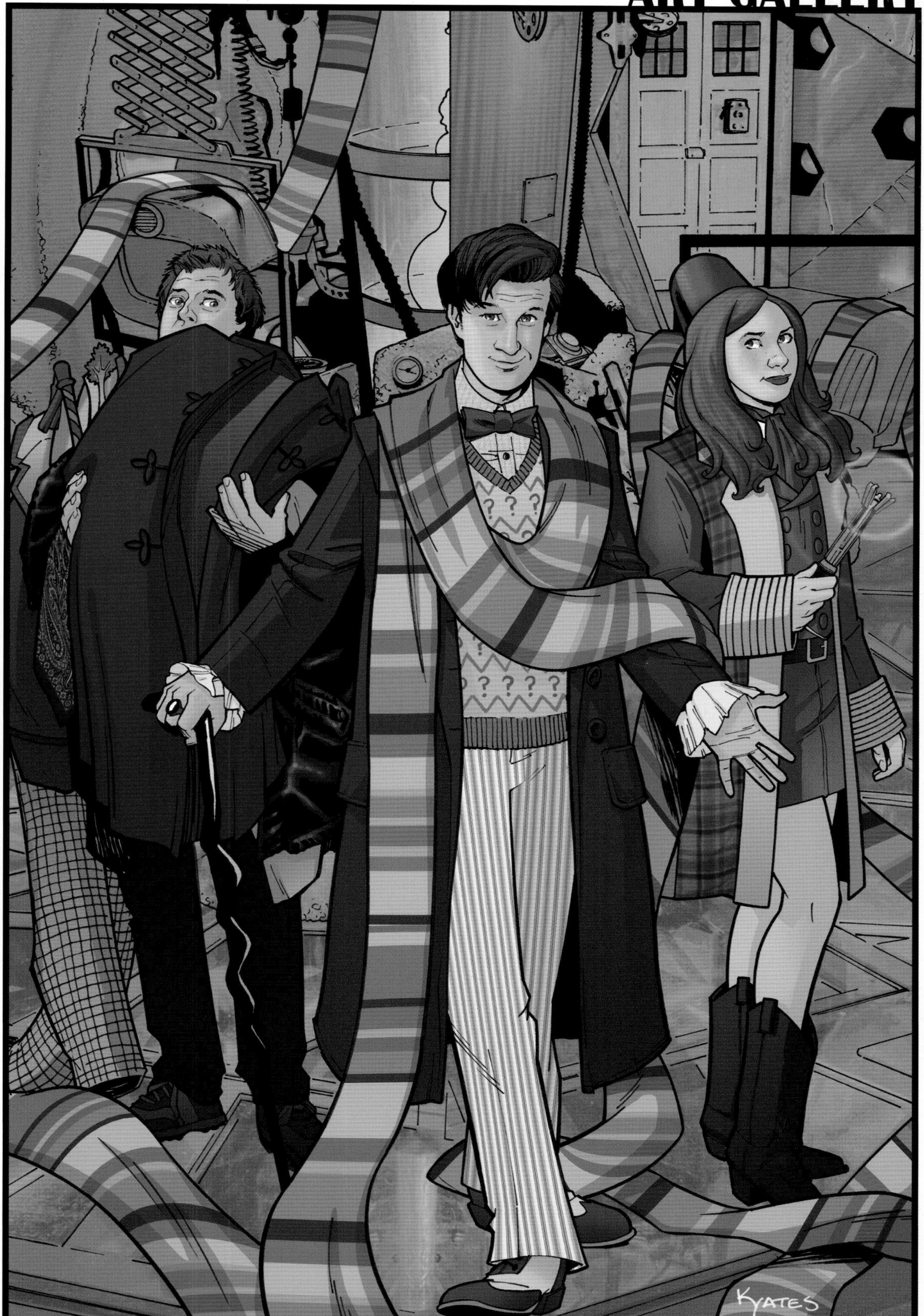
KYATES

Art by Kelly Yates

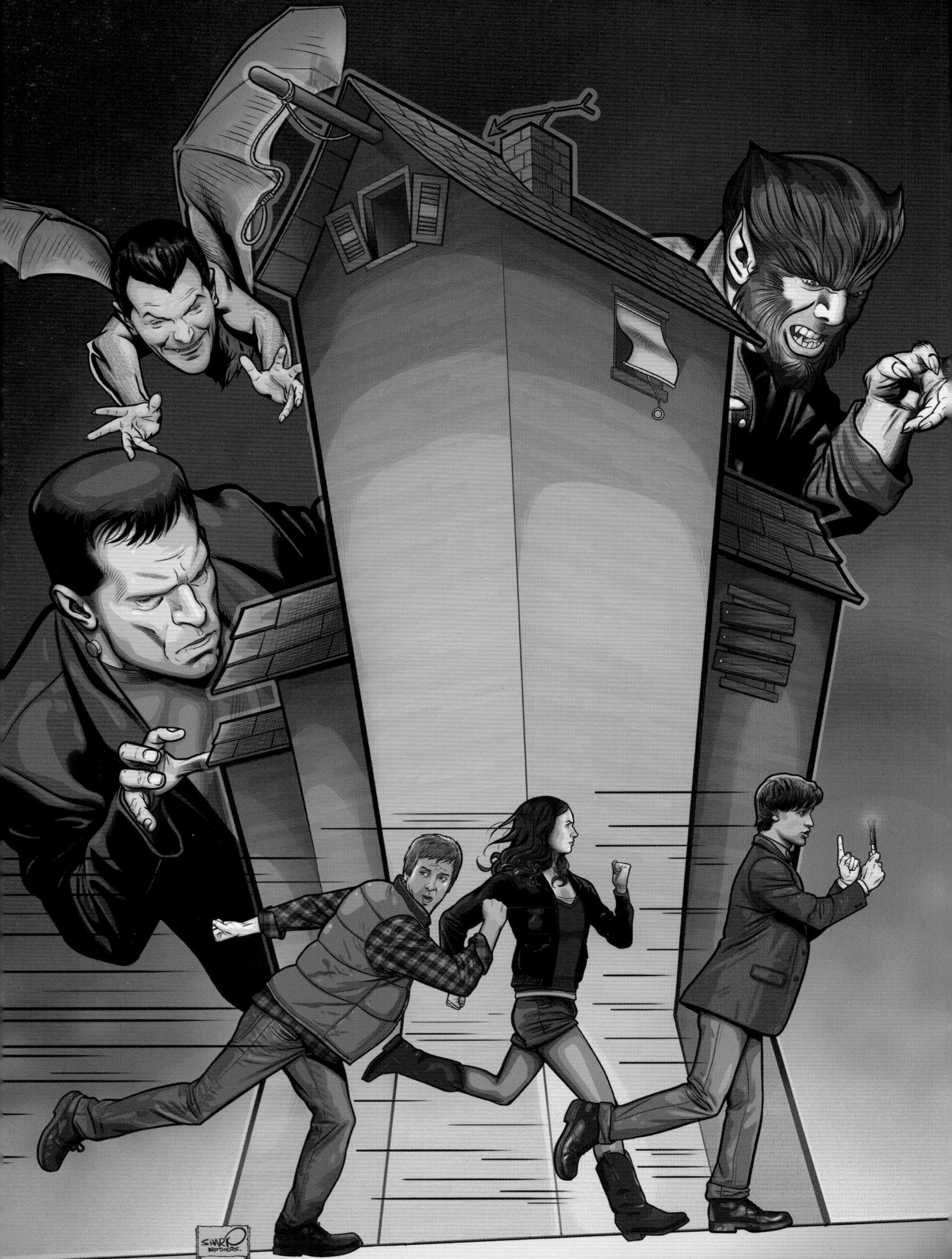
SHARP BROTHERS

Art by The Sharp Brothers

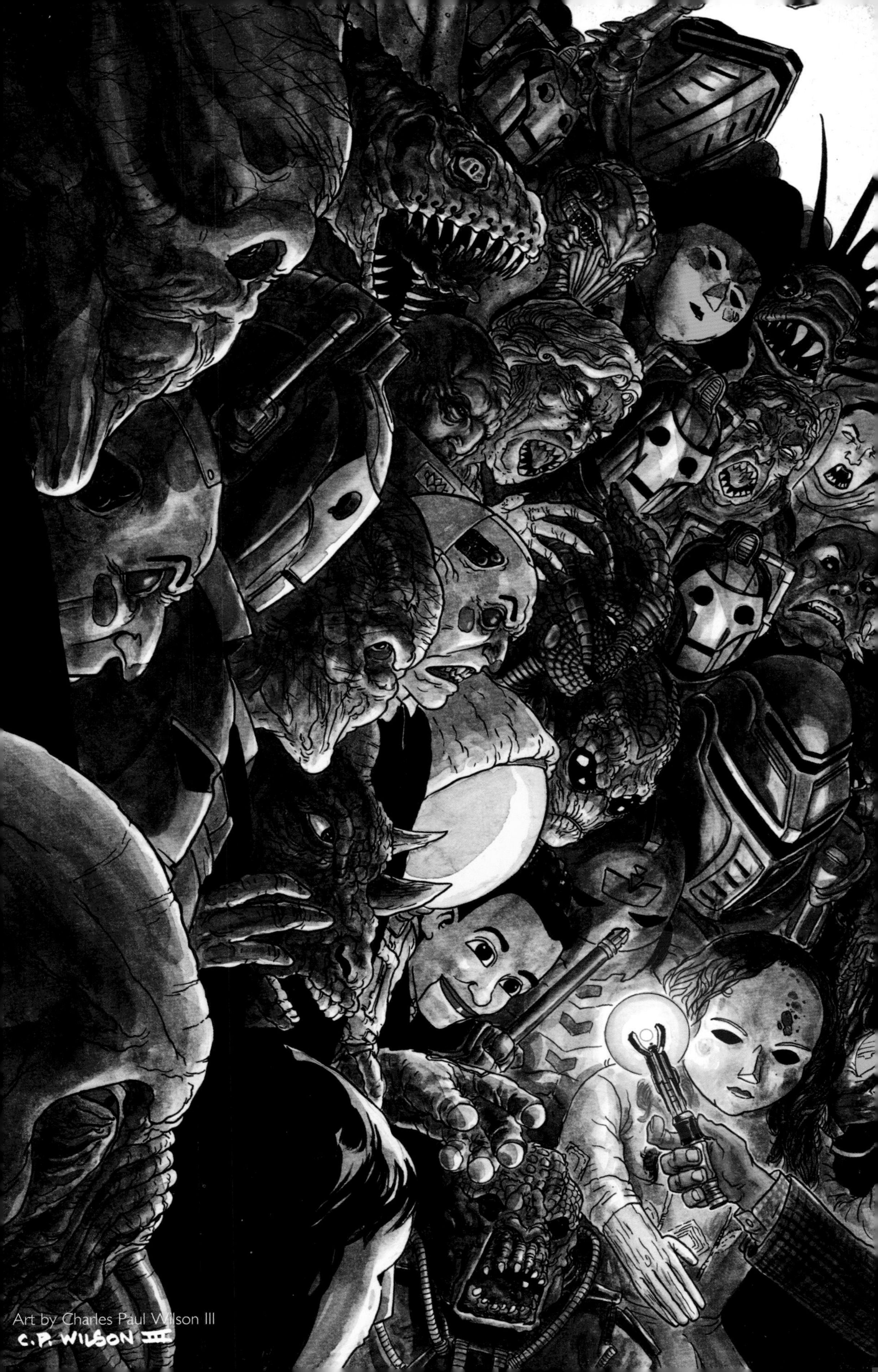
C.P. WILSON III

Art by Charles Paul Wilson III

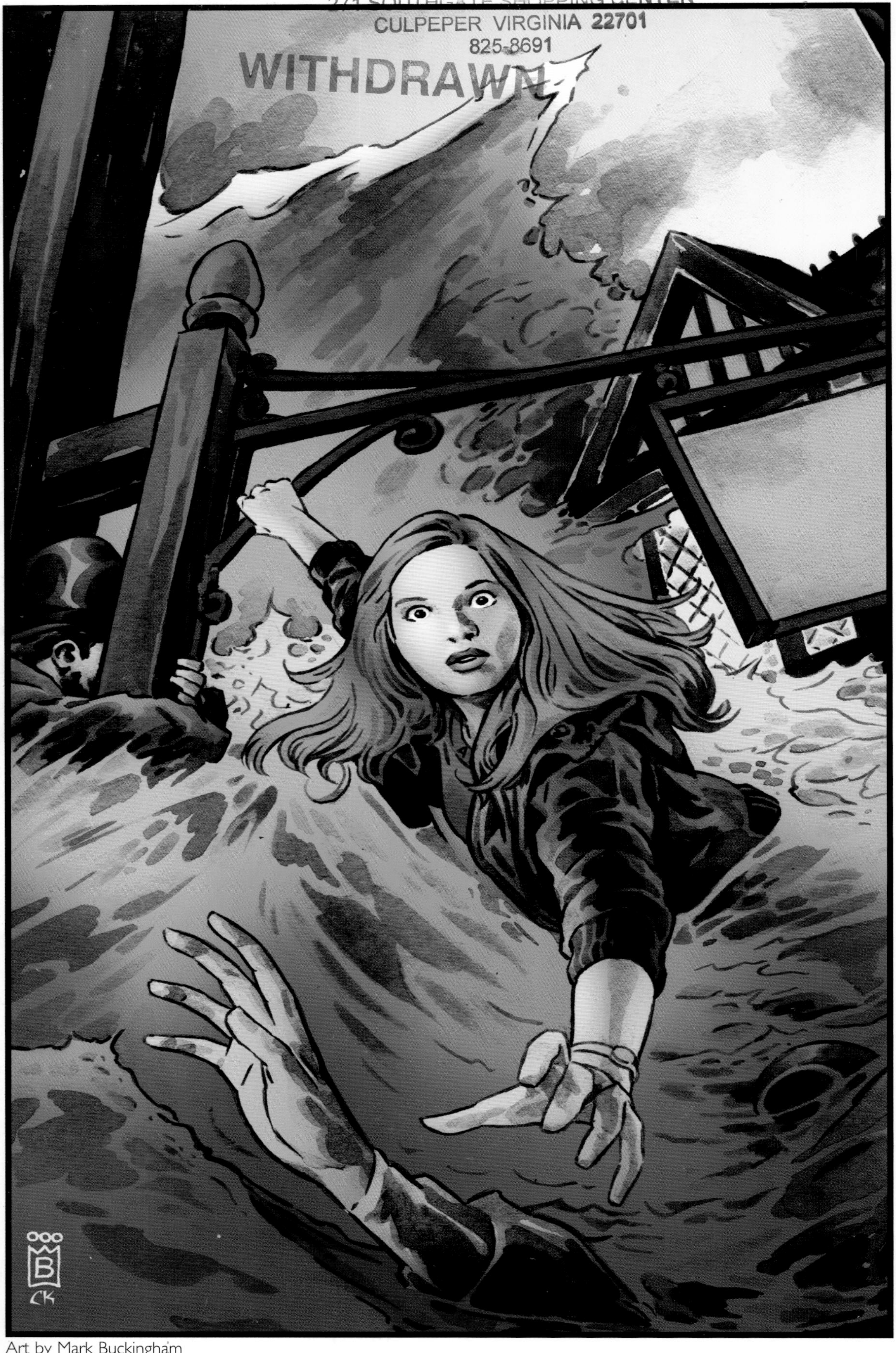

Art by Mark Buckingham
Colors by Charlie Kirchoff